S0-ACN-485

This book is born out of a desire to understand the way in which truth is conceived, developed and disseminated. The author worked for the BBC and each day would walk past *The Sower*, a sculpture by Eric Gill in the entrance hall of Broadcasting House. The sower is broadcasting the good seed, scattering it freely.

C.S. Lewis walked through the same entrance during the Second World War. There were ideas to be commissioned, truths to be examined and words to be broadcast to a wide and fascinated audience. This book tells that story.

Justin Phillips was a broadcaster. He worked for the BBC as a radio journalist. He loved it, and served the BBC faithfully and energetically for over twenty years. He worked in the World Service, produced *Today*, was deputy editor of *The World Tonight* and latterly worked in the management of Network Radio and Heritage. He was also a 'card-carrying Christian', as he put it. He was an elder at his local church and a frequent speaker and preacher about Christianity, the media, and the relationship between the two. His faith, work and life were finely intertwined.

This book was written in the midst of a busy family life. Justin would sit at the kitchen table, hitting the computer keyboard with one finger, listening to tapes of the Lewis talks on the stereo, and seemingly oblivious to the bustle around him. Our last family holiday in France, with our four daughters, was happily punctuated with cries of 'look what I've discovered!' We would celebrate at the local café overlooking the Gorges de Verdun when another chapter was successfully completed.

Justin took the finished manuscript to HarperCollins in December 2000 with pride and a flourish, hitting their deadline: a true journalist to the last.

In the early hours of Boxing Day 2000 Justin died suddenly, of an asthma attack. He would have been fifty a few weeks later. He died in faith, fully confident that his next destination was heaven. He achieved a great many things in his full life. This book was his last piece of writing. He was pleased with it, glad to have told the story and shed light. His oldest daughter, Laura Treneer, has acted as his editor and brought the manuscript forward to publication. He would have been thrilled that she could do this for him.

Gillian Phillips

C.S. LEWIS
at the
BBC

Messages of Hope in
the Darkness of War

JUSTIN PHILLIPS

HarperCollins*Publishers*

For
Gillian

HarperCollins*Publishers*
77–85 Fulham Palace Road,
Hammersmith, London W6 8JB
www.harpercollins.co.uk

This paperback edition 2003
First published by HarperCollins*Publishers* 2002
1 3 5 7 9 8 6 4 2

Copyright © Justin Phillips 2002

Justin Phillips asserts the moral right to
be identified as the author of this work

A catalogue record for this book
is available from the British Library

ISBN 0 00 710436 7

Typeset in Fairfield Light by Palimpsest Book Production Limited,
Polmont, Stirlingshire

Printed and bound in Great Britain by
Clays Ltd, St Ives plc

FOREWORD

C.S. Lewis once remarked that 'At every tick of the clock, in every inhabited part of the world, an unimaginable richness and variety of "history" falls off the world into total oblivion.' Well, here is a book that caught many hours of the history of Lewis's *Mere Christianity*. That great work originated as four series of BBC broadcasts and Justin Phillips could not have left behind a finer legacy than this story of how it happened. Everyone has known for years that *Mere Christianity* began as broadcasts over the BBC, but until now no one had shown them against the background of the Second War, nor explained how much the BBC's famous wartime broadcasts did to shape religious broadcasting.

C.S. Lewis was, of course, one of many talented authors nurtured by the BBC. His remarkable story, Justin Phillips explains, began in February 1941 when the Director of Religious Broadcasting, impressed by Lewis's *The Problem of Pain* (1940), invited the Oxford don to give the nation a 'positive restatement of Christian doctrines in lay language.' That has to be one of the most valuable invitations of all times! Lewis agreed, and thereafter things moved with great speed in what was, to Lewis, an unknown world. BBC's Eric Fenn took Lewis under his wing, and while Lewis was writing the first series of broadcasts the BBC made a record of his voice. 'About 3 weeks ago,' Lewis wrote to a friend, 'I had to make a gramophone record (not a song!) and heard it played through . . . I was unprepared for the total unfamiliarity of the voice; not a trace, not a hint, of anything one could identify with oneself.'

As unfamiliar as he was with the microphone, writing was for Lewis as natural as breathing. 'I don't know what I mean,' he once said, 'till I see what I've said.' But it wasn't simply a matter of expressing ideas clearly that was called for. Eric Fenn explained the severe restrictions imposed upon all broadcasters during the Second War and why all scripts had to be passed for security and then rigidly adhered to. Lewis was born with a talent for clarity, and an impatience with vagueness, but the BBC's contribution was requiring Lewis to write short, crisp sentences, each of which made a precise contribution to Christian theology.

Tutoring Lewis in clarity is not a job many would willingly undertake. But as Justin Phillips demonstrates, Eric Fenn's 'tutoring' was exactly what was needed. On reading the five fifteen-minute talks on 'What Christians Believe', Fenn said: 'There is a clarity and inexorableness about them which made me positively gasp!' But such clarity did not come as easily as it might look. After Fenn's criticism of the last series, Lewis admitted that, while it would be easy to conceal one's ignorance in a university lecture 'this d---d colloquial style is so intrinsically honest' concealment is impossible. This important lesson was never lost. Writing about it later, Lewis said, 'Any fool can write *learned* language. The vernacular is the real test. If you can't turn your faith into it, then either you don't understand it or you don't believe it.'

It often seems to me that writers with profound ideas find it difficult to be clear, while those with a catchy style have nothing profound to say. In this excellent history Justin Phillips helps us understand why, as a result of his collaboration with the BBC, *Mere Christianity* turned out to be the supreme example of C.S. Lewis's ability to make profound truths clear to everyone.

Walter Hooper

CONTENTS

AUTHOR'S INTRODUCTION

The phone rang. It was during the spring of 1997. Betty Baker, then administrator for the London Institute for Contemporary Christianity, wanted some help. A delegation of Americans was coming to London to join other scholars and admirers of C.S. Lewis to attend a special conference to mark the centenary of his birth. Would it be possible for the BBC to allow them to hold some sessions in the Radio Theatre (known during the war as the BBC Concert Hall) of Broadcasting House? I told her I'd see what I could do. Then Betty asked if by any chance I could obtain a recording of C.S. Lewis's voice that could be played to the delegates at the conference? It took only a few telephone inquiries to establish that the conference could be held there, that very few recordings had survived of C.S. Lewis and only one of the famous wartime *Broadcast Talks*. That is what happened. Unknowingly however, Betty had triggered a train of thought and if there is one quality that every journalist possesses in abundance it is curiosity. After the summer, I started to investigate how much of C.S. Lewis's BBC legacy had survived. To my surprise and delight, I found in the BBC's Written Archives Centre in Caversham numerous files containing all the correspondence between the BBC and C.S. Lewis from 1940 till 1963. All the staff there were really helpful (a full acknowledgement for all who have contributed appears at the back). The existence of this collection of letters was known to Walter Hooper, literary advisor to the C.S. Lewis Estate, who had drawn upon it, in part, for his authoritative *C.S. Lewis – Companion and Guide*. But much of it had never seen the light of the printed page.

As Head of Heritage for the BBC, I have responsibility for how the BBC captures and communicates its own history. This has enabled me to use some original source material from within the BBC's archives not published before. However, I should make it clear that this book is my own work and the views expressed in it, and any errors contained within it, are mine alone and not necessarily those of the BBC, my employer.

Most of the dozens of books written about C.S. Lewis tend to focus on his achievements as a Christian apologist, popular theologian, medievalist, literary scholar, writer of science fiction and children's books – creator of Narnia – poet and polymath. Many books look at his personal life through the lens of biography or interpretations of personal episodes in his life, such as *Shadowlands*. No broadcaster has, to the best of my knowledge, attempted to place Lewis firmly within the historical context of wartime religious broadcasting. Nor has his sometimes turbulent relationship with the BBC been explored in any detail. Nor has his role in the creation of contemporary Christian apologetics first through the medium of radio (and later the printed page) been fully assessed by a broadcaster. Lewis himself felt there was a book waiting to be written. At a particularly sticky point in the relationship with the BBC, he wrote to his producer saying . . .

> If you know the address of any reliable firm of assassins, nose-slitters, garotters and poisoners I should be grateful to have it. I shall write a book about the BBC – you see if I don't! gr-r-r-r !!

Lewis never wrote such a book but he was quite right in thinking that there was a tale to tell, even if a rather different one. What emerges is a story of wartime broadcasting – at times heroic in proportion and at other times bordering on the farcical. From it comes the re-invention of religious broadcasting and the breaking down of old taboos. C.S. Lewis and Dorothy L. Sayers were in the vanguard alongside other literary figures like J.B. Priestley, George

Orwell, T.S. Eliot and J.R.R. Tolkien. The BBC had its own pioneers in the Director of Religious Broadcasting and his Assistant Director – Rev. James Welch and the Rev. Eric Fenn – and in Drama, its head Val Gielgud. Recognition for their contribution to the re-invention of religious broadcasting and drama is long overdue. Without their efforts, C.S. Lewis would not have written the broadcast talks that were to become the multi-million-selling classic *Mere Christianity*. We should not allow his later reputation to overshadow the short but hugely influential broadcasting career of C.S. Lewis had between 1941–1944. Without the BBC's influence, Dorothy L. Sayers would not have written her most important religious drama *The Man Born to be King*. The great flourishing of Christian apologetics owes much to the BBC's role as facilitator and innovator.

Arguably the best appreciation of the power of radio as a medium was written by J.B. Priestley in his introduction to the published edition of his *Postscripts* in December 1940, when he said 'a mere whisper over the air seems to start an avalanche'. He became fully aware of the staggering power and effect of broadcasting. After twenty years 'hard at it' trying to get through to the public mind, Priestley discovered that as a medium of communication, broadcasting made everything else in comparison seem like a secret society. The only people unaware of this, Priestley reckoned, was the War Cabinet. In his view, they did not realise that in the BBC 'we have something as important to us in this war as an army or navy or air force'. It was not just a battle for the mind and morale of a nation at war. For the religious broadcasters, it was a battle for the soul. The story is complex and fascinating. It begins on Friday 1 September 1939.

Justin Phillips

CHAPTER ONE

1 September 1939

∾⊶∾

On Friday 1 September 1939, the Reverend James Welch was sitting in studio 3E on the third floor of Broadcasting House.[1] The BBC's Director of Religious Broadcasting was conducting the daily act of worship in the studio especially designed for religious programmes. *The Daily Service* was broadcast on BBC radio each morning between 10.15 and 10.20. A slip of paper was quietly passed to him with some breaking news: 'Germany invaded Poland early this morning'. Welch knew exactly what he had to do. 'That paper was the signal to alter our service, and especially our prayers, to meet the wartime needs of our people. We broadcast a prayer for the people of Poland. We added a prayer for trust in God in all that might lie ahead.'[2]

Broadcasting House is the headquarters of the British Broadcasting Corporation, the BBC, situated at the top end of Regent Street where it meets Portland Place, adjacent to All Souls Church. The building itself is shaped like the stern of a huge ship. The offices run along the outside facing the street and the studios are positioned off corridors along the middle, well away from the noise of traffic. Studio 3E is tucked away in the middle of the building on the same floor as the Director-General's office.

The Daily Service went out live. This means that, unlike a pre-recorded programme, it was possible to change the content even as it was being broadcast on the air. James Welch responded immediately to the words he saw. There was no time to reflect on them or lay them to one side. He led the nation in prayer.

By five o'clock that day the BBC's emergency plans were in operation. As different departments dispersed across the country, religious broadcasting was on its way to its first wartime home in Bristol. It now faced its greatest challenge and in James Welch had a leader willing to take risks and to test new ideas. Welch was fully aware that the traditional programming offered by his department would not be sufficient in wartime. Such radical new circumstances would demand programmes that would attempt to deal with the toughest questions facing listeners as the possibility of war became a reality.

Though the horrors of the Great War of 1914–1918 may have given a shocking taste of what was to follow, nothing could have prepared the British people for the total devastation of the Second World War. It was to be waged not only on the battlefields, but on the streets and in the homes of ordinary people as they found that no one was out of reach of the German bombs. One of the most precious commodities was up-to-date and accurate information. It is impossible to over-estimate the importance of the role BBC Radio played during the war years.

The invasion of Poland had triggered the implementation of a whole series of contingency plans and decisions. One of these was to evacuate over one million children from London to the countryside, to protect them from the anticipated bombing raids that it was assumed would follow from Hitler's act of aggression. The six o'clock evening news gave warning that the evacuation was about to begin. All over Britain, every BBC transmitter station and office was opening sealed orders. In between records, listeners heard the staff announcer repeat the warnings and tell listeners to retune their radio to two designated wavelengths. At 8.15 p.m. the nation heard the BBC's new 'on-air' identification for the first time: 'This is the BBC Home Service'.[3]

The children evacuate the cities

In London, twelve railway stations were packed with children. The BBC reported their departure and later broadcast interviews with some of them once they had arrived. One cheerful boy used the BBC to send a message to his parents left behind in the city. 'Mum and Dad, don't get worried about us, we're all very happy here and I don't think anyone wants to go home yet.'[4] An American broadcasting network, CBS, had sent over its esteemed news correspondent Edward R. Murrow to direct its news coverage. His vivid reporting spoke of a silent city without its children. For six days he had not heard a single child's voice and it felt very strange.[5]

One of the missing voices belonged to Jill Freud (at that time called Jill Flewett).[6] Her school had carried out a full dress rehearsal for evacuation a year before in 1938. She was living in Barnes and at age twelve was evacuated with her two sisters, aged five and fifteen. Jill's mother was given twenty-four hours to make up her mind whether to let all of her children go. Jill recalls that 'at that time, I had no awareness at all of what it must have meant to them. I mean, cheerily waving goodbye and getting homesick but not thinking that I had a mother who didn't have a job and whose whole life was looking after us.'[7] She found herself billeted with two Unitarian sisters. It was another two years before she joined an Oxford household – that of C.S. Lewis.

By 2 September, the first evacuees had arrived in Oxford. C.S. Lewis described them in a letter to his brother, Warnie, as 'very nice, unaffected creatures and all most flatteringly delighted with their new surroundings. They're fond of animals which is a good thing.' Within a week the pleasure of the evacuees was beginning to wane. 'Modern children are poor creatures. They keep on asking "What shall we do now?" After being told to have a game of tennis or to mend their stockings or write home, when done, they just come looking for more ideas. Shades of our own childhood!' Lewis tells his brother, who had already been conscripted.[8] All men between the ages of eighteen and forty-one were liable for conscription into military service. By the end of 1939, one and a half million conscripts were in uniform. Lewis suspected he was too old for military service himself. Besides, although not a pacifist, fighting didn't excite him in the least: 'the flesh is weak and selfish and I think death wd be much better than to live through another war.'[9] As it was, his profession teaching at Oxford meant that he was not conscripted. Although he was appalled to find England at war with Germany again, he had no doubt that this was a righteous war and that he would do his duty to assist the war effort. It would also shake him out of what was becoming a bit of a rut. He wrote to his lifelong friend Arthur Greeves: 'I daresay for me, personally, it has come in the nick of time: I was just beginning to get too well settled in my profession, too successful, and probably self-complacent.'[10]

Lewis's time in Oxford was successful. His academic works and lively lectures attracted a large student following. In 1938 he began to diversify with his first venture into science fiction. *Out of the Silent Planet* spawned two sequels. In the autumn and winter of 1939, as the war began, Lewis was writing *The Problem of Pain*. It was this book which was to catch the eye of James Welch at the BBC. In the years to come C.S. Lewis would, through the BBC and the encouragement of Welch and his team, discover an entire new audience eager to hear what he had to say about the Christian faith.

BBC Television closed down

On Friday 1 September, the BBC's Director of Features and Drama, Val Gielgud, was about five minutes away from Broadcasting House in a rehearsal room. Val Gielgud had been born into a family with the theatre in its blood. The Director of Drama could boast the great actress Dame Ellen Terry (1848–1928) as his great-aunt, partner of the great actor Sir Henry Irving. His brother was an aspiring actor with a formidable reputation already, John Gielgud. Val was fully pre-occupied rehearsing a Somerset Maugham play,

The Circle. This was a rare venture for him into television. It was due to be broadcast the following Sunday.

Gielgud had not produced a full-length play for television before so this was a considerable challenge. Later, recalling the day, he said, 'I doubt if any member of the rehearsal group had their minds on the job or much hope that the play would be performed on 3 September'.[11] It wasn't. None the less, it was quite a shock when the phone rang to tell him that not only had his play been scrapped, but the BBC Television Service was to close down as well. The transmitter at Alexandra Palace in north London turned off. The long-planned-for BBC 'emergency period' had begun.

As the receiver was replaced, the cast looked at one another quite stunned. At that moment a BBC messenger arrived with some props for the play, including two tennis racquets and some tennis balls.[12] Whether they were ever retrieved from the rehearsal rooms in Marylebone Mews or if they were left behind as the last artefacts of the first era of British television, nobody could remember and nobody cared. The invasion of Poland had changed everything.

One of the first casualties of the war was Britain's fledgling television service, its wings clipped before it could fly. At the Coronation of King George VI in 1937, cameras were not allowed inside Westminster Abbey but the procession out of the Abbey was broadcast on television, with Freddie Grisewood providing the commentary, to an audience of 10,000 viewers. Despite the impact of this outside broadcast, take-up of television sets was slow. The number of sets sold by the end of 1937 was just over 2,000 – only 1,600 more than at the start of the year, despite a fall in prices of new sets. In 1938 sales began to pick up, aided by a large exhibition at London's Olympia and the Munich Crisis. Chamberlain's trip to retrieve his scrap of paper which convinced him that 'peace for our time' had been achieved – the hollow triumph of appeasement policy – sold more sets in three months than in the previous history of television.

At this stage in the medium's development, Britain was still ahead of the United States in the service it provided. All that changed in 1939. On the morning of 1 September, the engineer in charge of the BBC's transmitter at Alexandra Palace in north London received a message that the transmitter should be closed by noon. It was too good a direction-finder for enemy aircraft. So the last item to be televised turned out to be a Mickey Mouse film. Professor Asa Briggs records that the last words were spoken in the style of Greta Garbo: 'Ah tahnk ah kees you now'.[13] There wasn't even any closing announcement. In the United States NBC had revealed in 1939 the launch of its television service, two hours per week, as the first step towards making 'the art of television available to the public'. American television never looked back. British television was put in the deep freeze for the duration of the war.

As shortages began to bite, newsprint became scarcer. This meant that not only were newspapers bringing news to their readers later than they could hear it on the BBC airwaves, but the space available for in-depth reporting had to be restricted. The only restriction on space available on the airwaves was what the broadcasters chose to put into the radio schedule. So a fifteen-minute news bulletin could cover a wide range of stories up to one day before the newspapers could report the same events. This gave radio a huge competitive edge. This was to become of vital importance. There was no television to watch. All cinemas, theatres and other places of entertainment were closed down until further notice. Cinema newsreels were to become a valuable source of news later in the war, but it was often a case of too little and too late. So radio came into its own. The family would gather around the receiver to listen to news bulletins for the most up-to-date dispatches. It was a war in which radio was to become a most potent weapon for delivering information and for the exchange of ideas, within clearly defined limits.

The BBC was well prepared for war. Under the emergency procedures plans were already in place, and many staff would be called into service and others would be moved to a new base to continue their work but under wartime conditions. It was assumed

London would be deluged with bombs and that broadcasting from city centres would be too great a risk. Most of the programme divisions were to be scattered about the country.

Drama transferred to Evesham

Val Gielgud's own department – Drama and Features – together with the BBC Repertory Company, was booked for Evesham, referred to by the code-name of Hogsnorton. Its identity was veiled in secrecy for some time, or so it was believed. A BBC engineer had a different tale. This man had been to Berlin during the early summer of 1939 for a German Radio Exhibition. He asked to see a new gadget and was refused, since all examples had been issued to secret German radio stations. 'And by the way,' added the Reich official, 'how is your little secret hideout in the Vale of Evesham getting along?'[14] Drama would come into its own in the war years, providing an increasingly popular service to listeners and giving playwrights like Dorothy L. Sayers the opportunity to re-invent religious drama.

At the time Sayers, already a celebrated novelist, was seeing the success at His Majesty's Theatre in Whitehall of her most recent play. This was a contemporary version of the theme of Marlowe's great study of good and evil, the story of Faust. Written against the background of the failure of Chamberlain's peace initiative, its resonance was powerful and prophetic. She was invited by the War Office to serve on the Authors' Planning Committee of the Ministry of Information. This was a small group built around three women writers – Dorothy Sayers and her friends Helen Simpson and Muriel St Clare Byrne. In forming this group they hoped that they would gain some opportunity 'for doing something to disseminate encouraging ideas about war aims, reconstruction and so forth'.[15] Three days after the declaration of war Sayers and Simpson wrote to *The Times*, urging that the churches stay open during the war, even if theatres were forced to close.

BBC overseas services

One of the most important roles the BBC was to play during the war was the work of its overseas services, broadcasting news of the conflict back to the occupied countries and to Germany itself. It was a key element of the propaganda effort, and in countries like France was to play a vital part in rallying resistance to Nazi occupation. One of the most talented producers within the German service was the idiosyncratic David Graham. He had made his name at Oxford University in the Union, where he had devised the notorious motion passed by the Oxford Union in 1933 'That this House will in no circumstances fight for its King and Country'. The Oxford Union debating society carried the motion by 275 votes to 173.

A group of Oxford undergraduates, spurred on by a national newspaper, ripped out the record of the debate from the minute book in protest. They needn't have bothered. David Graham, who had seconded the motion, reconstructed the minutes from memory.[16] Graham himself was no pacifist but he did have a fiercely independent spirit. His fluent German was of great value to the BBC who recruited him as a part of a small team to broadcast to Germany. David Graham recalled those days in September 1939 working alongside his colleague Maurice Latey.

> Of all that we ever did together what I remember most vividly is the week we spent together just before Hitler's war began, cooped in a small studio cubicle with one disc turntable in Broadcasting House, doing nothing else but listening hour after hour to the BBC's excellent recordings of Hitler's speeches, and marking the bits that sounded silliest and most obviously untruthful of all if we played them back to the Germans, probably all too soon.

Graham and Latey proudly played their first selection to the person seconded from the Foreign Office of the British Government to liase with the BBC. It went down a storm with him but not, alas, with their line manager in the BBC, the director of external broadcasting. Graham continues the story . . .

> On September 1st 1939, when Hitler's aircraft had been bombing Poland since dawn, Maurice Latey and Leonard Miall and I thought the time had now come to let the Germans have a first selection that evening, to encourage them to take Hitler's next bombast with a grain of salt. And the F.O. representative agreed heartily. Not so the BBC. The director of external broadcasting, who had not been near us for weeks, called in early on the evening of Sept. 1st, saying 'I thought I would like to see what you are planning today for Germany tonight'. He began to read my English translation and he frowned. 'Oh no,' he said. 'The BBC can't take responsibility for saying this kind of thing about the head of a friendly state.' 'But, Sir,' I said, 'the Foreign Office man likes it very much, and says it's just the thing for tonight.' 'But surely you know,' said my boss severely, 'the BBC does not take orders from the Foreign Office.'[17]

So instead of broadcasting the selected extracts of Hitler's speeches back to Germany, the BBC played Mozart because nothing else was ready. The government were too timid to broadcast it on the day Germany invaded Poland. But after war was declared, it was exactly what was wanted. The programme which showed Hitler making a fool and a liar of himself out of his own mouth came into its own two days later.

On 31 August, Adolf Hitler had issued his 'directive Number 1 for the Conduct of the War'. It determined that the attack on Poland should take place on 1 September. Inserted in red pencil was 'Time of attack – 04.45'. And that is how it happened. Poland was attacked by Germany at dawn.

The mobilisation of British forces was ordered during the morning. Prime Minister Neville Chamberlain told Winston

Churchill that he saw no hope of averting a war with Germany and that he would form a War Cabinet of ministers, without departments, to conduct it. He invited Churchill to join it. Churchill penned a note to Chamberlain after midnight pointing out that the War Cabinet was too old, averaging over sixty-four. Churchill proposed adding Sinclair and Eden, the first forty-nine and the second only forty-two, to bring the average down to fifty-seven. Churchill recommended there be a Joint Declaration of War at latest when Parliament met on the Saturday afternoon. He heard nothing from Chamberlain the whole day.

There was a 'short but very fierce' debate in the House of Commons that night.[18] The mood was one of united resolution not to fail in our obligations to Poland and therefore to declare war. A series of ultimatums had been presented to Germany at 9.30 p.m. on 1 September and a second and final ultimatum at 9 a.m. on 3 September.

The BBC broadcast early on the 3rd that the Prime Minister would speak on the radio at 11.15 a.m. As it now seemed certain that war would be immediately declared by Great Britain and also by France, Winston Churchill prepared a short speech appropriate for such 'a solemn and awful moment in our lives and history'.

At 11.15 the nation gathered around their wireless sets to hear the solemn announcement by Prime Minister Neville Chamberlain.

I am speaking to you from the Cabinet Room of 10 Downing Street. This morning the British Ambassador in Berlin handed the German government a final note stating that unless we heard from them by eleven o'clock that they were prepared at once to withdraw their troops from Poland, a state of war would exist between us. I have to tell you now that no such undertaking has been received and that consequently this country is at war with Germany . . . You may be taking your part in the fighting Services or as a volunteer in one of the branches of the Civil Defence. If so, you will report for duty in accordance with the instructions you received. You may be engaged in work essential to the prosecution of war for the maintenance of the life of the people – in factories, in transport, in public utility concerns, or in the supply of other necessities of life. If so, it is of vital importance that you should carry on with your jobs.

The Second World War had begun. There was no escape now from taking on the might of Nazi Germany. The British people half expected a replica of the 1914–1918 war. Millions of gas masks had been distributed to protect people from gas attack. Air-raid shelters were being built in back gardens. Cinemas, theatres and the BBC's television service were closed down. To find out what was going on, people listened to the radio and the programmes provided on the BBC's Home Service.

Notes

[1] BBC Year Book 1945, p. 41

[2] Ibid.

[3] Hickman, Tom, *What did you do in the War, Auntie?* BBC Books, 1995, p. 9

[4] BBC Radio Collection, *75 Years of the BBC*, CD1 track 35

[5] Finkelstein, Norman H., *With Heroic Truth – the life of Edward G. Murrow*, Clarion Books, New York, 1997, p. 67

[6] Jill Freud's full title is Lady Freud. She is married to Sir Clement Freud, writer, broadcaster, caterer and former Member of Parliament

[7] Interview with Jill Freud, 19 November 1999

[8] Lewis W.H., *Memoir of CS Lewis* contained in *Letters of CS Lewis*, revised edition edited by Walter Hooper, Harcourt and Brace edition, 1993, letter to W.H. Lewis, 18 September 1939

[9] Letter to Dom Bede Griffiths O.S.B. from Magdalen College 8 May 1939, in Hooper, *Letters*.

[10] 15 September 1939 in Lewis, C.S., *They Stand Together*, the letters of C.S. Lewis to Arthur Greeves (1914-63), ed. Walter Hooper, Collins, London, 1979, p. 485

[11] This next section draws heavily on Val Gielgud's two memoirs of wartime broadcasting, viz. Gielgud, Val, *Years of the Locust*, Nicholson & Watson, 1945, pp. 166–182, and his essay in the BBC Year Book 1945, pp.53–55

[12] Ibid.

[13] Briggs, Asa, *The History of Broadcasting in the United Kingdom Volume 3, The War of Words*, Oxford University Press, Oxford, New York, 1995, Appendix B, p. 666

[14] Gielgud, *Years of the Locust*.

[15] Letter to Dr J.H. Oldham, 2 October 1939, Reynolds, Barbara ed., *The Letters of Dorothy Sayers Volume II 1937–1943 From Novelist to Playwright*, St. Martin's Press, New York, 1997

[16] Obituary of David Graham from *The Daily Telegraph* 26 August, 1999

[17] This memoir comes from David Graham's notes for a tribute to his BBC colleague Maurice Latey, 1991, provided by his son Christopher Graham, the Secretary of the BBC until 2000.

[18] Churchill, W.S., *The Second World War* Volume One, *The Gathering Storm*, The Reprint Society edition, 1950, p. 328

CHAPTER TWO

The BBC's Early Vision

∾∾

From its foundation in 1922 as the private British Broadcasting Company by a small consortium of wireless manufacturers, and subsequent incorporation as the British Broadcasting Corporation in 1927, the BBC has grown to be a world leader with an unparalleled reputation for public service and impartiality. At the time of its birth many saw radio as merely a technical means to keep ships in touch with shore. Few could have foreseen the impact which broadcasting would come to have on the lives of people the world over, but the founders of the BBC sensed the unlimited potential of a whole new medium of communication.

Before the BBC was funded by a public licence fee, it generated income by selling licences. In its first two years, the new-born BBC attracted revenue by selling licences with the earliest BBC logo to manufacturers of crystal sets, the most popular domestic radio receivers. By 1927 the Company had established itself as an integral part of national life. It had built the biggest transmitter in the world at Daventry. From here it transmitted its signals to virtually the whole nation from a height of 160 metres.[1] The BBC broadcast King George V's words from the British Empire exhibition in Wembley in 1924. It became a vital, if then too progovernment, source of news during the General Strike of 1926, coming through a bruising conflict with the politicians. Five years after its birth, the BBC was granted its first Royal Charter and was no longer a company but a Corporation. There were then over 2 million people with licences to receive the broadcasts and more were signing up by up to one thousand per day.[2]

John Reith – creator of the BBC

The BBC began with only four members of staff led by a 33-year-old Scottish engineer called John Reith. From the day he started work, Reith became the architect of public service broadcasting in Britain. Until the day he left the BBC on 20 June 1938, the Corporation bore his indelible stamp. Rarely has the personality of one man been so closely identified with a national service as Sir John Reith was with the BBC. The service reflected his character and his views. His autocratic style, his high principles and his vision for the BBC as a civilising force in Britain gave the English language a new word – 'Reithian'. It stands for quality and integrity. *The Times* acknowledged his unique contribution: 'The BBC is not without its critics, and never should be; but Sir John can leave Broadcasting House with the knowledge that his pioneer work, now brought to maturity, has not to wait for the approval of posterity'.[3]

The Reithian – the three pillars on which the BBC was founded – are education, information and entertainment. As early as 1924, in a book called *Broadcast Over Britain*, John Reith wrote:

> I think it will be admitted by all that to have exploited so great a scientific invention for the purpose and pursuit of entertainment alone would have been a prostitution of its powers and an insult to the character and intelligence of the people.

For Reith, it was completely natural that a broadcasting institution that aspired to high ideals with a sense of public service should have what he called 'an instinctive sense of fitness'.[4] The earliest mention of these three aims of BBC broadcasting – education, information and entertainment – occurs near the beginning of the 1936 Royal Charter. After a paragraph mentioning that more than seven and a half million people in the UK held broadcasting licences, it states that

> whereas in view of the widespread interest which is thereby shown to be taken by Our People in the Broadcasting Service and of the great value of the Service as a means of information, education and entertainment, we deem it desirable that the Service should continue to be developed and exploited to the best advantage and in the national interest.[5]

Reith himself was a powerful figure. One of his successors as Director-General of the BBC, John Birt, was to describe him in a speech to mark the BBC's 75th Anniversary in 1999 as 'a zealous, high-minded, deeply religious, authoritarian, driven, unclubbable, difficult, battle-scarred, lonely, self-absorbed, inwardly-tormented but remarkable and visionary Scot'.[6] Reith shaped the character and ethos of the Corporation. He instilled his own values into the BBC and more than any other Director-General in its history, shaped the whole organisation. For him, religion was an integral part of the broadcasting mix. The early BBC fully adopted Christian values.

A good seed sown . . .

This is evident in the architecture and design of Broadcasting House, the world's first purpose-built broadcasting centre. To this day, the moment you walk through the heavy bronze swing doors, you are confronted with the explicit statement of its values. Look up and you will see the dedication of the building to Almighty God inscribed in gold letters in Latin on its walls. Christianity is central to the BBC's ethos.

DEO OMNIPOTENTI
TEMPLUM HOC ARTIUM ET MUSARUM ANNO
DOMINI MDMXXXI RECTORE JOHANNI REITH
PRIMI DEDICANT GUBERNATORES PRECANTES UT
MESSEM BONAM BONA PROFERAT SEMENTIS UT
IMMUNDA OMNIA ET INIMICA PACI EXPEL-
LANTUR UT QUAECUNQUE PULCHRA SUNT ET
SINCERA QUAECUNQUE BONAE FAMAE AD HAEC
AVREM INCLINANS POPULUS VIRTUTIS ET SAPI-
ENTIAE SEMITAM INSISTAT

The translation of the inscription in English (also displayed on a marble plaque in the right-hand corner of the entrance hall) is:

This Temple of the Arts and Muses is dedicated to Almighty God by the first Governors of Broadcasting in the year 1931, Sir John Reith being Director-General. It is their prayer that good seed sown may bring forth a good harvest and that the people, inclining their ear to whatsoever things are beautiful and honest and of good report, may tread the path of wisdom and uprightness.

The key word is 'whatsoever'. Underneath the BBC's coat of arms, or to give it its formal name, The Armorial Bearings and Badge of the British Broadcasting Corporation (1945), and on display in the Board Room of the BBC Governors, is the single Latin word 'Quaecumque', which means 'whatsoever'. Both the first Governors' inscription and the BBC's motto are inspired by the letter of St Paul: 'Finally, brethren, whatsoever things are true, whatsoever things are honest, whatsoever things are just, whatsoever things are pure, whatsoever things are lovely, whatsoever things are of good report; if there be any virtue, and if there be any praise, think on these things'.[7]

At the back of the entrance hall, adjacent to the lifts, is a magnificent sculpture of *The Sower* by one of Britain's most celebrated stone-carvers, Eric Gill. Below it is the Latin inscription for 'God gives the increase'. Seed-sowing is the earliest metaphor for broadcasting. Just as a farmer sows the seed, so the broadcaster sows seeds of ideas and imagination. Eric Gill used 'broadcast' in its original derivation. *The Sower* is one who 'broadly casts' the seed across the field, sowing ideas and reaping the crop of all those qualities described in the inscription taken from St Paul.[8] From its earliest days, British public service broadcasting was imbued with the idea of sowing the 'good seed' of Christian values as far as the radio waves would carry them.

'Ooh I luv 'em sir'

In the Thirties, BBC radio programmes began to branch out in many new directions. There was a concerted effort to reach new listeners and to broaden the base of the BBC. Entertainment was the key. For those who did not appreciate the extraordinary ambition of Sir Henry Wood's Promenade Concerts or the growing popularity of opera, briefly boosted by a government supplementary grant to the BBC from 1931 to 1932,[9] there was a galaxy of dance bands to explore. This was the heyday of the big-band leader. Conductors like Ambrose, Geraldo, Jack Payne, Henry Hall and others became household names.[10] Geraldo could easily fill the St George's Hall, just the other side of All Souls' Church from Broadcasting House and opposite the Langham Hotel. BBC Variety had come under Val Gielgud's leadership as well as Drama, until the two genres were separated in 1933.

In Eric Maschwitz, the BBC had someone to lead its variety programmes who was, in his own right, an impresario and writer of popular music of great distinction. BBC Variety ploughed a well-worn furrow with a heavy dependence upon music-hall entertainment. In Professor Asa Briggs' dismissive phrase, 'some of the programmes were not so much sowing seed as gathering the last harvest from the nineteenth-century music hall'.[11]

Maschwitz's heart was in popular music. He wrote the lyrics for *A Nightingale Sang in Berkeley Square* and *These Foolish Things*. The actress Hermione Gingold, Eric's wife, remembers rushing from the BBC where she was doing a radio play to catch the final curtain of Eric's musical *Balalaika*. 'I discovered Eric at the back of the stalls shouting "Author Author!" and having started it off, rushing round to take a bow.'[12]

Maschwitz was a legendary figure whose legacy includes many theatrical anecdotes. The most famous concerns his musical *Goodnight Vienna*. Maschwitz was driving back from Brighton and passed through Lewisham in south London and noticed that a production of *Goodnight Vienna* was playing at the Lewisham Hippodrome. He stopped the car and went in to see how well it was going down. 'So how's it doing then?' he asked the manager. The manager looked a bit crest-fallen.

'Well, how can I put it, Sir? *Goodnight Vienna* is doing as well in Lewisham as you'd expect *Goodnight Lewisham* to do in Vienna,' came the reply.[13]

Maschwitz went to MGM and Hollywood, leaving it to his successor John Watt to move light entertainment out of the music-hall era. He developed some of the most successful radio comedy formats in its history, most notably *Band Waggon*. This situation comedy starred Richard 'Stinker' Murdoch and 'Big-hearted' Arthur Askey. They broadcast from an imaginary flat on the roof of Broadcasting House, that many listeners were convinced was real. What they offered was quick-fire humour and hilarious characters – like the landlady's daughter Nausea Bagwash. It was a welcome antidote to the growing crisis in Europe in 1938. One of the regular features on *Band Waggon* was *Chestnut Corner* – with a succession of schoolboy humour. Here's a flavour of the quick-fire repartee and gags.

Murdoch: 'Ladies and Gentlemen. *Band Waggon* brazenly presents *Chestnut Corner*. Or the things we come out with'.

Murdoch: 'My wife's a decided blonde.'

Askey: 'I know, I was with her when she decided.'

Askey: 'Excuse me sir, but can you spare me a shilling for a cup of coffee?'

Murdoch: 'Shilling, that's lot for a cup of coffee isn't it?'

Askey: 'Listen, are you trying to trying to tell me how to run my business?'

Murdoch: 'What can be nicer than a nightingale in a tree?'

Askey: 'A lark in a field.'

Murdoch: 'How did you lose your hair?'

Askey: 'Worry.'

Murdoch: 'What did you worry about?'

Askey: 'Losing my hair.'

Murdoch: 'How are you getting on in your new house?'

Askey: 'Oh, fine. I've furnished one room by collecting coupons out of soap packets.'

Murdoch: 'That's a grand idea – why not furnish all the other rooms in the same way?'

Askey: 'I can't.'

Murdoch: 'Why not?'

Askey: 'They're full of soap.' (prolonged laughter)

Askey: 'I've come to change my name.'

Murdoch: 'That'll be an expensive business, what is your name?'

Askey: 'Harry Smells.'

Murdoch: 'Ooh I'm not surprised, what do you want to change it to?'

Askey: 'Charlie Smells.'

Murdoch: 'And that Ladies and Gentlemen concludes *Chestnut Corner* for this evening. Later on we hope to bring you some even better old jokes.'[14]

The other classic comedy that captured the imagination of the British public in that last pre-war summer was *ITMA – It's That Man Again*, starring Tommy Handley. This was devised over tea and coffee at the Langham Hotel across the road from Broadcasting House. The producer and script-writer got together with Tommy Handley to devise a gag show with lots of puns, often based around the armed services and innuendo. It gave the nation a host of catchphrases and favourite characters. For the next fifty years, cleaners and charladies were to be called Mrs Mopp, after the character portrayed by Dorothy Summers with her catchphrase 'Can I do you now sir?' A typical exchange went like this:

Handley: 'Here she is, Mrs Mopp the Private's enterprise . . .'

Mrs Mopp: 'Ooh I luv em sir . . .'

Handley: 'I know you do, you old camp follower. If you're not swinging the leg you're presenting arms . . .'

Handley: 'Well how are you getting on with your Sergeant Major Mrs M?'

Mrs Mopp: 'Ooh he's as saucy as ever sir. Why, only yesterday he wanted to see my work ticket.'

Handley: 'Then he expected you to pass out, eh?

Mrs Mopp: 'I repelled his invasion exercises.'

Handley: 'What did you do, take off your gas mask?'

Mrs Mopp: 'I've another follower now sir. He's a gunner.'

Handley: 'Is he? I expect you make him come out of his shell.'

Mrs Mopp: 'Oh yes sir, he says I'm a wicked little barrage!'

Pre-war BBC religion

Variety was to come into its own soon enough but in this pre-war period, religious programming still accounted for a larger share of weekly broadcasting than features or drama. There was no Sunday morning programming other than the religious service and the weather forecast. Sunday was set aside as a special day quite distinctive from the rest of the week. From April 1938 there was a slight loosening of the schedule in response to overseas competition. Both Radio Normandie from northern France and Radio Luxembourg were beginning to erode audiences. The Churches were consulted and the advisory body recommended that the BBC be allowed to change its policy. What James Welch was to describe as the 'strict Puritan Sunday' could no longer be enforced.[15]

Quite apart from its dominance of the Sunday schedule, religious broadcasting permeated weekday programming like a river. In peacetime, the BBC broadcast the *Daily Service* on weekdays, a talk to schools on the Bible or Church history on Mondays, cathedral evensong on Wednesdays, and a mid-week service on Thursdays. The weekday service was already one of the BBC's longest-running programmes. Choral evensong was also an established fixture. It was first broadcast live from Westminster Abbey on Thursday 7 October 1926.[16] Sunday was the big day but religious programmes in peacetime were almost entirely confined to the broadcasting of services, talks and church music.[17] Its contributors were invariably men of the cloth – vicars, priests and bishops. Occasionally there were religious plays. James Welch's predecessor as Director of Religious Broadcasting, the Reverend F.A. Iremonger, given that title in 1933, began to reduce the reliance on the omnipresent cleric and introduce lay speakers. The most notable of these was C.H. Dodd, who later went on to write such Christian classics as *The Apostolic Preaching and its Developments* and *The Founder of Christianity.*

Iremonger succeeded in establishing a very considerable degree of confidence with the Churches through very tactful handling of the Central Religious Advisory Committee. This was a representative body of senior churchmen from different denominations who acted as the BBC's advisors on religious broadcasting. The BBC's role at that time was essentially to 'eavesdrop' on church services. The function of broadcasting was simply to put a microphone at the front of a place of worship and to broadcast whatever it recorded, enabling those unable to attend to listen in.

The only exceptions to this were programmes broadcast from

studios or from the BBC's neighbouring Church in London, All Souls, Langham Place, like the *Daily Service*. The *New Every Morning* book of prayers and the *Epilogue* to close the day's broadcasts were other innovations. This was the inheritance received by James Welch, Director of Religion and his Assistant Director, Reverend Eric Fenn.[18]

Eric Fenn was a Minister of the English Presbyterian Church who had built up a formidable reputation before the war as an activist in the SCM – Student Christian Movement – and as an ecumenist, committed to bringing Churches closer together. He helped to set up the international Oxford Conference of Life and Work in July 1937 on 'Church, Community and State', from which was to emerge the World Council of Churches after the war. Fenn was then one of a whole young generation of highly capable Christians committed to the larger ecumenical cause.

Later he was to become C.S. Lewis's producer. Fenn was well aware of the suspicion with which many Church leaders viewed the new upstart of radio. It is no wonder that he was to forge such a close relationship with C.S. Lewis, who shared with him a desire to find the common ground in Christian belief which would unite rather than divide. The establishment consensus felt that the Church had a protected status beyond the reach of broadcasters. Christian belief should not be challenged on the air. The last thing expected of religious broadcasting was that it should question the status quo or stimulate controversy. Welch and Fenn rejected this retro-suppressive view. They wanted the Christian gospel to be a compelling force in changing lives. They believed that Christianity had something vital to say about the state of man and the future of society. They had no time for 'cosy Christianity'. In C.S. Lewis they detected a soul mate.

Eric Fenn attributed the Church's attitude to fear:

> It was partly that they were terrified of this new instrument.
> It was all very odd, you see. They were all brought up in
> the cat's-whisker era and didn't take broadcasting seriously

and then found it intruding into their own affairs and rather got paralysed by it. What Iremonger did was to persuade them that this was an instrument they could use.[19]

It was the appointment of James Welch as Director of Religious Broadcasting that paved the way to the renewal of spiritual pro-gramming Welch had much greater ambitions than his predecessor. He read anthropology at Cambridge University and then theology. He travelled to Nigeria and returned to complete a post-graduate course, culminating in a PhD in anthropology. Welch went to the Church of England's teacher-training college in York. There he became a close friend and devout follower of William Temple, the Archbishop of York, who was an inspirational leader and brilliant communicator. York itself became a centre for those who wanted to promote the ecumenical aspect of Christian faith and belief. Welch also became involved in the League of Nations movement just before the war, pre-cursor to the United Nations.

All of this gave him a burning conviction to get the people of the country to realise that the Church was 'more than just a pious institution, but had something to say to the life of the nation as a whole'.[20] If it had nothing relevant to contribute, then Welch felt it had failed. His passionate concern was that the Churches should make a much more vital and valuable contribution to society by using broadcasting in the right way.

The task and the tone were set on the first Sunday of the war. The religious broadcasters had been whisked out of London in 'a frantic state, a state of the jitters'.[21] Nobody knew what was going to happen and so everyone was prepared for the worst. The BBC's contingency plans worked on the basis that the first thing that would happen was that London would be bombed. That Sunday, the Archbishop of Canterbury, Cosmo Lang, was persuaded to come down to Bristol and to broadcast, much against his will. In the lis-tening room were the religious producers and some from secular branches of the BBC. All were hoping to hear a message to fit the crisis, one that would lift the spirits.

Alas, their hopes were in vain. No such message came. What Archbishop Lang had to say was, according to Fenn, 'completely vapid and totally irrelevant, we were very much disappointed'.[22]

It was a difficult if not disastrous beginning. Here was the BBC's religious department facing its toughest challenge and finding that on perhaps the most important act of worship broadcast for many years, for which they anticipated a massive audience, they felt badly let down by the Archbishop of Canterbury.

For the next two days the team discussed what they could do to try to make amends. It was more than damage limitation, it was a question of establishing the credibility of the department to respond to the mood of the nation. Fortunately for Welch and Fenn an early opportunity arose. The usual weekly film preview slot was vacant. The closure of public entertainment centres, cinemas and theatres, meant the BBC had nothing left to review. Welch made up his mind. 'Eric, you must do something on Thursday.'

So Eric Fenn took over the film slot and gave a short address. 'I tried to say some of the things I felt the Archbishop should have said, which was a bit of an impertinence, but there it was.' Fenn's starting point was that the British people might now feel that God had let them down. They might feel that . . .

> because this war has come, faith is in vain. *That* we must put right. Secondly, we know that we're going to be faced with large-scale sudden death. We must, therefore, come to terms with death if we're going to survive at all. And thirdly, because of the enormous increase in understanding between Christians across national barriers, we must hang on to this ecumenical vision of the church as somehow spanning even the most awful division of war and coming out the other side in some way.[23]

What was happening to BBC religious programmes was a microcosm of a much bigger problem. All the contingency plans and preparations in advance of the declaration of war had assumed that from the first day, there would be fighting. Therefore, with the expectation of immediate hostilities from day one, the BBC's programme producers had been dispersed across the country. Government restrictions were in full force. People walked around with gas masks ready expecting imminent air raids. The blitzkrieg was expected to be followed up by air and sea invasion. In reality, nothing happened. The war was taking place somewhere else, but not yet in England. A state of war existed all right, but at home, life seemed to be continuing as normal. What was abnormal was that places of public entertainment were closed. The writer and playwright George Bernard Shaw was scathing in his criticism of this decision, calling it a 'masterstroke of unimaginative stupidity'.[24] Only churches and pubs stayed open.

This was the great opportunity for BBC radio to step into the vacuum. Instead, it found it was driving away listeners because of restrictions on output and the first impact of censorship. The schedule was pared down to the bare essentials, it seemed at the time. The two wavelengths were kept clear for continuous light music, interrupted only by news bulletins, *The Daily Service*, which was to provide spiritual comfort and, rather curiously perhaps in the circumstances, *Children's Hour*. At this moment, one week after war had been declared, only four people were allowed on the air to fill religious slots. James Welch and Eric Fenn were two of them. The others were the Dean of Bristol and the Rev. Swann of St Mary Redcliffe, a local vicar in Bristol. It was only a temporary measure until it was clear what was going to happen.

For the first months of the War, a nation reliant on radio for information, with nine million radio licences issued (about 73 per cent of households), was stuck with a dull diet of government public information, religious and children's programming and some music.[25] It doesn't take a lot of imagination to realise that many of these radio sets would be on all day in the background so that nobody missed the latest public service announcement such as, in the worst-case scenario, a report of a German invasion of Britain.

The sinking of a passenger liner in the Irish Sea by a German sub-marine the day after Chamberlain's broadcast did little to steady people's nerves.

Not since the Norman invasion in the eleventh century had Britain suffered occupation by enemy forces. England enjoyed a long history of repelling the invader from the Spanish Armada of Elizabeth's reign to the forces of Napoleon in the first decade of the nineteenth century. But this time, the danger seemed real enough. Yet the ten news bulletins each day struggled to fill the air-time. This period, known as 'the phoney war', lasted for seven months. And the BBC was in danger of killing its audience by boredom.

The listener had to endure at least one hour of public announcements every day, pep talks by Ministers, hundreds of gramophone records and undiluted doses of organ music. In the Concert Hall in the basement of Broadcasting House, the BBC pipe organ was given its sternest test – 23 sessions of organist Sandy Macpherson in the first week of war and 22 the following week. If it was tough for him playing to fill up time, often without scores, it was even tougher on the listeners. The *Radio Times*, with classic understatement, noted that 'Sandy Macpherson is having a busy time at the BBC Theatre organ'.[26]

It did not take long for the press to turn against the BBC. The Sunday papers in September started the backlash. The *Sunday Times* accused the BBC of pouring into the air 'an endless stream of trivialities and sillinesses, apparently labouring under the delusion that in any time of crisis the public becomes just one colossal moron'. The *Sunday Pictorial* was harsher still. 'For God's sake, how long is the BBC to be allowed to broadcast its travesty of a programme which goes under the name of entertainment?'

Soon other journals joined the campaign. The *Musical Times* declared: 'No emergency could justify such programme poverty'. By the end of September even Parliament was joining in, but doing nothing to help. 'I am not a habitual listener,' future peace-time Prime Minister Clement Atlee confessed, 'but I must say that at times I feel depressed when I listen in.'

Having gone onto a war footing, the BBC found it harder to go into reverse. Listeners' goodwill and BBC staff morale were both suffering. It was exasperating for staff to be compelled to wait for an explosion of listener indignation in the press to confirm what they were already saying before any change in attitude took place. Non-news staff were frustrated that the broadcasting of plays would be considered superfluous. When the department complained, it received the less than pleasing response that space might be available occasionally for a play not lasting more than half an hour 'rather along *Children's Hour*' lines. But attitudes did change within the BBC hierarchy. The Governors recognised that the BBC was failing in its duty to inform, to educate and to entertain and persuaded the government to loosen its control. The programme balance was eventually restored.

Notes

[1] Cain, John, *The BBC: 70 Years of Broadcasting*, BBC, London, 1992, p. 17
[2] Ibid., p. 21
[3] BBC Handbook 1939, p. 9
[4] Briggs, Asa, *The BBC: The First Fifty Years*, Oxford University Press, Oxford, New York, 1985, p.131
[5] Researched by BBC Written Archives Centre, Caversham Park
[6] Birt, John, speech 21 January, 1998
[7] Philippians, 4: 8
[8] This follows the same biblical imagery that the first Governors derived from Paul's epistle. Eric Gill's *Sower* is based upon the parable told by Jesus Christ in Mark 4: 1-9.
[9] Briggs, op. cit. p. 125
[10] Confirmed by Douglas V. Osborne in interview 29 May 2000
[11] Briggs, op. cit. p. 128
[12] Sherrin, Ned, *Ned Sherrin's theatrical anecdotes*, Virgin Books, 1991, p. 177
[13] The author first heard the story brilliantly told by another BBC luminary, James Moir, Controller of BBC Radio 2, himself a former BBC Light Entertainment executive, at the Radio Festival in 1994. As it is a story passed on from generation to generation of BBC light entertainment heads, I've given the definitive James Moir version.

[14] BBC Radio Collection, *75 Years of the BBC,* CD1, track 31

[15] Briggs, op. cit. p.130

[16] The first broadcast was on the National Programme. It celebrated its 70th anniversary with a live broadcast from Westminster Abbey on 9 October 1996. It was then the longest-running outside broadcast radio series in the history of broadcasting. For 70 years, after an initial period of a repeated weekly broadcast from the Abbey, worship had been relayed both live and recorded from cathedrals, college chapels, parish, collegiate and monastic churches throughout Britain and in recent years from overseas as well. Since 1982 it has been broadcast on BBC Radio 3 and continues to this day.

[17] Welch, James, *Religious Broadcasting in Wartime,* BBC Year Book 1945, p.42 ff.

[18] The BBC staff list of 1939 refers to James Welch as the 'Director of Religion', and Eric Fenn as his assistant. Internally and in correspondence this title was referred to either as 'Director of Religious Broadcasting' or 'Director of Religious Programmes' (abbreviated to 'DRP').

[19] Interview with Eric Fenn by Frank Gillard for the BBC Oral History Archive, 4 July 1986

[20] Ibid.

[21] Ibid.

[22] Ibid.

[23] Ibid.

[24] Briggs, op. cit p.176

[25] Hickman, Tom, *What did you do in the War, Auntie?,* BBC Books, 1995, p.14

[26] Briggs, op. cit

CHAPTER THREE

Censorship Kicks In

The BBC took its time to respond to rapidly changing events. However, when it did defend itself from the growing public criticism, it acknowledged that it was failing to entertain. Even its news service was struggling to meet expectations. One of the difficulties was that the flow of news was not coming through official channels as promised. Censorship was 'petty, absurd, tyrannical' according to one American journalist.[1] The BBC's own correspondents were managing to get news through from France and from neutral countries. However, by the end of 1939, a more recognisable schedule of wartime broadcasting was being established with increased emphasis on entertainment and live reports.

Outside broadcasts added a welcome dimension. They introduced more live concerts and entertainment and religious worship services. BBC broadcasting in foreign languages began to expand as well, giving the government a potential propaganda tool and providing the BBC with more outlets. The work of the external services is not without its share of mystery as well. One of the issues historians face today is why, as the war progressed, the general public was not better informed by press and broadcasting about the systematic extermination of the Jews of Europe under Nazism? There are a number of contributory factors identified by Professor Jean Seaton of the University of Westminster.[2] There was an in-built scepticism towards atrocity stories, a legacy of the First World War. The style, stance and tone of the BBC's broadcasting militated against it. There was resistance to broadcasting what might sound like overt and exaggerated propaganda. Seaton explains . . .

> The dominant style that evolved of the British at war was one of level-headed, stubborn endeavour. The emphasis was on 'humble, everyday heroism'[3] . . . This was self-consciously pitched against Teutonic images of romantic heroism. Such a style was singularly unsuited to the transmission of knowledge about the kind of horrors that were taking place in the ghettoes. If the war was not exactly a game of cricket, too much accusation of beastliness on the other side seemed to offend against decent, wholesome, British good taste.[4]

In fact, the BBC's language services were among the first to learn what was really happening. The German service under Hugh Greene, later to become Director-General, recalled that from 1940 the service received information of a 'quite unequivocal kind' from debriefed prisoners and information analysis that was immediately broadcast back to Germany. The Polish service was one of the main sources of news about the slaughter of the Jews. They even received two postcards indirectly from the death camps themselves sent by Jews and written in Yiddish. The Director-General sent a memo to senior staff with directions for a 'constant reiteration of atrocity stories in Poland, without exaggeration and with full statistics'.[5] Some attitudes prevailed which today would be regarded as 'evidently anti-Semitic' within the BBC, but were not untypical of their time. One odd internal BBC paper argued that the Corporation did not want to accept 'pro-Semite' programmes because 'anti-Semites would demand the right to reply and it would be difficult to refuse'.[6]

There was anxiety within the BBC and the Ministry of Information about the growth of anti-Semitism within the British public. Another memo from the Director-General instructed the BBC to confine itself to reporting 'and indeed giving prominence to the facts of Jewish persecution . . . as well as any notable achievements by Jews, particularly in connection with the war effort'. At the same time, the BBC should not promote or accept any propaganda in the way of talks or discussions with the object of trying 'to correct the undoubted anti-Semitism which is held very largely throughout the country'.[7]

Another way in which the BBC used its foreign language services to good effect in the bigger cause was to provide a conduit for exiled leaders to stir up resistance in the occupied countries. The recruitment of such outstanding talent to broadcast to France and Poland in particular, was one of the great achievements of wartime broadcasting. It was not just Charles de Gaulle speaking to his fellow countrymen from June 1940 who stirred up the Free French and helped to inspire the resistance to occupation, but a whole team of 'free' French. Those broadcasting to Germany and to Poland also had a powerful impact in countering propaganda and, as the war progressed, in delivering a less partial account of the activities on the ground and in the air. By December 1939, the BBC was transmitting internationally in 16 languages.

Over Christmas the King broadcast to the nation once more, popular entertainer Gracie Fields gave a concert in France and the Archbishop of Canterbury preached at Lambeth Palace. Within a month the BBC launched the Forces Programme, aimed at entertaining the troops. This brought much-needed diversity to the output.

There were constitutional issues at stake in all of this and the BBC had to reassert its independence before it found itself becoming the mere poodle of the Ministry of Information. Frank Gillard, the distinguished BBC war correspondent, who, after his retirement, created the BBC's Oral History Archive, knew exactly what was at stake. Had the Corporation's independence not been maintained then 'it would have been a propaganda instrument for all time, in the hands of the government in power. And, thank

God, it never happened, but it was a near thing, and it had to be fought most resolutely.'

The BBC maintained its independence in theory, by retaining its Board of Governors, though reduced in number. In practice, however, the Government ensured it was a compliant BBC. 'Every word the BBC put out was censored both for security and for policy,' Frank Gillard recalled. 'There were plenty of powerful voices within the Government, Parliament and outside saying that the wartime BBC should be regarded as a department of the Ministry of Information.'[8]

The BBC's handling of the various political crises in the three years before the war had not helped its cause. The BBC did little to question the policy of appeasement or Chamberlain's Munich venture. As one of the few voices warning of the dangers of Nazi Germany and its real threat, Churchill found the BBC unwilling to put him on the air. He never forgave the BBC for that. He described it at various times as 'one of the major neutrals' and as 'the enemy within the gates'. But he also understood its immense power to raise morale and to lift the nation, especially during the darker times.

The BBC was independent constitutionally but not free from government influence over what it broadcast. News editor Patrick Ryan reported to the Ministry of Information each morning to receive the full government briefing before heading up news operations for the rest of the day.[9]

News bulletins were safeguarded by a double line of defence against the inclusion of reports which might, if broadcast, give useful information to the enemy. This censorship was seen as not just a necessary evil but of real help to a responsible news editor in wartime. The second line of defence used by the BBC was to ensure that listeners received a thoroughly accurate service. Some news might be censored or held back, but at least what was broadcast was reliable. The BBC was able to tell its listeners that it took no chances with the news. What it said about the progress of the war had official knowledge and opinion behind it.[10]

According to Leonard Miall, who joined the BBC in March

1939, journalists and writers in the German service always worked on the assumption that all the raw material they received had already been vetted by government. 'The material that one received in the BBC had already been censored – anything you got from the news agencies or sources of that sort. The only things not censored were things that the BBC commissioned. And there the censorship was essentially one of policy censorship not security censorship. There were various people in the BBC who were delegated powers of censorship.'[11]

The area most affected by this was broadcast talks. These were single-speaker commentaries on current events or opinion pieces. Usually these were broadcast live, the script having been vetted first, so as not to give any information damaging to morale or helpful to the enemy. This hit the religious broadcasters quite hard. The religious department found that it became more difficult than ever to broaden the agenda, let alone question assumptions or air controversy. Indeed, Eric Fenn later recalled that 'everything had to be scripted, every script had to be submitted to the censor and could not be broadcast until it bore his stamp and signature. And thereafter, only that script – nothing more or less – could be broadcast on that occasion. Not a single syllable could be added to it when it was broadcast.'[12]

It was not just a matter of content alone. Another part of the reasoning behind this was to prevent any unforeseen silences or gaps appearing within a broadcast. The fear was that it might enable a German transmission on the same wavelength to break through – perhaps even the German propagandist Lord Haw-Haw. On one occasion, an eminent Free Church minister was broadcasting and added an extemporary comment in the middle of a paragraph. He had to be taken off the air until he came back to his script again. Not understanding why, he was very angry.[13] Studio managers were under strict instructions to follow the script very closely and to cut off the speaker if there was any departure from it.

Not only were religious broadcasters carefully censored, some were banned altogether. Before the war when the pacifist movement was proving very popular, organisations like the Peace Pledge Union gained respectability. With the advent of war, however, the BBC was required by government to keep all pacifists off the air. Therefore a number of people who had been high-profile religious broadcasters before 1939 found themselves banned from the wireless. They included the Methodist leader Lord Soper, the distinguished naturalist Canon Charles Raven, who used to give talks on bird-watching, and George MacLeod, founder of the Iona Community.

For Welch and Fenn this caused a great deal of anxiety. Fenn recalls: 'James and I were very worried about it, not because we wanted people to preach pacifism. That was quite irrelevant. But we felt that from the common gospel, people do reach different conclusions.'[14] They felt that there should be no restriction on which churchmen were allowed to broadcast and so proclaim the gospel of Christ, whether or not the broadcaster concerned happened to be a pacifist.

The pair were pushed to the point of resignation from the BBC when they had to drop a book review of a biography of Dick Sheppard. The review was written by Welch's predecessor, Iremonger. Dick Sheppard was well-known as the vicar of St Martin-in-the-Fields just off Trafalgar Square. He was a pillar of the pacifist Peace Pledge Union and a distinguished speaker and Church leader. Iremonger found it impossible to write a review that did not refer to Sheppard's allegiance to the Peace Pledge Union but the Director-General of the BBC ordered him to delete the reference. In January 1940, the issue went before the Central Religious Advisory Committee. The committee stood firm and Iremonger walked out of the meeting in disgust. The Bishop of Winchester, Dr Garbett, was in the chair for the meeting and he persuaded Welch and Fenn not to do anything rash as he would take the matter up elsewhere, using his other channels. They accepted that and followed the Director-General's ruling.

Other pacifists were soon being banned from the air as well. Sir Hugh Roberton and the Glasgow Orpheus Choir found themselves excluded from the BBC because of his pacifist leanings.

Fenn recalls the composer Vaughan Williams writing a furious letter to *The Times* saying that he forbade the BBC to use any of his works so long as the bar remained. The issue was finally resolved by an intervention by Winston Churchill in the House of Commons, after he had become Prime Minister in May 1940. 'Reprehensible though this gentleman's views may be [Vaughan Williams], I do not see this to have any bearing on how he may play the fiddle.'[15] The matter was dropped from then on, and slowly, permission was granted to begin to reintroduce some of the banned speakers, so long as they did not use the airwaves to support pacifism. Some they were unable to reintroduce – the ban on Charles Raven and Lord Soper lasted throughout the war.

Despite these restrictions, James Welch had a sense of mission. He was determined that religious broadcasting should break with its past dependence on church worship and dull, anodyne religious talks. Its role, as he has described it, was 'to speak a word of God in and to each changing situation of peril, suffering, anxiety, victory, and hope – a word of God, not a word of the State, not even, necessarily, a word of any one churchman or of any one branch of the Christian family'.[16]

Welch felt strongly that the divisions of war did not diminish the relevance of the word of God or its direction. If anything, it made the gospel more important than ever. Christ's offer of forgiveness to all who turn to him in repentance and faith is universal. The claim of Christ to be the route to God himself – the Way, the Truth and the Life[17] – applied in all times and all places. It applied equally to men and women of all nationalities. Germany might be the enemy, but the Christian gospel had equally to speak to Germans as to the English. Religious broadcasting 'has had to speak the word of God who is Lord, Judge, and Father of all men, of Germans equally with British, of Japanese equally with the Americans. For religious broadcasting is, fundamentally, the broadcasting of the truth about God and of the truth given by God.'

For Welch, there was one question above all others which nagged away at him. 'How can we be true to the word of the living God of all the nations, and at the same time meet the needs and terrible anxieties of a nation responding to the demands of a total war?'[18]

Sunday broadcasting re-invented

One of the bastions of religious broadcasting fell at the first Christmas of the war. The Board of Governors decided on 22 December that the BBC's Sunday policy should be relaxed for the Forces Programmes, in recognition that the troops in the field needed to be entertained and diverted, not simply uplifted. A line was drawn at broadcasting new variety shows on a Sunday, but repeats were allowed alongside the inclusion of dance music and sport to make Sunday programmes more popular and inclusive. James Welch was not present at the discussions and had considerable doubts about this pragmatic erosion of the traditional BBC Sunday. 'I cannot see,' he wrote, 'why we should assume that because a few listeners have put on uniform and crossed the Channel they should be considered different persons religiously.'[19]

In the debate that followed internally Welch won some points – that no variety would be broadcast live for instance. Reith's successor as Director-General, Frederick Ogilvie, confirmed that Sunday programmes would still be different from the rest of the week, high in quality and 'fortifying to the individual and strengthening to the home'.

Within weeks of the launch of the new radio network for the armed forces, the audience research 'listener reports' from the troops confirmed that the BBC was getting to grips with what the British Expeditionary Force in France wanted to hear. News came top of the list and the troops eagerly tuned into the French language lessons. *Sandy's Half Hour*, a music programme in which the organist Sandy Macpherson played specific tunes selected by soldiers, received 1,500 requests in under a fortnight.[20] It seemed that his single-handed efforts to fill the airwaves in the 'phoney war' had not dimmed his popularity after all. One of the high points of the new service was a Franco-British concert broadcast from the Paris Opera House on 16 April. Gracie Fields and French entertainer Maurice Chevalier topped the bill.

James Welch realised this was the thin end of the wedge. The logic of breaking the pre-war mould was that religious programming would now have to compete with the output of variety, drama and entertainment programmes. He knew too that once the religious monopoly on Sunday programming had been broken, there would be no turning back. Listeners could return home from church services to catch their favourite variety shows on the Forces network. He realised that the needs of wartime had shifted the broadcasting sands for good.

Audience research offered little encouragement either. The response to religious broadcasts at this stage was unexpectedly low and the public felt over-saturated. This cut both ways for Welch and the religious broadcasting team. BBC Religion could no longer rely upon its privileged position within the schedule. It was only a matter of time before the Forces Programme became a service on its own not dependent on scraps from the existing production departments. He could not have foreseen that when wartime was over, the popular programmes of the Forces network would provide the basis for a new service of light programmes.[21]

The situation also presented Welch with a golden opportunity. If religion was to compete in the broadcasting market-place against more popular programming, it had to become more accessible and less traditional. It had to explore new formats and to push out the boundaries. Why not religious drama? Why not produce more provocative programmes that captured the public imagination? Why not broaden the range of contributors to include those who could make religion more accessible? In this apparent set-back, the abandonment of the traditional Sunday policy, the seeds of renewal were sown.

In April 1940, James Welch went on a five-day tour of the British Expeditionary Force in France. It enabled him to find out from the soldiers themselves how well the new Forces programmes were going down. He was relieved to find that the BBC had won over the soldiers and had their goodwill. It had proved right to give the Forces a programme that was light, entertaining, and asked little of the listeners in the middle of what was a cold and miserable winter.

Welch also discovered that the BBC was still falling short of their expectations. The half a million troops were 'young, surprisingly literate (long, daily letters home are the rule), intelligent not cranky, unbiased, not wedded to the familiar and reminiscent, ready and eager for arguments in broadcasting'. He observed that the longer the troops were in France, the more British they felt. Soldiers told Welch that they appreciated the British Sunday more and more and wanted it to be a different day from the rest of the week. 'Sameness is the thing we hope to fight against, so for heaven's sake make Sunday different without making it dull.'[22]

James Welch returned from France with first-hand awareness of the vital importance of getting away from one-dimensional broadcasting and treating the audience with the utmost respect. A BBC that was responsive to the needs of its audience was one that would serve its audience best. The rules of broadcasting were being rewritten by the day. Religious output was no exception. Competition for airtime was increasing. Privileged positions were eroding.

The religious climate

James Welch considered that listeners in Britain fell into three broad categories.[23] First were those who approved of religious broadcasting. This group asked little more than the traditional presentation of the Christian gospel through services and talks. But they expected them to be good and not to stray into the unconventional or controversial. The second group consisted of those who were indifferent and apathetic towards it but not unfriendly. In the third camp were those who were overtly hostile. The three groups were about equal in size. This meant that Welch and his religious broadcasting department were faced with two-thirds of an audience for whom religion had next to nothing to say to their lives.

The language of Christianity was obscure. It was largely the language of the King James Authorised Version, rooted in the beauty of early seventeenth-century English but still problematic to the ordinary listener. Like the works of William Shakespeare, the King James Bible offered eloquent, sometimes familiar and at times wonderfully memorable phrases and turns of speech, but by and large, it went in one ear and out of the other.

What of God himself? He was conspicuous by his absence from many people's lives. Two-thirds of BBC listeners, according to Welch, were living without any reference to God. God was simply not a factor. Religious programmes were a 'given' part of the broadcasting landscape but one of little everyday relevance. Understanding of the Bible and knowledge of the gospel stories was minimal. Those responsible for religious broadcasting considered that 'everywhere, there was great ignorance of the Christian faith'. Of one group of men entering the British army, only 23 per cent knew the meaning of Easter. One bright youth thought Mark's gospel was written by Karl Marx, author of *Das Kapital*. At the same time, there was widespread dissatisfaction with materialism and a leaning towards a spiritual interpretation of life. Welch credited even the two-thirds unresponsive or hostile to Christianity, with 'an almost unanimous consensus of opinion that in the man Jesus lay the key to many of the riddles of life'.

So with an arid spiritual landscape, a tradition of religious broadcasting unhealthily dependent upon traditional rebroadcasting of church services, it would be an uphill battle to make programmes relevant. Another emerging difficulty was the effectiveness of German propaganda.

The propaganda threat

William Joyce broadcast from Germany and became known as 'Lord Haw-Haw'. At first, he proved attractive to both troops and home listeners as his bulletins came with a different twist, a subtle mix of propaganda, boastfulness and also hints of another war, the full extent of which might not be known in Britain. His broadcasts were a curious mixture of what passed for news and comment, but with innuendo and a firm suggestion that listeners in England were not being told the full story of the German advances. Part of Haw-Haw's success arose from the acknowledgement that this was probably true. He presented a German perspective on the unfolding war. But the listener had little way of knowing what was truthful and what was not. It was an intoxicating mix and began to build an audience of its own. There were also concerns about Lord Haw-Haw cutting across BBC transmissions.

Over time, Joyce's idiosyncratic accent – his exaggerated upper-crust vowels with a hint of Irish – were hugely appealing for all the wrong reasons. The opening gambit 'Germany calling, Germany calling', pronounced as 'Jairmony calling, Jairmony calling', became a catchphrase. It fed British comedians with ample raw material for satire. But the popularity of his broadcasts also caused concern. One listener wrote to the Ministry of Information expressing his disquiet that thousands tune in just to 'relieve the boredom'.[24]

The BBC resisted suggestions from the Ministry that it should come up with an on-air refutation of Lord Haw-Haw's claims. In a memo written on Christmas Eve 1939, the Head of Talks, Sir Richard Maconachie, argued that 'the success of false propaganda with any audience which has access to facts would be a "short-term affair"'. The best antidote remained better programming to draw audiences away from him and news that was reliable and trustworthy. You don't fight lies with more lies but with truth.

The BBC was still having difficulties with the Ministry of

Information over the supply of news. On Boxing Day 1939, the BBC Director-General Frederick Ogilvie complained to the Government in writing that 'if the Air Ministry continues trying to disguise losses on the wireless or if the Admiralty begins trying to disguise them (in the apparent interests of airmen or sailors or the home front) it will play straight into Haw-Haw's hands'.

In January 1940, an internal BBC document revealed that nearly one-third of all adult listeners in Britain were tuning in to German broadcasts from Hamburg. A typical main evening BBC news bulletin at 9 o'clock would attract sixteen million listeners, over half of the listening public. This was the most popular news bulletin of the day. It was followed by a talk heard by an audience of nine million. This meant that some seven million people were either switching off their radio sets after the news or re-tuning.

In reality, an estimated six million listeners were re-tuning from the BBC's main evening news to listen to Lord Haw-Haw. So the BBC's proposed solution to reduce his popularity was not a counterblast but a simple classic scheduling trick. It moved peak entertainment programmes into the 9.15 slot in direct competition with Lord Haw-Haw. This might be *What's on Tomorrow,* one of the most popular programmes on the Forces Programme, the comedy *Band Waggon* or even Gracie Fields.

Over the coming months, the BBC slowly began to come round to the idea of a more serious counterweight to Haw-Haw. The BBC's Home Service board approved the idea, early in 1940, of appointing a weekly commentator. They wanted to avoid any sense that this was overt counter-propaganda though its purpose was just that. There was much debate within the BBC Talks Department about who would produce the programme.

Ironically, the team entrusted to come up with the British response to the challenge of German propaganda included Guy Burgess, then a mere BBC producer but later one of the notorious Russian Communist spy-ring. The combination of Kim Philby, Burgess and Maclean and art historian Anthony Blunt supplied the Soviet Union with invaluable British secrets until their exposure during the post-war years. It is a delicious irony that one of the creators of the most important programmes developed to counter German Nazi propaganda should be Guy Burgess. No doubt such an act was entirely compatible with his Communist ideology, but it also served the cause of Great Britain supremely well. This was the birth of one of the most famous wartime programmes. It was called *Postscript*.

After six months and more of war, radio was now finding its true place in the front line in the battle for the minds of the listeners. It was to shape how they perceived the war to be going. It was already a powerful tool in maintaining morale and in the dissemination of information. The listener was becoming increasingly sophisticated in working out what was propaganda and what was truthful. Although operating under strict controls that ensured that information helpful to the enemy would not get on the air, the BBC news bulletins had developed their own style of conveying bad news. The Home Service was becoming a vital instrument for disseminating information about how to live with war and about the events of the conflict. The government did not try to prevent news of serious defeats being published, as it had in the First World War. It was not, however, averse to using the airwaves to underplay disasters, to reinterpret defeats and show them in the best possible light.

For the Christians within religious broadcasting, there was the wider challenge of looking reality hard in the face and of seeing how well the old eternal truths of Christianity stood up to the test. There was no fudging of the issue. Religious broadcasting had to respond to the crisis of faith that threatened to engulf the country if the war continued to go badly. No hiding place was available. If the Christian faith had something to say to the nation in its time of greatest need, every Christian of influence had to play their part. In broadcasting, that responsibility fell squarely on the shoulders of James Welch, Eric Fenn and their colleagues.

Notes

1 Quentin Reynolds quoted in Briggs, Asa, *The BBC:The First Fifty Years*, p. 178
2 Seaton, Jean, *The Media in British Politics, Reporting atrocities: the BBC and the holocaust*, pp. 154-182
3 G. Dyson (ed.), *Heroes of the House*, London, London, BBC Publications, 1942, p.43
4 Seaton, op. cit. p. 161
5 Ibid. p. 164. Director-General memo dated 5 February 1941, BBC Written Archives Centre file R34/702/3
6 Seaton, op. cit. p. 169, memo dated 7 June 1943
7 Ibid. p.170, memo dated 19 November 1943
8 Gillard, Frank, *Auntie: The Inside Story*, transmitted 28 October 1997
9 Ibid.
10 The BBC Diary 1942, p.20
11 Interview with Leonard Miall, 23 February 2000
12 Interview with Eric Fenn by Frank Gillard for the BBC Oral History Archive, 4 July 1986
13 Ibid. Fenn does not identify the Free Church minister involved.
14 Ibid.
15 Ibid.
16 Welch, James, *Religious Broadcasting in Wartime,* BBC Year Book 1945, p. 41ff.
17 Gospel of John 14:6
18 Ibid.
19 Letter of James Welch to Basil Nicolls, 2 Jan 1940, quoted by Briggs, Volume 3, p. 120
20 Ibid., p. 124
21 After the war, BBC Radio divided into three services: Home, Light and Third Programme. This was sustained until 1967 when they were reconfigured and renamed Radio 1 (contemporary music), Radio 2 (the old Light Programme), Radio 3 (classical music and culture), Radio 4 (news, speech and entertainment) and later in 1995 Radio 5 Live (News and Sport).
22 Welch, James, *Report on visit to the Western Front*, April 1940
23 Welch, James, introduction to Dorothy Sayers, *The Man Born To Be King*, Victor Gollancz, London, 1943, p.11 ff.
24 Letter sent by H.J. Ormerod, 12 Jan 1940.

CHAPTER FOUR

The Radio Talk

∞∞

The return of the broadcasting services to a more recognisable pattern of programme at the start of 1940, albeit within the confines of censorship, made a huge difference. The BBC was free to lift the spirits of the nation. This was badly needed in the face of a succession of bad news from the front line. The Corporation's home news editor, R.T. Clark, appreciated the dilemma. How do you raise morale when the news is so bad? 'It seems to me that the only way to strengthen the morale of the people whose morale is worth strengthening, is to tell the truth, and nothing but the truth, even if the truth is horrible' was his response.[1] But this was not considered wise according to the BBC's critics in parliament. They wanted a compliant BBC that simply did as it was told. There were questions about 'the tone' of news bulletins. There was disapproval of commentaries that were independent and not supplied or approved by Government.[2] The BBC has never taken kindly to being told by elected members of Parliament that they must toe the government line. The heavier the criticism, the more the BBC resisted pressures on it to comply.

Through the first months of 1940 the German onslaught continued with attacks on Norway and Denmark and an advance through Holland, Belgium and Luxembourg towards France and the Channel.

On 14 June Paris fell to the Germans. During the spring of 1940, the BBC decided to deploy its own weapon, the broadcast talk. Losses in the land war could so easily lead to a defeatist frame of mind among the British people. It was important to keep the spirit of the nation defiant in the face of overwhelming odds. Already well-established before 1939, this simple broadcasting device was now to be deployed with more depth and range than before. The radio talk had many virtues: it was low in cost, easy to produce, could be prepared in a matter of hours, and was high in talent and deadly in its aim.

Few understood its potential better than the BBC's Director of Radio Talks, Sir Richard Maconachie. He was head of the Home Division of the BBC. This included the home talks and news departments, the editorial direction of the *Radio Times* and *The Listener* magazines and other publications, and the Press Department.

Although the wireless had long been a familiar piece of furniture and equipment in the British home, this was the first great war in which broadcasting had played a part. As Maconachie saw it, writing at the start of 1941, the producer of wartime broadcasts was 'treading an unblazed trail which he can trace only as he goes along – largely by trial and error – and of which he cannot as yet see the end.'[3]

'Unblazed' it may have been and the outcome certainly was unknown then, but already he had identified a very clear definition of the role of the radio talk as a weapon of war. Its contribution to the national effort was:

> to explain the significance of events as they occur; to keep the essential issues clearly before the nation; to inspire determination to see the war through; to reflect the personal experience of the man and woman in the front line; and to tell the ordinary citizen what he must do, and how and why, to cope with the practical problems that confront him in the new conditions of 'total war'.[4]

These practical problems were as fundamental as ensuring that people had enough to eat. With shipping convoys having to run the gauntlet of the German submarines and much of Western Europe occupied by Germany, Britain had to be self-sufficient in food production. In late 1941, heavy losses were being sustained by the Atlantic convoys. Given the British were already a nation of gardeners, it was a relatively simple matter to urge the people to use their green fingers to assist the war effort. Back gardens were already being dug up to house the Anderson bomb-shelters. What grass was left was turned over to create vegetable patches. Listeners were inspired to cultivate and to grow.

The gardening journalist Cecil Henry Middleton became one of the BBC's most popular presenters. Listeners knew him simply as Mr Middleton. Born in 1887, he followed his father, a head gardener on a large estate, into horticulture and began his career in the nursery trade in London.[5] After the First World War he became an inspector for the Ministry of Agriculture and joined Surrey County Council in 1926. He was recommended to the BBC as a broadcaster on gardening by the Royal Horticultural Society and so began in 1931 an outstandingly successful broadcasting career on radio and television that lasted until his death in 1945. Mr Middleton's fifteen-minute talks, *In Your Garden*, came from a studio at the BBC's Midlands base at Wood Norton. The programme went out on Sunday afternoons after lunch and attracted between three and four million listeners. As the nation aimed to become self-sufficient in food supplies, he became an important contributor in the *Dig for Victory* campaign, both as a broadcaster and writer. His plain speaking, direct advice, gentle humour, love for his subject and common sense won him an immense and affectionate following. His contribution is remembered today by a memorial gate, which leads to the garden of the BBC's Written Archives Centre in Caversham.[6] *Dig for Victory* was a hugely successful campaign, its legacy still evident in many gardens to this day.[7] That Sunday afternoon gardening slot became so well-established that sixty years later the BBC continues to broadcast its evergreen *Gardeners' Question Time* on Sunday afternoons on Radio 4.

Alongside talks on gardening were instructions on how to prepare meals from home-grown food. The five-minute *Kitchen Front* cookery talks began on 13 June 1940 and went out at 8.15 a.m. By the end of the war, there had been almost 2,000 wartime broadcasts on food. These short talks were an extremely popular innovation. Their major role, from the government viewpoint, was to supplement food rationing. *Kitchen Front's* slot in the schedule, just after the breakfast news bulletin, guaranteed it a huge audience. In the first week after it went on the air, the BBC was bombarded with cakes and gifts from listeners who had tried out the recipes.

Some of the concoctions became almost surreal in the attempt to bring some variety into the nation's diet. Women across the country were making pastry and egg flans out of carrots. Parsnips became the substitute in banana in 'banana cake'. The tongue was firmly in the cheek with some of the recipes. 'Skinflint's Joy' was a dessert, baked potatoes and sausage was called 'Pigs in Clover'. One had the grand name of 'Connaught Pie', but its resemblance to one of London's smartest hotels stopped with the name. 'Another disguise for parsnips?', the programme joked. In fact it was simply a way of making a portion of meat go further, by adding oat flakes and water to bulk it up and then giving it a fancy name.[8] Even the presenters acquired culinary nick-names. Freddie Grisewood had to suffer the indignity of being called 'Ricepud'.[9] Those who delivered the talks quickly became household names and personalities.

The people who deserved the credit for keeping the nation healthy on this meagre diet of potatoes and parsnip, cabbage and carrot was the scientific partnership of nutritionist Elsie Widdowson and Professor Robert McCance, a specialist on the chemical composition of food. The diet they devised has been widely acknowledged since as probably the healthiest ever enjoyed by the British population. It formed the foundation of the austerity diet promoted by the Ministry of Food under Lord Woolton and promulgated by the BBC during the war. So-called 'Woolton Pie' was made of vegetables and breadcrumbs. Their joint research was published by the Medical Research Council in 1940 as *The Chemical Composition of Foods*. It ran into six editions.

What they did was to come up with an experimental diet based on bread, cabbage and potatoes. These, they decided, contained all the nutrients the nation needed for its survival, however great the food shortages became. Both the vegetables were in plentiful supply and could be relied upon whatever happened to the convoys of ships bringing in food across the Atlantic. They tested the diet upon one another, living off it for three months and then doing some vigorous fell walking in the Lake District to test their physical fitness. They found themselves perfectly fit and healthy, so it was adopted by the Ministry of Food.

The government later added chalk to bread-making after the pair identified calcium as an essential to prevent rickets. McCance and Widdowson continued to give nutritional advice well after the war.[10] Perhaps the greatest testimony to the achievement of these two is not simply that the nation was sustained by this diet for the war years, but their own long and healthy lives. The professional partnership lasted for sixty years until McCance died in 1993. Elsie Widdowson died in June 2000 at the age of ninety-three. She, however, attributed her long life not to her healthy eating but to her genetic inheritance. Her father lived until he was ninety-six years old and her mother died aged one hundred and seven.

What C.H. Middleton had done for gardening and therefore for eating, Dr Charles Hill did for health. As the Radio Doctor, his participation in a programme could boost the audience from six to fourteen million. Hill was a brilliant communicator and dispensed his medical wisdom with a warmth and humanity that made him every listener's best friend. His advice was eminently sensible and down-to-earth. Not identified on the air, the Radio Doctor spoke with common sense. 'Don't give Father extra butter, Mother, that's your ration.' He waged war against constipation, urging listeners to embrace 'that humble black-coated worker, the prune'. He was a doctor and talked to the listener with a bedside manner, as if each individual at home was his personal patient. He liked to pose questions like a doctor in his surgery, probing to check the symptoms. His broadcast at Christmas in 1943 began . . .

But how are you today? How's your tongue? Is it smooth and red or knobby and beige with an overcoat of a muddy hue? And how's the stomach? Is it firm and steady or somewhat warm and a little wobbly and a trifle windy? Or was your Christmas Day so spartan that you're fighting fit with no twinge of remorse?[11]

After the war, Charles Hill continued to be a major force in broadcasting, serving both as Chairman of the Independent Television Authority and of the BBC itself, by which time he sat in the House of Lords as Lord Hill of Luton.

All these variations of the radio talk format were to prove successful. James Welch began to realise that if he could find his own radio celebrity to champion religion, in the same way in which C.H. Middleton had become the BBC's voice of gardening and Charles Hill the voice of medicine, then the cause of Christianity could be much advanced. The man for the job turned out to be C.S. Lewis – not a name Welch was familiar with at this stage, but one that would come to mean a great deal.

Lewis had been brought up with his brother in the Church of Ireland. From an early age 'Jack' and Warnie were close. The death of their mother when Lewis was only ten years old disrupted what had been a happy childhood. His father stayed in Northern Ireland but sent Lewis to England to continue his education, with mixed results. An unhappy start at a school in Watford run by a cruel headmaster was followed by happier times at another school in Malvern. Here C.S. Lewis lost his faith. Under the influence of a private tutor W.T. Kirkpatrick in Surrey, Lewis's intellect prospered but his increasing doubts about the existence of God had hardened into atheism. By 1916, he had reached the position of believing that all religions are merely man's own invention. For Lewis the educated and thinking ones had stood outside old beliefs and superstitions in every age. He stood with them. After a brief period of service during the First World War, Lewis left Oxford with a triple first and by 1925 was a Fellow at Magdalen College.

He was also on his journey back to Christian faith, influenced by friends and colleagues, among them the academic and writer J.R.R. Tolkien. His spiritual odyssey ended when in 1929 he 'gave in and admitted that God was God, and knelt and prayed: perhaps, that night, the most dejected and reluctant convert in all England'.[12]

'By snatching glory out of defeat . . .'

News played its part in encouraging the development of radio talks. War came home with a vengeance in 1940 with the Battle of France, the retreat from Dunkirk and the Battle of Britain fought in the skies. The BBC came into its own. 'The greatest thing in any war is news, news, news. People want to know what is happening,' as Frank Gillard put it.[13] The news became the staple diet of radio listening and was the point in the schedule when the BBC could guarantee its biggest audience. Everybody wanted to know what was going on. They didn't want to wait to read it the next day and newspapers were fearfully thin in any case because of the shortage of newsprint. The BBC had to be the voice of the whole nation in a time of war.

Some companies broadcast the lunch-time bulletins to factory workers. The headlines across the Tannoy public address system at the steel-makers McCalls would signify lunch-time[14]. This practice was to continue after the war. Other programmes, such as *Music While You Work*, provided upbeat background music in the factory. It boosted morale and increased productivity. *Workers' Playtime* took entertainers to a different factory every lunch-time. It was introduced by Wilfred Pickles, whose strong Northern accent was one of the first to be heard regularly on the BBC.

New opportunities for the radio talk as a format were developing all the time. *The Kitchen Front* had already demonstrated the value of placing a talk strategically within the schedule after a significant news bulletin in the morning. The same was to be the case with the main evening news bulletin at 9 o'clock, which attracted the biggest audience of the day. The news commentary *Postscript* followed it.

This five-minute slot straight after the news had to be good to hold the audience. Sir Richard Maconachie was ambitious in his choice of speakers, not hesitating to introduce Americans if they had something to say, or Hollywood film stars for that matter. Among those who delivered talks were the actors Robert Donat and Leslie Howard, who starred as Clark Gable's rival for Vivien Leigh's affections in her role as Scarlett O'Hara in *Gone with the Wind*.

Finding good contributors was not easy. Maconachie observed dryly that 'heroes are seldom remarkable for their powers of self-expression and proficiency in broadcasting is not yet recognised as a qualification for promotion in the public services'. That meant that candidates who, from their experience or official position, might appear on paper to be ideal commentators for a slot like *Postscript*, only too often disappointed. Such people 'too often demonstrate, under the fierce test of the microphone, how narrow is the line which divides the teacher from the bore and the prophet from the prig'.[15]

One who passed the microphone test with flying colours was the writer J.B. Priestley. His work was already familiar to listeners. He had read the various instalments of his novel *Let the People Sing* on the Home Service, one of the few drama productions to survive unscathed by the cutbacks of the first few months of war. He faced a challenge of an altogether different scale when his first *Postscript* came to be written. The date was Wednesday 5 June 1940. A week earlier in Westminster Abbey, a service of Intercession and Prayer had been held to pray for the nation. The war was going badly and the British Expeditionary Force was in retreat as the German advance across France pushed the Allied troops back towards the sea. The invasion of Britain seemed a real possibility.

One of those who attended the service in the Abbey was Winston Churchill. 'The English are loath to expose their feelings,' he recalled, 'but in my stall in the choir I could feel the pent-up, passionate emotion, and also the fear of the congregation, not of death or wounds or material loss, but of defeat and the final ruin of Britain.' Within days the War Cabinet was meeting to discuss the imminent evacuation from Dunkirk.

Churchill remarked casually that whatever happens at Dunkirk, 'we shall fight on'. There was a spontaneous demonstration of support from his closest colleagues in government. He was in no doubt that had he faltered at all in the leading of the nation, he should have been 'hurled out of office'. Churchill was convinced then that every Minister was ready to be killed and to lose everything rather than give in to Hitler and that the nation felt the same. 'It fell to me in these coming days and months to express their sentiments on suitable occasions. This I was able to do because they were mine also. There was a white glow, overpowering, sublime, which ran through our island from end to end.'[16]

Within a week Dunkirk had brought the rescue of an estimated 338,000 British, French, Dutch and Belgian troops to fight another day. There were 693 British ships involved in the evacuation altogether. The number of small British craft, omitting ships' lifeboats and some other privately owned craft of which no record is available, amounted to 372 boats. There were 77 trawlers alone. This far outnumbered the 39 naval destroyers, 36 mine-sweepers and 8 hospital ships.[17]

At one level the evacuation of Dunkirk was a catastrophe. A humiliating retreat in the face of a more powerful enemy. But one of the reasons why it has gone down in history as a legendary example of heroism, plucking victory from the jaws of defeat, is the way it was portrayed on the BBC. What was a well-organised but massive retreat in the face of an advancing enemy was described as 'the miracle of Dunkirk'. This not only made it sound less like a disaster, but suggested there was some religious significance to the escape. The robust plain-speaking of J.B. Priestley, so characteristic of a Yorkshireman, left an indelible mark in this respect. In his first *Postscript* he singled out the role of the pleasure-steamers, found on every river and around every English holiday resort.

> To my mind what was most characteristically English about it – so typical of us, so absurd and yet so grand and gallant that you hardly know whether to laugh or to cry when you read about them, was the part played in the difficult and dangerous embarkation – not by the warships' magnificent though they were, but by the little pleasure-steamers. We've known them and laughed at them, these fussy little steamers, all our lives . . . They seemed to belong to the same ridiculous holiday world as pierrots and piers, sandcastles, ham and egg teas, palmists, automatic machines and crowded sweating promenades. But they were called out of that world – and, let it be noted, they were called out in good time and good order. Yes, these 'Brighton Bells' and 'Brighton Queens' left that innocent foolish world of theirs – to sail into the inferno, to defy bombs, shells, magnetic mines, torpedoes, machine-gun fire – to rescue our soldiers. Some of them – alas – will never return. Among those paddle steamers that will never return was one that I knew well. For it was the pride of our ferry service to the Isle of Wight. None other than the good ship 'Gracie Fields'. . . . But now – look – this little steamer like all her brave and embattled sisters is immortal. She'll go sailing proudly down the years in the epic of Dunkirk. And our great grand-children, when they learn how we began this war, by snatching glory out of defeat, and then swept on to victory, may also learn how the little holiday steamers made an excursion to hell and came back glorious.[18]

After the initial Dunkirk broadcast on Wednesday 5 June, he broadcast each Sunday evening until 20 October. The press turned against him after a suggestion that those who had left Britain should have their property confiscated. Priestley, who was often critical of the war effort, proved a popular broadcaster, but was eventually taken off the Home Service. He went to great trouble to tell listeners in his last *Postscript* that it was his decision to stop:

> This is my last Sunday postscript for some time, perhaps the last that I shall ever do. The decision was mine and was in no way forced on me by the BBC. My relations with the BBC are excellent. But I had some good reasons for wanting to stop; in the first place people get tired of hearing the same voice at exactly the same time each week, and I'd be the last man to want to add to the boredom and tedium of the war. Then again, there's another more subtle reason . . . the whole situation of the country and also the mood of the country have changed, and so it might be better if these were interpreted for you on Sundays by another speaker . . . Stupid persons have frequently accused me in public of – I use their own words – taking advantage of my position to bring party politics into my talks. This is extremely ironical because I am not a member of any political party.[19]

Priestley explained his deeply-held conviction that what was at stake was civilisation itself. He hoped the British example would ensure that 'a reasonable liberty along with a reasonable security can be achieved'. He predicted, foolishly, that this would not even be a long war and he signed off defiantly, making no apology to listeners who from their 'impregnable fortresses of stupidity' assured him of their hostility. He promised to go on disliking more and more everything they stood for. But to the large majority of other listeners, he offered apologies for the irritations and thanks for the thousands of pleasant letters and expressions of gratitude.

J.B. Priestley was, in effect, taken off air by the Ministry of Information, but continued to be heard on the BBC's overseas services. He went on to broadcast regularly and successfully to the United States via the North American Service of the BBC from July 1941 to September 1942 and again from December 1942. He attracted unwelcome attention in the House of Commons, however, where some Conservative members of Parliament accused the BBC of 'giving excessive preference to Left Wing speakers such as Mr Priestley'. A counter-motion applauded the BBC for its 'expression of varied points of view on matters of public interest' and congratulated the Corporation on the 'revival of broadcasts' by J.B. Priestley.[20] However, the motions were never debated and sole responsibility for selection of speakers for *Postscript* was handed over to the BBC by 1943.

Churchill and the BBC

The Prime Minister himself used the BBC sparingly but with huge impact. Churchill had little time for the BBC. In the five years between 1934 and 1939, despite his long-standing opposition to the government's appeasement policy, he broadcast only four times. That was partly because the BBC, in its efforts to stay on-side with the government, gave Churchill next to no air time to express his opposition to Chamberlain. As his own history of the Second World War testifies, he was far more interested in the military aspects of war than in the role of information and propaganda. The BBC is barely mentioned in his own wartime history. His view, expressed in one of his first wartime broadcasts on 12 November 1939, was that if words could kill then Britain would be dead already.

Nevertheless, Churchill did recognise radio's importance as a direct means of speaking to the nation. So when he did broadcast – and on at least nine occasions he turned down invitations to speak – it was to great effect. In the views of another broadcaster, the American war reporter Edward R. Murrow, 'he mobilised the English language and sent it into battle'.[21]

Less than a fortnight after J.B. Priestley's epic tribute to the Dunkirk spirit, Winston Churchill made arguably his greatest broadcast. It was on 18 June 1940. The prospects for Britain had never seemed so bleak. Paris had been occupied just four days earlier.

Dunkirk was fresh in the memory. On 13 May 1940, Churchill had told Parliament that he had nothing to offer but blood, toil, tears and sweat. As he spoke to the people he made it clear the war was about to enter a new and most perilous phase. Half the adult population, some 16 million listeners, tuned in to hear what their leader Winston Churchill had to say to them. The nation stood still. The records of the public utilities showed that scarcely anyone used the telephone, put on the kettle or even went to the toilet during the broadcast. Nobody wanted to miss a single word. This is how Churchill rallied the nation to face its greatest fear:

> What General Weygand called the Battle of France is over. The Battle of Britain is about to begin. Upon this battle depends the survival of Christian civilisation. Upon it depends our own British life and the long continuity of our institutions and our Empire. Cold fury and might of the enemy must very soon be turned on us. Hitler knows that he will have to break us in this island or lose the war. If we can stand up to him all Europe may be free. And the life of the world may move forward into broad sunlit uplands. But if we fail, then the whole world, including the United States, including all that we have known and cared for, will sink into the abyss of a new dark age made more sinister and perhaps more protracted by the lights of perverted science. Let us therefore brace ourselves to our duty and so bear ourselves that if the British Empire and its Commonwealth last for a thousand years, men will still say 'This was their finest hour'.

General de Gaulle

In June 1940, when France surrendered to Germany, a young and little-known Brigadier-General in the French army arrived in London. Churchill's personal envoy to France, Brigadier-General

Spears, had chosen this man to lead French resistance and flown him to England. His name was Charles de Gaulle. He was taken to studio 4B in Broadcasting House, which survives to this day, to speak to his countrymen at home. 'I, General de Gaulle, invite French officers and soldiers who are on British territory or who are coming here, with or without arms, to join me . . . Whatever happens the flame of the French resistance must not go out and it will not go out.' Leonard Miall was de Gaulle's producer. The memory burns vividly in his mind sixty years later.

> Nearly everything was broadcast live. There were six different recording channels for the whole of Broadcasting House domestic and overseas – six altogether. They had to be booked weeks in advance. When de Gaulle turned up at the last minute we had to put him on the air. He asked me the next day if his talk had been recorded and I had to tell him it had not and I became the first British recipient of the famous de Gaulle temper. He tore strips off the BBC in general and me in particular for failing to appreciate the historical significance of this occasion. We decided to repeat the main point of his appeal. That was recorded. When de Gaulle died, radio stations around the world played what they said was the original recording and only I and one or two others knew it wasn't true.[22]

The broadcast was the start of the creation of the Free French movement out of the scattered groups and individuals in London from both civil and military backgrounds. Others had fled further afield to North America or gone south to wait and hide in North Africa. De Gaulle had to bring the dispersed Free French together into an organised movement of resistance and to stir internal defiance within occupied France. It took time for de Gaulle's appeal to the Free French to drive home. But within one month, nearly 2,000 had responded to his call to arms.

Those who had escaped Nazi occupation travelled far to hear

him speak. One meeting at the Kingsway Hall in London in March 1941 was so packed that every seat was taken and people were standing at the back and down the aisles to hear de Gaulle. The self-declared leader of the Free French, later to become the President, was in exile in England waiting for the liberation of France. Over time, the Free French became Fighting France, and came together with the Resistance so that France could eventually claim its share of credit in the liberation of its occupied homeland. It was another three years before de Gaulle could walk the streets of a liberated Paris. However, for a time, he lived at the Langham Hotel just across the road and minutes away from the studios of the BBC.

Notes

[1] Quoted by Hickman, Tom, *What did you do in the war, Auntie?*, p. 23

[2] Briggs p. 283 in reference to House of Commons debate, 24 April 1941 Hansard volume 371 col. 257

[3] BBC Year Book 1941, p. 60

[4] Ibid.

[5] Researched by Jacquie Kavanagh and Geoff Jones at the BBC's Written Archives Centre

[6] Middleton died in 1945 and in 1954 money was raised by public subscription for a memorial gate in his honour. The gate, designed by O.H. Parry of the BBC Building Department, cost £175. It stood, set in the wall of the garden from which he had broadcast later in the war at the side of the BBC's offices in the old Langham Hotel until the BBC sold the building. The gate was transferred to Caversham in 1990 and now leads into a garden designed using some of his favourite ideas and planted with the trees, shrubs and flowers he most admired. His niece, Mrs French, attended the opening ceremony.

[7] The author can testify to its success in his own garden. The previous owners of his West London home dug up a square in the lawn eight metres by five metres to grow vegetables. Sixty years later it is still, in part, a vegetable patch. All over England, allotment societies enable gardeners who prefer to keep their garden for recreational use to use a plot of land at a peppercorn rent in order to grow vegetables.

[8] *The Kitchen Front*, 27 May 1942

[9] Hickman, op. cit. p. 74

[10] When the army had concerns over the weight of officer cadets, the problem was identified as lack of bread, not lack of meat. *Daily Telegraph* obituary Elsie Widdowson, 22 June 2000.

[11] BBC Radio Collection, *75 Years of the BBC*, CD1 track 42

[12] The full story is told in Lewis's book, *Surprised by Joy.*

[13] Gillard, Frank, *Auntie: The Inside Story*, transmitted 28 October 1997

[14] Interview with Douglas V. Osborne, 29 May 2000

[15] Maconachie ibid. p. 63

[16] Churchill, Winston, *The Second World War*, p. 96

[17] Ibid. All numbers from Churchill's chapter on the Deliverance of Dunkirk, p. 97

[18] 5 June 1940, Priestley, J.B., *Postscript to the News*, BBC Written Archives scripts and published in Priestley, J.B., *Postscripts*, William Heinemann, London, 1940, p.3

[19] Ibid. p.96 ff.

[20] Briggs, Asa, *The History of Broadcasting in the United Kingdom, Volume 3, the War of Words 1939-1945*, Oxford University Press, New York, 1995, p. 558 ff.

[21] Finkelstein, Norman H., *With Heroic Truth – the Life of Edward G. Murrow*, Clarion Books, New York, 1997, p. 69

[22] Interview with Leonard Miall, 23 February 2000

CHAPTER FIVE

Broadcasting House Bombed

∞∞

The first broadcast of writer and academic C.S. Lewis was still some time away. During the autumn of 1939 and the spring of 1940 he had been occupied with writing and with the new experience of sharing his home with evacuees from London. His first theological work, *The Problem of Pain,* was nearing completion.

On 3 December 1939, Lewis and his friends met for their usual informal evening gathering in the rooms of J.R.R. Tolkien. This group, The Inklings, met weekly from 1930 to 1949 in various college rooms. Over convivial conversation and a drink, there was serious discussion as each participant might share or read aloud whatever any of them was writing. They had a very pleasant evening drinking gin and lime juice, with readings from 'the new Hobbit' and *The Problem of Pain.*

This was Lewis's first venture, unless you include his science fiction, into Christian apologetics. And he was nervous about it. The preface to the book tells the story. Ashley Sampson, owner of Centenary Press, suggested the writing of the book. Lewis wished to write it anonymously for fear that he would make 'statements of such apparent fortitude that they would become ridiculous if anyone knew who made them'.[1] There is a confessional quality to the preface, aware as he is that he has not known some of the pain he describes. However, he defends himself against one criticism:

No one can say 'He jests at scars who never felt a wound', for I have never for one moment been in a state of mind to which even the imagination of serious pain was less than intolerable. If any man is safe from the danger of under-estimating this adversary, I am that man.

The preface also includes a carefully inserted theological disclaimer. Lewis describes himself as 'a layman and an amateur' of little reading. Self-effacing though this preface is, it is also misleading. The new reader, unfamiliar with the power of Lewis's intellect or his skills as a teacher, might think it was the work of an amateur theologian. It is nothing of the sort. Simply by virtue of the fact that it had been debated by such a close-knit intellectual circle as The Inklings ensured it had undergone considerable scrutiny.

In the words of Walter Hooper, a leading authority on C.S. Lewis, this was the forum in which most of Lewis's books went through the fire.[2] This was the test. 'It must have been exactly the type of criticism that an author might really want if he's spent a lot of time thinking about it. You really do hope that somebody would be really honest with you.'[3] Such was the calibre of this group of men that they felt that there was no point in offering criticism unless it was sincerely meant.

One of those deeply impressed by *The Problem of Pain* was James Welch. He made a mental note that this academic might one day make the transition from lecturer and writer to broadcaster. Here was someone prepared to grapple with the tragedy of war – the inexplicable loss and suffering at the hands of evil.

London blitzed

The Problem of Pain carried a strong resonance at a time when so many were suffering from grief or personal loss of every kind as a result of the war. In July 1940, Hitler gave Reichsmarschall

Hermann Goering the task of destroying British air power. Until this had been done, the German High Command refused to contemplate any attempt to invade Britain. Goering's immediate tactics were to attack shipping in the English Channel dividing England from continental Europe. His intention was not just to sink ships but to lure the planes of Britain's Fighter Command into battles over the Channel. He counted on the German Messerschmitts winning the dog-fights against Spitfires and Hurricanes. The German intelligence reports suggested that the British were short of trained pilots so the attacks were intended to deplete Britain's air defence. German shipping was being assembled in support of a projected invasion, providing another target for British planes across the Channel.

By August, the German Air Force, the Luftwaffe, had switched its attacks to targets in southern England. The Battle of Britain had begun. Churchill realised that Britain's fate depended upon victory in the air.[4] It became obvious that the German leadership recognised that all their plans for the invasion of Britain depended on winning air supremacy over the Channel and securing their pre-selected landing places on the south coast. By mid-August, the Air Ministry reckoned that more than one thousand German planes were being sent over Britain daily. In the ten days since the mass raids began, the Royal Air Force claimed to have destroyed 694 German planes against losses of 150 aircraft. Nearly 60 pilots had survived being shot down, critical to the battle as pilots were far harder to replace than aircraft. Other pilots from countries as far apart as Canada and Poland supplemented the RAF's recruitment from the UK.

One of the factors in the success of the RAF in blunting the impact of the Luftwaffe's offensive was the still-secret use of radar detection. This allowed the Spitfires and Hurricanes to remain on the ground for longer instead of using up fuel in lengthy patrols. With the enemy aircraft detected seventy-five miles away, the RAF still had plenty of time to get its fighters in the air before the Luftwaffe appeared. The superior agility in the air and speed of the British planes more than made up for the enemy's strength in numbers.

The birth of *Screwtape*

In Oxford, C.S. Lewis was fully aware of developments in the war. He had not been called up and was doing his best to support the RAF by visiting bases and camps where he gave stirring talks, many on theological themes. Despite a confession to his friend and correspondent Dom. Bede Griffiths[5] that he suffered from 'laziness', Lewis had a mind and imagination constantly alert to new ideas. In July 1940 he writes to his brother to tell him of a startling idea he has had at church after Holy Communion:

> Before the service was over – one cd wish these things came more seasonably – I was struck by an idea for a book wh. I think might be both useful and entertaining. It wd be called *As one Devil to Another* and would consist of letters from an elderly retired devil to a young devil who has just started work on his first 'patient'. The idea wd be to give all the psychology of temptation from the *other* point of view.[6]

So began in the imagination of C.S. Lewis one of his most successful works of popular Christian apologetics, *The Screwtape Letters*. The fact that he should first formulate the idea during a church service after taking Communion would be more than sufficient evidence for any Christian believer that the idea came from God himself. Lewis made no explicit connection between the timing of this inspired conception and what was going on in the war. But again, the idea that he should devise an entertaining way in which to subvert the devil and all his works in the middle of the Battle of Britain is itself more than intriguing. To what extent Lewis made any connection in his mind between the attacks of the German enemy by air and the work of the devil in attacking the soul, must remain a matter for speculation alone. We simply do not know. But what is transparent is the parallel of Lewis writing his most convincing books dealing with evil, pain and the devil and all his works at the moment in the war when Britain was taking its biggest battering and was most at risk of enemy invasion. It was as if the overt aggression of war had its spiritual counterpart in Lewis's grappling with the dark side of faith – the spiritual powers unleashed against belief and believers. While Lewis was developing the *Screwtape* idea, the battle being waged in the air was to take a sinister turn for the worse.

The Blitz

In September 1940, Goering changed tactics once again. He had failed to destroy the RAF over the Channel and the attacks on airfields and radio installations had also failed to soften up England for invasion. Without command of the skies, it was too dangerous for Germany to proceed with a sea-borne invasion. Their ships would be too vulnerable to air attack. Shortly after tea-time on 7 September, in broad daylight, the East End of London witnessed an incredible sight. Nearly 1,000 aircraft including 300 bombers were flying up the River Thames towards the heart of London. They bombed a power station, the Woolwich Arsenal, a gas works, the docks and the City of London itself.

Two hours later another 250 bombers appeared and the raid continued through the night. German pilots reported back that London was an ocean of flames. London's Docklands was ablaze. More than 400 Londoners were killed and 1,600 badly injured. According to the Air Ministry, the Luftwaffe lost 99 planes and the RAF 22.

The BBC's head of drama, Val Gielgud, had been due to spend the weekend in the Thames estuary. If he had done so it is unlikely he would have survived the air raids that night on London's Docks and the East End. Instead he stayed in Sussex where there was a steady roar of German bombers passing overhead en route to

London. By pulling aside the blackout curtains he could see the whole sky a vivid salmon pink deepening to angry red as London was ablaze some forty miles to the north.

It was not his first narrow escape. While producing a play called *Three-Cornered Room*, Gielgud was dining with an American actress in the cast. They were eating privately in the flat of a friend near Marble Arch, a 15 minute walk from Broadcasting House. As they headed back to the studio with twenty minutes before the live transmission, the siren sounded, anti-aircraft guns opened up and the streets were deserted. About one-third of the way along Wigmore Street the shrapnel began to patter down. They had one helmet between them. Bombs fell around them, one just behind the Cumberland Hotel they had passed five minutes earlier. They made a run for it, reaching Broadcasting House with five minutes to spare.

By the end of September 7,000 people had been killed and over 9,000 injured. This was the Blitz. At its height, those who had no bomb-shelters in their gardens sought refuge in public shelters. When those were full they went into the tube stations of London Transport's underground railway. Sleep was almost impossible with the sound of bombs, anti-aircraft guns and the sirens of fire engines and ambulances.

There is evidence that the government did try to disguise the full effect of the bombing on London and Londoners, so as not to encourage the enemy. Newspapers published stories of people being brave and standing up to the effects of air-raids. They avoided photographs which might cause distress to the victims of the raids. Balham Underground station took a devastating direct hit but the pictures were not published until after the war.[7]

Even today, many Londoners have stories to tell of the Blitz. The author's late father, John Phillips, was assigned to directing anti-aircraft guns in Blackheath while his wife Vera took cover with her first-born daughter Linda in an Anderson shelter in her garden in Chiswick. In the hallway of the house there was a row of containers and watering-cans full of water in readiness for any fire.

Sure enough, that night an incendiary bomb landed on the house. She watched it penetrate the roof and rushed out of the shelter blowing on her tin whistle to summon help. Within minutes the fire brigade was fighting the fire, using the water-containers she had prepared, and managed to save the house[8].

Within days of the loss to Germany of somewhere between 60 and 180 enemy aircraft on 15 September 1940,[9] the long-planned invasion across the English Channel was postponed. But in place of daylight raids by the Luftwaffe, night attacks by Dornier and Junkers aircraft began, intended to bomb England into submission and surrender.

Despite the chaos, London continued to function as a commercial centre. Each morning, the red double-decker buses picked their way through the bomb craters and wreckage to get Londoners to work. Shops and businesses, even when glass had been blown out and wooden boards covered shop-fronts, carried the sign 'Business as Usual'. The English approached all this with their traditional sangfroid and stoicism. There was no evidence of wholesale looting and the public did its best to assist the emergency services dig through the rubble in search of survivors.

Bombs show no partiality. Nobody was safe. Buckingham Palace was hit by a bomb and 10 Downing Street, residence of the Prime Minister, suffered damage. Winston Churchill took refuge in his underground Cabinet War Rooms.

London's West End bombed

One area of London that was to become a key target after the East End was the West End. At the north end of Regent Street, where it becomes Langham Place and Portland Place, was a unique cluster of buildings. One lady who stayed regularly at the hotel is said to have remarked: 'That part of London in the late Thirties had everything – a Regency Church for the soul, the Victorian Langham for the body and the brand-new Broadcasting House for the mind. Then there was music at the Queen's Hall. In just that one corner was a complete civilisation.'[10]

Whether reporting from the front line or from the bowels of Broadcasting House, BBC staff faced the same dangers as everybody else. They also carried out fire-watching duties on the roof. The BBC's Tom Chalmers describes the scene:

> I can see practically the whole of London spread round me. The whole of the skyline to the south lit up with a ruddy glow. The flames are leaping up into the air now. The dome of St Paul's Cathedral is silhouetted blackly against it. It's almost like the day of judgement.[11]

The United States received eye-witness reports from Edward R. Murrow, among others. He had been based in London since 1937, living at 84 Hallam Street just along the road from Broadcasting House and the CBS European Office. He directed from London the European war-reporting of CBS. Murrow aimed to undermine the isolationism of the US and bring home to Americans what life in London was really like.

After Dunkirk, to convey the traumatic experience of the British serviceman, Murrow reported the story of a young airman he had met at an RAF base. In conversation, the man did not speak normally, every response was shouted loudly. Murrow asked why. 'Oh,' was the reply, 'he was shot down over Dunkirk, landed in the sea, swam back to the beach, was bombed for a couple of hours, and came home in a paddle steamer. His voice sounds that way because he cannot hear himself. You get that way after you've been bombed for a few hours.'[12]

Murrow reported the courage of the British troops and airmen and the everyday resilience of the people. He stayed in London throughout the Blitz. Although he could have reported with relative safety from the basement studios of the BBC, he preferred to commentate from high vantage points during bombing raids, often broadcasting live to the United States from the roof of BBC headquarters as the bombs fell all around him. In one report he admitted there were no words to describe what was happening: 'A man pinned under wreckage where a broken gas main sears his arms and face . . . the stench of air-raid shelters in the poor districts'. The determination which Londoners demonstrated to continue life as normally as possible found its way into Murrow's reports. He described the race as the bomb squads attempted to remove the bombs that had already fallen before the next batch fell from the sky 'but the milk and morning papers continued to arrive' at his flat each morning.[13]

Broadcasting House was sand-bagged all around its perimeter and heavily guarded. Although an obvious target for the German bombers, the London Blitz had continued for two and a half weeks before the BBC sustained its first damage. St George's Hall, adjacent to All Souls Church, Langham Place, was gutted by incendiary bombs and its theatre organ destroyed.

The Langham Hotel, across the road from Broadcasting House and facing All Souls Church, was hit just after ten o'clock at night on 16 September 1940. The high-explosive bomb struck one of the towers. Much of the west wing was destroyed. The bomb completely removed one of the bedrooms which had been taken over for the use of the programme announcer on late duty. Half an hour later he would have been sleeping there. Ed Murrow was in the restaurant at the time and wrote to his wife Janet, then in Somerset, instructing her to stay where she was. 'Under no circumstances return to London till I say so. Corner of Langham Hotel hit by a small bomb last night . . . I was dining with Dick Marriot at Langham when bomb fell – plenty of glass blown in and pillars staggered but no damage to us . . . West End took a pretty heavy hammering last night.'[14]

Another broadcaster who narrowly escaped death that month was J.B. Priestley. While he was writing and presenting *Postscript* after the evening news, he took up residence in the hotel. In September 1940 he had finished two broadcasts on a Sunday and was due to give another the following Tuesday. He had planned an early night but with great reluctance 'growling and cursing' accepted an urgent call from Canada House asking him to go into Broadcasting House to deliver a talk to Canadian listeners about the Blitz.[15] Priestley later told listeners what happened.

> Last night I had a very lucky escape. You might as well hear about it because after all it's part of the war, and in any case until I've got this story off my chest I'm quite incapable of talking about anything else. The night's air-raid began and the bombs sounded loud and near . . . A little later I heard that my hotel had been hit, not all of it, apparently, but one wing. I spent some odd moments then wondering which wing had been hit.

When daylight broke, Priestley wandered across the road to discover that his own room was one of those destroyed. A calm but deeply apologetic hotel manager in morning suit and striped trousers told him the news. 'I'm afraid you won't be able to return there. Well, no, sir, there's no breakfast but we hope to be able to arrange some lunch . . . Certainly, sir, the barber's shop is open.' It was a good example of the English at their finest.

During the first half of the war the team of newsreaders for the Home Service consisted of Frank Phillips, Alvar Lidell, Joseph McLeod, Alan Howland and Bruce Belfrage. Frederick Allen filled in for absentees and John Snagge read selected bulletins. Having so few newsreaders with such instantly recognisable voices, identifying themselves on the air, was one of the security measures to prevent impersonation in the event of German invasion. When invading Holland, Belgium and France, the Germans had taken over the radio stations and, during the confusion, when no one knew precisely how matters stood, they had impersonated the local radio announcers and broadcast false instructions to civilians to add to the confusion and disrupt the defence. Had Britain been invaded, there were locations prepared from which the BBC's news announcers could have continued to broadcast. The fact that the names and voices were so well known would have quickly exposed any attempt at impersonation.

On 15 October 1940, radio listeners heard a bomb hit Broadcasting House. It happened in the middle of a news bulletin. Announcer Bruce Belfrage was at the microphone reading the nine o'clock news when the building received a direct hit. At about 8.15 p.m. a cluster of bombs began to fall. One destroyed the International Broadcasting Company's premises in Portland Place. Another hit The George, a pub a few minutes away on the corner of Great Portland Street and Mortimer Street. The third bomb hit Broadcasting House. It had a delayed-action fuse and did not explode on impact.

The 500-pound bomb had crashed through a window on the seventh floor, fallen through two floors, through some swing doors and come to rest in the Music Library on the fifth floor in the heart of the building. The unexploded bomb was discovered at around eight-thirty. According to Bruce Belfrage's own account, shortly after nine o'clock 'somebody with more courage than sense tried to anticipate the arrival of the bomb-disposal people and to shift it to the outer corridor where, if it decided to explode, it would do less damage to the central structure'.[16] This brave but foolhardy person had acted on their own initiative. The building had not yet been evacuated. The bomb exploded and seven people were killed and many more injured.

Bruce Belfrage was in the basement studio when the incident occurred. Listeners heard the thud of a falling bomb and an explosion. The building shook, but the announcer's voice, after a barely perceptible pause, went on without a tremor. Behind the scenes was darkness, the crash of falling masonry, choking smoke and dust. People were flung against walls or pinned under wreckage. Belfrage recalled that 'apart from the descent of a good deal of plaster and soot, nothing happened to me except a severe attack of old claustrophobia. Had the great battleship collapsed into Portland Place?'

One of the most curious things is that a series of remarks were attributed to Belfrage by some of the millions who heard the whole episode through their loudspeakers as it happened. Some comments attributed to him were, in his words, 'brilliantly witty and others purely obscene'. They included the full range of expletives and swear-words to the calm assertion 'It's all right'. Belfrage though has put on the record what really happened: 'I am afraid it shows great lack of originality and enterprise that, in fact, I made no comment at all, but hurried on with the bulletin with the fixed idea of finding out at the earliest possible moment whether it was still possible to get out into the street.'[17] Here are the words of that news bulletin . . .

> This is the BBC Home and Forces Programme. Here is the news and this is Bruce Belfrage reading it. Tonight's talk after this bulletin will be by Lord Lloyd the Colonial Secretary. [There follows the sound of a massive explosion lasting around ten seconds before Belfrage continues without any reference at all to the interruption]. The story of recent naval successes in the Mediterranean is told in an Admiralty communication . . .

That one night destroyed thousands of precious gramophone records, wrecked the news library and reduced the telephone switchboard to a tangle of splinters and broken wire.[18] The explosion on the fifth floor had a devastating effect on many floors above and below. Studio 3E, where James Welch had first announced the invasion of Poland by Germany two days before war was declared, was severely damaged. This was always intended for religious services and broadcasts. It had a golden cross painted on the ceiling and alcoves to give the appearance of a church. Though not consecrated, it served in effect as a chapel. The bomb left the studio burned out, the ceiling damaged and the alcoves destroyed.[19]

At six in the morning after the explosion, the news librarian was trying to salvage the remains of important files from the wreckage and was nearly arrested for looting by a policeman. Losing the switchboard was a catastrophe. Nearly every internal telephone was out of action, a disaster for a broadcasting and news organisation. Small emergency switchboards were brought in which carried eight exchange lines instead of seventy. Working in a tiny gallery in the basement, the telephone girls coped as best they could handling eight calls per second. Nerves were strained to breaking point and it proved impossible for anyone to work more than an hour at a stretch in such conditions.

Overnight, Broadcasting House became a fortress. Beds were provided at this stage for staff working late or overnight. Corridors were littered with mattresses and the Concert Hall became a giant dormitory at night. A curtain stretched across the huge floor under the balcony separated men from women to maintain a semblance of privacy. The Director-General slept at first alongside commissionaires and support staff, sharing their discomfort. Later he had a bunk installed in his own room; 'to my shame', as he said later.

Another bomb, a very large one, completely demolished the block of houses behind the BBC which had been taken over as offices. A colleague of Bruce Belfrage was passing in his car just after the all-clear. He noticed, among the scattered office furniture in the road, a typewriter. He said to himself, Belfrage recalls:[20]

> 'This is justice. I have to work ceaselessly at my press articles in order to make my BBC salary up to a living wage. Let the corporation now give me some practical help.' So he quickly got out of the car, pushed the typewriter into the back and drove home in a hurry. It was a sad matter that it turned out to be the only Arabic typewriter in the BBC.

Not all the office equipment was destroyed. A BBC staff member wrote this from Broadcasting House:

Dear Old Thing,

I think I'd better take back my invitation to you in the last letter! What a night! They say it was the heaviest yet and I can believe them, although of course first thing next morning always seems hopeless. I think Margaret slept right thro' it. At any rate there wasn't a sound or a sight from her room the whole time. I went to bed about midnight, during a lull in the gunfire, and was wakened just before 2 by a terrific barrage. Then all our guns went quiet and our fighters went up and there seemed to be a terrific air battle going on just over our heads. The wretched things were dive-bombing which made it sound much worse. Then about 2.15 a plane zoomed down close to us – I thought it sounded as if something was wrong with it – then it roared up again and a few seconds later there was a sickening thud and the whole world seemed to shake, followed by several explosions. It was a Heinkel down on Camden Hill, just behind Patrick's place.

Hammersmith suffered badly again, up by the Broadway, and Oxford Street is closed from Marble Arch. BH [BBC Broadcasting House] building is all right, but all round it again caught it badly. Our building structure seems to have stood firm, but the inside is just blown out. We clambered up to our offices, over blown down walls and doors, and floors littered with glass and rubble, and have spent the morning salvaging. I got busy with brooms and duster and actually our office doesn't look so bad. The telephone had been blown right out of the window, hanging down its cord, and then I rescued it and put the receiver back on and it rang – still working! It was Patrick to know if I was all right. The City apparently didn't get it so badly, altho' it was pretty widespread. They're still digging for people under a pub just opposite our windows – it's rather sickening but how those A.F.S. [Auxiliary Fire Service] men do work.

Mrs M. Fawcett-Barry
Secretary to the Editor of the *Listener*[21]

The BBC studios at Maida Vale, a few miles west of Broadcasting House, received another direct hit. It was here that the reserve news announcers spent the hours of darkness, on standby to take over should Broadcasting House be put out of commission or destroyed. There was one deputy on standby for every thirty-five foreign language newsreaders as well as for the Home and Overseas services. The only fatality suffered was the German announcer.

On another evening, the bomb-spotters on the roof of Broadcasting House watched as a large object descended. They called the Defence Office in the basement to alert them. 'There's something coming down on a parachute – can't quite see what it is – it's quite close now – it's passing me – I can almost touch it!'. At this point there was a tremendous explosion. A large landmine had fallen and blown in part of the right-hand flank of the building. The voice of the Defence Officer rebuked the watchers on the roof: 'Butter-fingers!' The bomb had landed gently but carried a deadly payload of one ton of dynamite. It turned out to be a magnetic mine. It tore a huge hole in Langham Place, opening up the stonework in the side of Broadcasting House and flooding the basements of the Langham Hotel. The bomb that caused most damage to the hotel had drifted down into the roadway where its parachute caught on a lamp-post; then exploded. Four floors of the eastern bay of the hotel were swept away.

After this explosive barrage had continued for several weeks, the water tank on the hotel roof developed a fracture and burst. 38,000 gallons of water poured down through the seven-storey hotel. Most of the public rooms were flooded. It was no longer fit for paying guests but continued to act as home from home for BBC staff and visitors. One BBC Duty Officer was called in to investigate a complaint that one of the BBC staff had locked his room at night, a breach of wartime regulations. The offender was the talks producer Guy Burgess who occupied room 316 of the hotel. Burgess had broken out of the room with a fire extinguisher which had gone off damaging the door and carpet.

Part of Broadcasting House had to be evacuated. The staircase was a waterfall and the lobby a swimming pool. From an upper gallery a Canadian journalist looked down into what was normally the newsroom and saw that the desks were almost floating. The walls had broken into fissures from which burst spurts of water. In the kitchens, catering staff were choking from soot and dust and were then flooded. Electricity was gone and so the cooks evacuated. They had only two picnic primus stoves working. Yet by six in the morning, they somehow managed to serve 500 breakfasts amongst the wreckage. In spite of every kind of breakdown, the broadcasting service carried on unbroken.

Of those four buildings that the hotel guest had suggested provided 'a complete civilisation' in one corner of London, every one was hit directly and indirectly by bombs. Three were to survive the war. One did not. On the last night of the Blitz – 10/11 May 1941 – the world-famous concert venue The Queen's Hall was totally destroyed. BBC producer David Graham watched the incendiary bombs fall in clusters. One lodged itself on the roof. He was one of the fire-watchers. He raised the alarm, but the fire-fighters could not get there in time. He stood on the roof of Broadcasting House watching helplessly as the home of the Promenade Concerts burned to the ground. Sir Henry Wood had conducted what had been agreed would be the last season of concerts in The Queen's Hall in September 1940 because it was proving impossible for audiences to return home in the blackout. When he wandered through the charred ruins of what remained of the Hall the next day, Sir Henry Wood wept openly.[22]

Notes

[1] C.S. Lewis, *The Problem of Pain*, Preface, Geoffrey Bles: The Centenary Press 1940, now published by HarperCollins

[2] Walter Hooper was secretary to C.S. Lewis in the last year of his life and a member of The Inklings. He is one of the leading authorities on the life and work of Lewis and is literary advisor to the author's estate.

[3] Interview with Walter Hooper, 28 October 1999

[4] Churchill, Winston, *The Second World War, Volume II: Their Finest Hour*, p. 263, Cassell, London, 1949

[5] Alan Griffiths joined the order of St Bernard, and as a Benedictine monk was given the name Bede, by which he was known.

[6] 20 July 1940 in Hooper, *Letters*, p. 355

[7] *Modern World History: Propaganda* on the BBC's website: www.bbc.co.uk/education/modern/

[8] Source Vera C. Phillips now living in Ealing, West London.

[9] These figures are disputed. On 15 September 1940 after a massive daylight air raid on London, the BBC announced that according to official figures, 180 German planes had been shot down. In fact the number was about 60, according to the BBC's education website today. People believed that the BBC was telling the truth as far as possible and relied upon it for information. This helped the government maintain morale.

[10] Steel, Tom, *The Langham, A History*. London, 1990 (published privately by the Langham International)

[11] 7 September 1940, BBC Radio Collection, *75 Years of the BBC*, CD1 track 39

[12] Finkelstein, Norman H. *With Heroic Truth – the Life of Edward G. Murrow*, Clarion Books, New York, 1997, p. 69

[13] Ibid.

[14] Steel, op. cit.

[15] Steel, ibid.

[16] Belfrage, Bruce, *One Man in his Time*, Hodder & Stoughton, London, 1951, p.111–4

[17] Ibid.

[18] White, Antonia, *The BBC at War*, BBC pamphlet, p.9

[19] Studio 3E was returned to use but in later years became a general studio and was home to Radio 4's *Today* programme in the early 1980s. At present it has been decommissioned as a studio, divided in half and turned into two conference rooms.

[20] Belfrage, op. cit. p. 113

[21] This letter can be seen on display at the Imperial War Museum in London.

[22] The Proms moved to the Royal Albert Hall. Queen's Hall was never rebuilt. It was replaced by an office block, appropriately named Henry Wood House and still occupied to this day by the BBC.

CHAPTER SIX

Lewis Approached: *Right and Wrong*

～⌘～

James Welch had no choice. The war was going badly with England experiencing mounting loss of life at the hands of a ruthless enemy. Many hundreds were losing their lives. People dreaded the knock on the door that could herald the bearer of tragic news. The prospect of facing sudden tragedy was all too real. When the radio was switched on for the evening news bulletin, people braced themselves for what might follow. Death was becoming a daily companion for so many.

Welch himself had a narrow escape in Bristol. One Sunday evening there was such a severe raid going on that the religious *Postscript* could not be broadcast from its normal studio. The orchestra could not cram itself into the small emergency studio, but Dr Welch was determined that listeners should not go without their music that night. The microphone was placed under a table, and with bombs crashing all round the building, Dr Welch delivered his talk, announcer Stuart Hibberd read quietly from the Bible and Paul Beard played the violin on his knees.[1]

Welch was undeterred by such experiences. It brought him closer to the audience. He was going through the same as his listeners. He was facing the same questions. He recognised that the BBC's religious broadcasters must either respond to events or rapidly become utterly irrelevant. He also knew the questions that they had to address on air. Four stood out to him. 'Why has it happened? Whose fault is it? How can we prevent its happening again? What kind of world are we fighting for?' Welch was not a person who suffered from self-doubt. To him, all these problems presented a unique opportunity for religious broadcasting to assert itself. His resolution was unwavering. His response was assured:

> In a time of uncertainty and questioning it is the responsibility of the Church – and of religious broadcasting as one of its most powerful voices – to declare the truth about God and His relation to men. It has to expound the Christian faith in terms that can be easily understood by ordinary men and women, and to examine the ways in which that faith can be applied to present-day society during these difficult times.[2]

For those who were unable to be in their churches for whatever reason, including military service, radio could fill the spiritual vacuum. Via the medium of radio, people could join in worship both on Sundays and during the week. Welch hoped that these programmes would be attractive to those – to use his characteristically tactful phrase – 'on whom church membership sits lightly'. He hoped they would gain a better understanding of the meaning of worship. The regular Sunday services, the daily morning service and the midweek service on Thursdays, well established before September 1939, carried on during the war.

The best formats to deal with these four fundamental questions were discussion programmes and the scripted single-person broadcast talk. These provided an effective means to air such great issues. In February 1941, Welch experimented by running four discussions on successive evenings, with a panel of three laymen and one clergyman. They thrashed out as honestly as they could questions about the Christian gospel and the Church and their relevance to a world at war. It was also time to find some new names to reach the ordinary man and woman looking for answers to the big questions. The 'regulars' were familiar to the listeners. Welch wanted to do something original – to develop the broadcast talk within religious programme output as the main way to tackle the tough questions listeners faced from day to day.

The generous sprinkling of worship spread through the radio schedule was not enough to stand against the waves of questioning and the doubt. Welch added a regular Tuesday evening service with a theme relevant to the needs of the time. A shortened version of choral evensong crept into the Saturday schedule; and once a month, eight male voices sang Compline, a short service to close the day.

Like all great commissioning editors, Welch was prepared to seek out new talent and to nurture it, however raw. He knew that the microphone required skills different from those of public-speaking or teaching or lecturing. The best broadcasters sound as if they are speaking directly to you. It is intimate and personal. Yet to carry conviction, the words must have an authority and gravitas that command respect but also engage with the mind as well as the spirit. Where could Welch find a novel approach? Where could he find someone who could broadcast from a Christian perspective and deal with the doubts?

Welch found the solution where he least expected. The answer was not to turn to the tried and trusted names familiar to listeners. Nor would he seek out the rising stars in the Church of England or the non-conformist Churches. He had stumbled across a refreshingly different lay communicator in another genre altogether – a writer who earned his bread and butter as an Oxford don. Welch had just completed reading a book of Christian apologetics. It had made a huge impression upon him. He decided to write out of the blue to the author – a man he had never met. The book was called *The Problem of Pain*. The author was C.S. Lewis. Welch wrote to him at Magdalen College on 7 February, 1941.

Reference P/JWW   7th February 1941

Dear Mr Lewis,

I address you by name because, although we have never met, you cannot be a stranger after allowing me – and many others – to know some of your thoughts and convictions which have been expressed in your book *The Problem of Pain*. I should like to take this opportunity of saying how grateful I am to you personally for the help this book has given me.

I write to ask whether you would be willing to help us in our work of religious broadcasting. The microphone is a limiting, and often irritating, instrument, but the quality of thinking and the depth of conviction which I find in your book ought surely to be shared with a great many other people; and for any talk we can be sure of a fairly intelligent audience of more than a million. Two ideas strike me:

1) You might be willing to speak about the Christian, or lack of Christian, assumptions underlying modern literature, treating modern writers as those who feel they have something they must say and which expresses, sometimes in advance, the mood and values of our people, passing from description and analysis to something more positive and helpful.

2) A series of talks on something like 'The Christian Faith As I see It – by a Layman': I am sure there is a need of a positive restatement of Christian doctrine in lay language. But there may be other subjects on which you would rather speak.

The whole idea of broadcasting may be unattractive; but if it is not, I wonder whether it would be possible to meet and talk sometime? My colleague, Eric Fenn, looks after the talks of this department and he is often in Oxford; or I could come over specifically sometime, as I have a long overdue engagement to stay with D'Arcy at Campion Hall.

Even if you feel you cannot help us in our work, may I take the opportunity of thanking you for *The Problem of Pain*?

Yours sincerely

J.W. Welch (Rev.)

Director of Religious Broadcasting

Welch deserves great credit for making this offer to C.S. Lewis without ever having heard his voice. Although he could be fairly confident that an Oxford University lecturer would be able to acquit himself with honour in front of a microphone, there was a degree of risk. Not every writer turns out to be a good broadcaster, George Orwell being a classic example.[3]

Welch was keen to secure Lewis's talents as a communicator and was prepared to take a gamble on his voice. It would be misleading to suggest that Lewis responded to the invitation with unbridled enthusiasm. He could see the difficulties. He had never broadcast or written for radio, a quite different technique to writing for the printed page or for an audience of students in an Oxford lecture hall. He was also extremely busy with speaking engagements, including many to members of the armed forces. Then there was the university. How would they look upon one of their teaching staff broadcasting on the BBC?

Lewis replied within two days of receiving the letter, on 10 February. His reply was positive but cautious, hand-written in black ink with small lettering, squeezing in fourteen words per line. Where he can use a simple abbreviation he does – 'wd' for 'would', for example. All the correspondence between C.S. Lewis and the BBC is preserved in the BBC's Written Archives Centre at Caversham.[4]

Lewis thanked Welch for his kind remarks about *The Problem of Pain*. His preference was to write a series of talks as suggested, provided they were broadcast in his vacation. The first proposal of Welch – a critique of contemporary writing – holds no appeal. Lewis dismisses it in a sentence: 'Modern literature wd. not suit me'. Instead he comes up with an idea of his own, which picks up on some of the themes he had recently explored in *The Problem of Pain*. He wanted to talk about the Law of Nature – that is, objective right and wrong.

> It seems to me that the New Testament, by preaching repen-
> tance and forgiveness, always <u>assumes</u> an audience who
> already believe in the law of nature and know they have dis-
> obeyed it. In modern England we cannot at present assume
> this, and therefore most apologetic begins a stage too far on.
> The first step is to create, or recover, the sense of guilt. Hence
> if I gave a series of talks, I shd mention Christianity only at
> the end, and would prefer not to unmask my battery till then.[5]

Lewis makes the running in what turns into a long-drawn-out process of finding the right title. What should this series of Broadcast Talks be called? Lewis could have no idea that this first seed sown in his broadcasting career was to germinate into a successful radio series that would itself generate another three series of talks, let alone a book bringing all the talks together a decade later, the best-seller *Mere Christianity*. But this is how this famous book came into being. *Mere Christianity* began its life because James Welch had found *The Problem of Pain* intriguing. Through it he identified C.S. Lewis as a potential new broadcaster. The timing was also auspicious.

The shackles go on

Despite the best efforts of the government and the BBC, religious broadcasting was 'as much caught up in controversy as politics'.[6] The elevation of Archbishop William Temple from York to Canterbury in 1942 further blurred the lines between politics and religion. Whereas Archbishop Garbett of York saw the war as fundamentally a religious war over 'the right way to order human life',

Temple saw it as an opportunity to reshape the future. He was accused of openly preaching socialism.

Temple's view was that 'neutrality in religion is impossible, because religion covers the whole field of human thought and conduct'.[7] This view was not confined to Temple. The Malvern conference of clergy and laymen in January 1941 advocated a Christian social programme to build a new post-war society. Temple's own book *Christianity and the Social Order* published by Penguin Books in 1942 sold 139,000 copies. What added to the pressures on Welch was that Temple's close links with the BBC were well-known. His predecessor as Director of Religion, Iremonger, was Temple's biographer. William Temple himself was a regular broadcaster.

Talks took place within the BBC to try to protect the religious broadcasting programmes from getting caught in the cross-fire between government and Church. There had been complaints in Parliament about religious talks on the BBC descending into 'controversial political diatribes'.[8] The Minister of Information, Duff Cooper, told the House of Commons that it was not considered 'desirable that politics should enter into religious broadcasts'.[9] The issue was how much control the BBC should exercise over its contributors.

Pacifists were already beyond the pale. Was the ban to extend to those with overtly socialist ideas? Where would such a move leave the Archbishop of Canterbury? As always when faced with charges of impartiality or bias, the BBC established its own guidelines to protect its independence. Richard Maconachie was closely involved and James Welch fought his corner with customary vigour. The outcome was what came to be called within the BBC 'the Concordat' of August 1941. This laid down that ministers of religion 'had no competence to speak on the working out' of economic or political issues, but only on the 'moral and religious principles and criteria by which political and economic situations, proposals and policies should, according to their beliefs, be decided.' Speakers with known competence in economics and politics had to state on air whether they were speaking as experts or declare if their views were controversial. It was a typically effective BBC compromise. The Governors approved it in September and the Central Religious Advisory Committee, CRAC, added its acceptance of the Concordat in October 1941.

All of this made it more important than ever for Welch to look beyond the restraints placed upon ordained clergy to develop more lay talent. While all these religious-political discussions were going on, he was continuing to develop the BBC's relationship with C.S. Lewis. The only question would be, was Lewis good enough to cut the mustard as a broadcaster?

'The art of being shocked' – the search for a title

The correspondence between Lewis and the BBC shows how gingerly and slowly the relationship developed between them. Relatively unimportant aspects – such as the title of the first series of broadcast talks – dragged on without resolution for many months. The BBC invested considerable time in nurturing C.S. Lewis as a broadcaster. And for Lewis himself, it was as if he was learning a new trade, finding himself in the unaccustomed position of being a pupil once again studying the art of broadcasting. But when it came to the contents of the talks C.S. Lewis, although open to suggestion, would concede editorial control to no one.

For Lewis, of course, the BBC's invitation was simply an opportunity to reach a new audience. Lewis rarely turned down any invitation to speak if he could reasonably fit it into his schedule. He could have had no perception of how the talks would be received, let alone that they would provide the basis for arguably the most important work of Christian apologetics he was ever to produce. But he had already discovered that war-time provided other opportunities to serve beyond his role as a university lecturer and tutor, including talks for the RAF.

In his first letter to James Welch accepting the invitation to write a radio series, Lewis suggested the titles *The Art of Being Shocked* or *These Humans*. These were the two titles that Lewis first came up with. James Welch replied by return of post on 11 February 1941. He thanked Lewis for his 'hopeful letter' and promised to pass it on to his BBC colleague, Eric Fenn, who was in charge of the religious talks. Welch said that he would leave it to Fenn to write to him about the suggestion. The Director of Religion expressed a preference for *The Art of Being Shocked* over *These Humans* but this could be settled later. He agreed to arrange these broadcasts to suit Lewis's vacation plans and suggested that he or Fenn would come to see him at Oxford.

Three days later Eric Fenn wrote the follow-up letter. Using the formal greeting 'Dear Mr Lewis', Fenn's letter was warm in tone and gave Lewis some breathing space:

I am very glad to see from your letter of February 10th that you would be prepared to do a series, and I like the general sketch of what you want to do very much indeed. We are booked up (unless any catastrophe happens in the way of a breakdown of plans) until the end of July.

Eric Fenn offered Lewis a series of four Wednesday evening talks to be broadcast live between 7.40 and 8.00 p.m. in August or September. He continued:

I would be so grateful for draft scripts about a month in advance of the broadcasts so as to have the time to discuss these with you and to arrange for a microphone rehearsal and things of that kind. The process of getting a series of talks 'on the air' is rather more laborious than it appears from the other side of the microphone – but that of course you will understand . . . I think the best thing is to come over to Oxford and talk the matter over with you in the fairly near future.

One of the first things that strikes one in handling the original correspondence for the first time is Lewis's attitude to paper. There is no standard size of paper or style of writing. Lewis is very frugal, ever-mindful of the shortage in paper supplies, and he used anything and everything to write upon. Sometimes it was a small corner of a post-card, other times strips of paper or a college correspondence card cut into sections. Lewis would send a strip of paper with the letter on it. He would never post a whole sheet. He'd always been like that and apparently did not throw paper away even as a young boy.[10] He coveted every scrap of it.

It became worse for Lewis during the war because it was difficult to get paper. When his American friends offered him things like hams and asked him what he would like, he would suggest paper. Occasionally, he would jot down his reply on the letter he had received and return it by post. One of his letters to Dorothy Sayers was written at the bottom of her letter to him. Lewis's handwriting is meticulous, uncorrected and minuscule. The size is appropriate to the amount of paper to hand.

Lewis told Eric Fenn, in hand-written blue ink on a small piece of card dated 17 February, that broadcasting in August would suit him very well. They finally met at the end of April, having rescheduled an earlier meeting. Meanwhile Fenn had booked the talks into the schedule for four weeks beginning 6 August 1941.

Early in May, Lewis had his first microphone test. He described the shock of hearing the sound of his voice in a letter to Arthur Greeves, his friend from childhood.

> I was unprepared for the total unfamiliarity of the voice; not a trace, not a hint, of anything one could identify with oneself . . . But don't any of you crow; wait till you hear yourselves and then talk if you dare![11]

Within days of Lewis's microphone test, London was going through the worst night of the Blitz so far – May 10 and 11, 1941. Over 500 planes took part in the mission. This was a reprisal for Allied bombing of Berlin and other cities. This single raid killed 1,400 people including the Mayors of two London boroughs. The bombs reduced the chamber of the House of Commons to a pile of rubble. Members of Parliament had to meet in the House of Lords, although its chamber also suffered some damage. The roof of Westminster Hall was destroyed above the place where Thomas More had stood trial. Part of the tower of Westminster Abbey collapsed and St Paul's Cathedral was hit once again. The city's four main railway terminals all suffered damage. Hundreds had to be pulled out of the rubble of shattered buildings by the fire services. London was not alone, although it took the brunt of the air assault. Other cities, notably Coventry, Hull, Liverpool, Belfast, Glasgow, Southampton, Portsmouth and Plymouth had also suffered huge damage and loss of life.

Two days later, Lewis had completed an initial outline of the talks and sent it to Eric Fenn. Fenn's reply could not be described as exactly bursting with enthusiasm. He reserves judgement:

> I think this will at any rate do to be going on with. We don't need to settle exact titles until July. Between now and then one of us may have a better idea. Your title is good and descriptive, but if I may say so, a little dull. Anyway, I will try it on my colleagues and see what the result is.[12]

Already Lewis was discovering the difficulty of trying to appeal to such a diverse radio audience that ranged in understanding from those who were totally ignorant to those well-versed in Christian thinking. He approached the task of writing for the radio with the same thoroughness and conviction he brought to all his speaking opportunities. When *Broadcast Talks* was first published in July 1942, Lewis emphasised that his qualifications to speak were as a layman and someone who had been a non-Christian for many years. This, he felt, was what helped him understand how the ordinary person felt about the subject.

At this time he had begun to correspond regularly with an

Anglican nun called Sister Penelope. She was a prolific writer herself and was preparing some talks. C.S. Lewis explained to her what he hoped to achieve in his broadcast work for the BBC. The purpose was pre-evangelistic rather than direct appeal. Writing to her on 15 May 1941, Lewis was keen to discuss his scripts with her:

> Mine are *praeparatio evangelica* rather than *evangelium*, an attempt to convince people that there is a moral law, that we disobey it, and that the existence of a Lawgiver is at least very probable and also (*unless* you add the Christian doctrine of the Atonement) imparts despair rather than comfort.[13]

By 3 June Fenn had received the first two scripts for the series and this time the response was far more emphatic:

> I think they are excellent and there is very little that any of us wish to suggest about them. But, it would be a help I think, if I could see you while I am in Oxford for a further talk.

The content was good but Fenn was becoming aware that Lewis was struggling with getting the length right. Writing for radio is a precise discipline. It is not enough to read through a script afterwards to time it or to count the lines and multiply by three seconds per line. Much will depend on the reading speed at the time of broadcast and the complexity of thought involved. Unlike with a book, a listener cannot turn back the page to grasp at the second attempt what was not understood at the first reading. So a presenter might read a complex, difficult script more slowly than one that is readily understood at first hearing.

Lewis was not accustomed to writing to fit a broadcast timeslot. This was also 'live' broadcasting so cuts in duration had to be made in advance, not afterwards. Producers rarely let a script pass their eyes without a degree of re-writing to improve the flow and sharpen the delivery. There was no possibility of filling in the silence left by a script that was too short. Silence was an invitation for German transmissions to try to break in.

Lewis was delighted with Fenn's letter. The scripts were excellent. This was a huge shot in the arm for Lewis who was beginning to recognise that broadcasting was a lot more demanding than he could have appreciated just three months earlier when first approached. So with his confidence brimming, he decided it was time to move away from the formal business relationship to something closer to friendship. On 4 June, Lewis began his letter: 'Dear Fenn, (May we drop the Mr?) If you can come and lunch at 1 o'clock on Saturday, that would suit me admirably'.

This was a busy time for Lewis with his many extra-curricular activities. His life was already full well before the broadcast talks came along. On top of his teaching schedule and tutorials, outside engagements and writing the scripts of the programmes for the BBC, Lewis had also accepted an invitation to preach in the church of St Mary the Virgin, in Oxford, on 8 June. The sermon was later published in the journal *Theology* in November 1941 and by SPCK in 1942. It was called *The Weight of Glory*.

The Weight of Glory reveals how Lewis's mind was occupied at the time of the writing of the first series of Talks. Given that it was delivered to an Oxford congregation packed with students, in June 1941, its central theme stands the test of time remarkably well. Lewis begins by asking what men consider to be the highest of virtues. He asserts that where great Christians of the past might have named love as the highest virtue, contemporary man would say unselfishness – a negative term substituted for a positive. Why should this be the case? Positive desire for its own good and for the enjoyment of it is thoroughly Christian, he argues.

> If we consider the unblushing promises and staggering nature of the rewards promised in the Gospels, it would seem that Our Lord finds our desires, not too strong, but

too weak. We are half-hearted creatures, fooling about with drink and sex and ambition when infinite joy is offered us, like an ignorant child who wants to go on making mud pies in a slum because he cannot imagine what is meant by the offer of a holiday at the sea. We are far too easily pleased.[14]

This provided the spring-board for Lewis to explore ideas of paradise and of glory, the consummation of our earthly discipleship as he sees it. How we think of God is of no importance, compared to how God thinks of us. The promise of glory is only possible by the work of Christ. For Lewis, just the notion of not only pleasing God, but delighting him, 'seems impossible, a weight or burden of glory which our thoughts can hardly sustain. But so it is.'[15]

Lewis ends with an appeal to see our fellow humans as God sees them, with the full potential to attain glory in relationship with Christ. All day long – in all our dealings – we can help each other to that destination. Those we know are not just ordinary people or mere mortals. 'Nations, cultures, arts, civilisations – these are mortal, and their life is to ours as the life of a gnat. But it is immortals whom we joke with, work with, marry, snub, and exploit – immortal horrors or everlasting splendours.'[16]

Lewis appealed to his congregation to demonstrate that real and costly love to others. After the blessed sacrament, your neighbour is the most holy thing we can encounter. In a Christian neighbour, Christ himself is hidden.

One of those who heard him was Eric Routley, an undergraduate at Magdalen College from 1936 to 1940. He had first heard Lewis on the second Sunday of the first term of the war in October 1939. He saw that Lewis was billed to preach at the university and went along out of curiosity, because it was so odd not to have a clergyman in the pulpit. For *The Weight of Glory*, the church was packed solid well before the service began. The sermon took forty-five minutes to deliver, to 'stunning effect'.

Lewis read every word – there were no 'rhetorical tricks'. Routley credits Lewis with 'a superbly unaffected delivery – a deep voice that went well with his cheerful and bucolic appearance'. He was 'captivated by its uncanny combination of sheer beauty and severe doctrine'. Here was a man who was 'laid hold of by Christ and who enjoyed it'.[17]

It is hard to escape the conclusion that *The Weight of Glory* was an important influence on Lewis's own thinking at this time of creativity as he discovered the possibilities of a new medium in radio. To please God, as his sermon had argued so cogently, was a burden of glory that was almost too rich to bear, yet the impact it has on our relationships was impossible to escape. This train of thought must surely have reinforced in Lewis's mind that he was himself engaged in helping those with little or vague faith to reach another destination. Through the talks he was writing for the BBC, it would be possible to enter into a dialogue with a new audience. In doing this he would himself be demonstrating that real and costly love to others which he advocated.

By the second week of June, Lewis and Fenn had agreed upon a title for the series. *The Art of Being Shocked* and *These Humans* were firmly rejected. Over lunch in Oxford they settled on a new title. On Monday 9 June Fenn wrote to confirm what they both came up with:

> This is just to confirm the titles we discussed as follows:–
> 'INSIDE INFORMATION?'
> Four talks on the meaning of Right and Wrong
> August 6   Common decency
> August 13   Scientific Law and Moral law
> August 20   Materialism or Religion?
> August 27   What can we do about it?
> Whether or not we make use of the subtitles will depend on how it proves best to bill the talks. I think that if we can insert a short summary of the previous talk it may not be necessary to use a sub-title . . .'

Fenn asked Lewis to set aside 1 October as a possible time for him to deal with correspondence and questions that might arise out of the talks. The best-laid plans are so easily set aside in broadcasting by the unforeseen. Just when it looked as if the series was right on track, authorities within the BBC were having grave misgivings over Fenn's and Lewis's proposed series title *Inside Information*. It was described as 'unseemly' with perhaps the implication that in wartime, such a phrase might refer to sensitive information or even the fruits of espionage, not to profound Christian verities.

The matter was settled finally by an internal memo from Harman Grisewood, Assistant Director of Programme Planning (ADPP) to James Welch, Director of Religious Programmes (DRP).

BBC Internal Circulating Memo
From Assistant Director of Programme Planning
To DRP cc DPP

15 July 1941

Subject: Your talk series: 'Inside Information?'
I have been asked to let you know that we don't greatly care for the title 'Inside Information?'. C.(P) had thought that you had changed the title to 'Right and Wrong?' and was therefore rather surprised to see the old title turn up in your suggested arrangements for the week beginning 31st August, week 36.
It may be that the title for this particular week was given in error, and that (p)'s impression is correct. I simply write to let you know that he feels 'inside information?' is a rather unseemly title and would like to hear whether you press for it strongly.
H. Grisewood

Fenn reopened the debate with C.S. Lewis and they came up with a fresh title.

ADRB Bristol to ADPP London through DRB copy to C
(P), London
22 July 1941
RELIGIOUS TALKS SERIES: CS LEWIS
In the light of your memorandum of July 15th and after
consultation with C.(P), I saw CS Lewis on Saturday and
agreed with him to rename this series as follows:
RIGHT AND WRONG
A clue to the meaning of the universe?
1. Common decency
2. Scientific Law & Moral Law
3. Materialism or Religion?
4. What can we do about it?

The question of the title resolved, the next test for Lewis was the
broadcast itself.

Notes

1 White, Antonia, *The BBC at War*, BBC pamphlet 1942, p.11
2 Welch, James, BBC Handbook 1942, p. 59
3 Although none of Orwell's broadcast talks for the BBC have survived, it
   was known that his voice was not good. A contemporary described him as
   a poor and halting speaker (John Morris, quoted in an article by Peter Hill
   in the BBC's *Prospero* magazine), reprinted in the journal *Tune into Yesterday*
   Issue 33, journal of the Old-Time Radio-Show Collectors Association
   (ORCA), who can be found on the internet at www.eurekanet.com/~orca/.
   There were mitigating circumstances in Orwell's case. He had been
   wounded in the throat by a sniper in the Spanish Civil War and was a
   heavy smoker, killed by lung disease when only 46.
4 The BBC Written Archives Centre holds thousand of documents. As
   well as being a resource for programme-makers, it is able to help bona
   fide researchers, but they must first contact the Centre in writing to
   make arrangements for access to the documents. These can seen in the
   Reading Room under supervision. The bulk of the correspondence
   between the BBC and C.S. Lewis can be found in files 910 Talks File:
   1a covering 1941-43 or 1b covering 1944–1962. Other documentation

can be found in Copyright files File 1 1946–63 and Script Writer File 11: 1948–63.

[5] 10 February 1941

[6] Briggs, Asa, *The History of Broadcasting in the United Kingdom Volume 3, The War of Words 1939-1945*, Oxford University Press, Oxford, New York, 1995, p. 561 ff.

[7] Ibid. Letter from Temple to the BBC 15 January 1943

[8] Hansard vol. 370 columns 569–70

[9] Ibid.

[10] Disclosed by Walter Hooper in interview, 28 October 1999

[11] Hooper (ed.), *They Stand Together*, p. 489

[12] 13 May 1941

[13] Hooper (ed.), *Letters* p. 359

[14] Lewis, CS, *The Weight of Glory*, found in *Transposition and other Addresses*, Geoffrey Bles, London, 1949, p.21

[15] Ibid. p. 29

[16] Ibid. p. 33

[17] Routley, Eric, *A Prophet* – essay within Como, James (ed.), *CS Lewis at the Breakfast Table and Other Reminiscences*, Harcourt Brace & Company, New York, 1992 edition p.33 ff.

CHAPTER SEVEN

Life in Oxford

∽◌∾

While Lewis was working for the BBC, he lived in a rambling house called The Kilns, built in 1922, adjoining a set of brick kilns at the base of Shotover Hill on the outskirts of Oxford, in a secluded wooded area. Lewis's brother Warnie fell in love with the garden at first sight. In his diary it is described as 'such stuff as dreams are made of'. He lovingly recalls the lawn and tennis court at the front of the house and the large natural pool behind. The back garden rises up the hill, 'a steep wilderness broken with ravines and nooks of all kinds runs up to a little cliff topped by a thistly meadow.'[1] Beyond that are more trees, a small wood and glorious views. That was how it seemed, in 1930 at least.

The only surviving eyewitness to live with the Lewis brothers in Oxford in the war years is Jill Freud, born Jill Flewett[2]. She stayed with the Lewis family for two years from 1943. Jill was one of the evacuees sent from London to the comparative safety of Oxford. Before joining the household at The Kilns, she had lived with the three unmarried 'Miss Butlers' and their mother, at that time aged ninety-nine and kept in the dark that there was a war on. The 'Miss Butlers' were three of the little girls to first hear *Alice in Wonderland* from their friend Lewis Carroll. Freud remembers playing games devised by Carroll on Sundays.

In the summer of 1942 when Jill Freud knew she wouldn't be

going back to the Butlers' the following September, she went up to The Kilns to be vetted as a billetee by Lewis's close friend, the widoweded Mrs Jane Moore.

> I went along and she was lying on a sofa and she talked to me and seemed satisfied. We liked each other and I wrote her a thank you letter and so on, it was agreed she would take me the following September. That July it was decided that the school would return to London so I didn't go.[3]

It had already been agreed that her ration allowance would be transferred to Mrs Moore and that chicken food would be supplied on the ration instead of eggs because Mrs Moore kept hens. Mrs Moore didn't want to go through all the palaver of getting it back and losing the chicken food so the arrangement was continued. She said she would send Jill Freud's family eggs, so once a month they received twelve wonderfully fresh new-laid eggs which they would never have got otherwise from the 'miserable ration books' in London. After Jill completed her School Certificate she left school the following July. Mrs Moore invited her to come to Oxford for a vacation. She went for two weeks' holiday and stayed for two years.

She recalls her impression of The Kilns and its garden with similar pleasure to that of Warnie thirteen years earlier:

> The Kilns was lovely because there was this wonderful garden. There was a tennis court which of course we couldn't keep up. There was a great garden going right up the hill, really almost to the top. We had a huge pond which he cleared when he could. The Lewis brothers would swim in it and then go for long walks. They had created walks by placing planks across places where you wouldn't normally be able to walk. There was a lovely walk right up to Headington Hill – to the top and then down again through the woods – and that was all their land. The household had

a full-time gardener called Paxford who lived in a hut in the garden. He'd been called up to work in a sizeable munitions factory in Oxford and he was there. He did what he could in the evenings when the light was good enough.

By this time, the garden was beginning to resemble a farmyard. The household was short of domestic help and there was much to do. 'There were twenty-five chickens, there were rabbits, there was a huge garden, the house and there were these two men' to look after. During this period, Jill Freud went up to the Royal Academy of Dramatic Art (RADA) and took her entrance exam, returning immediately on the train to help with the hens that evening. The family encouraged her to go to the Oxford Playhouse where she saw plays like *Androcles and the Lion*, but only the first two acts because she always had to leave the theatre in order to cycle up the hill and get back to shut up the hens before dark, when the foxes came looking for them. Although offered a place at RADA, she did not take it up at that time.

The atmosphere in the house of an Oxford don was inspiring. Lewis encouraged her to use his account at Blackwell's to buy books and she was stimulated by the intellectual conversation at The Kilns. Although Lewis had something of a reputation for being fierce with his students, for being very caustic, and for sometimes cutting people down, Jill never experienced anything of that kind herself. 'If he was cross with me or I said something really stupid he just didn't answer. That was the worst I ever had from him. I got a telling-off once which pulverised me. I couldn't speak to him for a week.' At first she had no idea in whose house she was living. Lewis was away from home to deliver one of his lectures and he came back two or three days later. 'I didn't know that the Jack that they were talking about was C.S. Lewis. I thought his name was Jack Lewis by that time but I hadn't put two and two together. It wasn't really until I saw a whole lot of his books on a shelf that I suddenly [realised] . . . I was pole-axed.'

Displaying an early precociousness, Lewis had marched up to

his mother in the course of one family holiday, 'put a forefinger on his chest and announced "he is Jacksie". He stuck to this next day and thereafter, refusing to answer to any other name: Jacksie it had to be, a name contracted to Jacks and then to Jack. So to his family and his intimate friends, he was Jack for life.'[4] Although he never called himself Clive again, in his writings and broadcasts he remained C.S. Lewis.

Chaplain to the RAF

Most weekends, Lewis was away doing what he called his war work. This was an important role as lecturer in theology to staff in the Royal Air Force, though that is barely the right description for what he did. After the Battle of Britain, many young people preferred to volunteer for the Royal Air Force rather than wait to be conscripted into the Army or Navy. For a time, the RAF was able to attract more than its fair share of the cream of the nation. The Dean of St Paul's considered that the Chaplain-in-Chief of the RAF would benefit from having at his disposal a lectureship and proposed that C.S. Lewis 'should fill it and help with his great intellect some of the finest youth in the country'.[5]

So on a rainy night in 1941, the Chaplain-in-Chief, accompanied by Charles Gilmore, his advisor, went to Magdalen College Oxford to try to persuade C.S. Lewis to take up this honorary role as visiting lecturer to the men and women of the RAF in the many camps and training establishments across the UK. Lewis's first reaction was one of interest but diffidence. With the way the war was going, Lewis had not entirely ruled out the possibility of being conscripted himself. As the negotiations continued, Gilmore could see Lewis 'slowly but surely "taking off" and promising to soar'.

This represented a new assignment for Lewis. Gilmore's concern was that he would be hesitant to commit himself to lecturing to an audience of those who had left school at sixteen and rejected further studies at university. As Gilmore puts it, 'he was a teacher to his bones . . . but I don't think that he was, for all his kindness, the plodder's teacher'.

His first outing was relatively local, to the RAF base at Abingdon, in April 1941. Lewis reported in a letter to one of his regular correspondents, Sister Penelope, that as far as he could judge the talks were a complete failure.[6] The fact that the Chaplain-in-Chief kept the invitations coming suggests Lewis was being characteristically hard on himself. Charles Gilmore thought it had gone far better than Lewis did. Over three-quarters of his listeners were civilians temporarily in uniform with time to think about who would have a stake in the post-war world. They would be the ones attracted to his talks. The non-thinkers, Gilmore reckoned, would stay away.[7]

Lewis quickly 'grasped the position' and adjusted his speaking script accordingly. Lewis's impact was profound – it was neither 'striking nor startling . . . but as a result of hearing Lewis there were handfuls of young people all gaining quite new concepts of how they fitted into the life that immediately lay before them'.[8] Among those who heard Lewis speaking to the troops was a young man who went on to become Bishop of London, the Rt. Rev. Graham Leonard.

Lewis's RAF lectures appealed beyond the young service personnel to the chaplains as well, a cluster of twenty-six to forty-six-year-olds, whose role it was to offer pastoral and spiritual support to RAF staff. Their skills varied hugely – from doctors and clergymen to former combatants from World War One. They were in the front line of dealing with the horrors of war. They had to face the grief and despair of pilots returning from missions with brothers-in-arms left behind, killed by the enemy or missing in action. When Lewis came to address the chaplains, his selected topic was less than ideal. He chose to speak on 'Linguistic Analysis in Pauline Soteriology'. The talk was not going down at all well. Lewis seemed to be struggling for words and one of the chaplains was visibly bored and started filling in *The Times* crossword.

The skills of the lecture hall did not desert Lewis – sensing he was losing his audience rapidly, he changed tack. He dropped in a reference to prostitutes and pawnbrokers being 'pardoned in heaven, the first by the throne' and he grabbed their full attention. The rest of the session was punctuated with serious debate and laughter. As Gilmore remembers, linguistic analysis was an early casualty but Lewis had done his job. After that he always came to the last day of the chaplains' training course, held in Cambridge, where Lewis was to take up his chair as Professor years later.

The RAF talks continued and Lewis was to give up many weekends on a regular basis to visit RAF camps to speak on theology. For a while Lewis thought that it might turn out to be a full-time job. This didn't happen, but it did involve significant time away from The Kilns. Throughout the vacation of 1941 Lewis writes of how he would be at home for only two to three days at a stretch before going off to lecture. The RAF talks took him all over the country, from Cumberland in the north to Aberystwyth in Wales and Perthshire in Scotland. They took their toll too: 'One felt all the time as if one had just played a game of football – aching all over'.[9]

Lecturer & Tutor

For over thirty years, Lewis earned his daily bread as a college tutor at Oxford and later at Cambridge. It was what he did for a living. It was his working preoccupation and arguably what he did best of all. Everything else including the talks, the books – academic, fiction, apologetics and children's – the innumerable articles and the interminable correspondence that followed, was secondary to his role as university tutor and lecturer. He was every inch the Oxford don. He did not always particularly enjoy it, the heavy workload of daily tutorials was a burden, but Lewis was at his best speaking to a packed lecture theatre or listening to a student essay read aloud in a tutorial and giving his verdict upon it.

Derek Brewer, undergraduate at Magdalen College, Oxford 1941–42 and 1945–47, was one of Lewis's tutorial pupils. In later life he became a university lecturer himself, a writer on medieval English literature and Master of Emmanuel College, Cambridge. He does not claim to have known Lewis well as a friend but he gives us an insight from one of his brighter students. For Brewer, Lewis was a good example of the ideal. Learning was to the good Oxford don 'a way of life, exemplified by the bachelor Fellows'. They did not strictly teach but were visited in their rooms by their students who 'read the subject with them'. So despite all the differences between a student of eighteen and 'this distinguished, jolly man, we were nevertheless of the same kind, engaged in the same pursuit'.[10]

Lewis treated his pupils as more or less equals without thinking about it. Brewer puts this down to a nineteenth-century attitude in Lewis, 'of which Lewis and I were natural inhabitants' that prevailed in English universities until 'the disturbances of the late sixties and early seventies'. According to Brewer's portrait, C.S. Lewis enjoyed personifying the stereotype of an English don.

> . . . He felt, and even, I suspect, took a pride, in being old-fashioned – typical again in this respect. In his Inaugural Lecture as First Professor of Medieval and Renaissance Literature in Cambridge [29 November 1954], he referred to himself as one of the last examples of Old Western Man, almost as antiquated as a dinosaur. There is in this self-dramatisation an apocalyptic touch not uncommon in his generation, but he was right. Changes in university, society, and in the Western world and the developing professional-isation and fragmentation of literary studies on the model of science have eroded the old ideal. But it was strong in Lewis.[11]

His lectures left the impression of Lewis being 'sharp and school-masterly' in Brewer's mind, 'deriving from his conviction, energy, and clarity of mind, not from any desire to dominate'. The breadth of Lewis's knowledge was beyond question. He covered the whole of the Oxford syllabus for English literature, from Old English to 1830, including more theoretical papers on the history of the English language itself. His reputation as a scholar had been established by his masterly volume *The Allegory of Love: A Study in Medieval Tradition*, published in 1936. And his lectures were packed to the gunnels.

Those of Lewis's students who shared their reminiscences with James Como for his volume *C.S. Lewis at the Breakfast Table* describe him in almost identical terms.[12] Dom. Bede Griffiths became an undergraduate at Magdalen College, Oxford, in 1925, soon after Lewis had become a Fellow and tutor in English literature. They were later to become lifelong friends but, curiously, it was not until after Lewis's death in 1963 that Griffiths read the Narnia books and appreciated the full extent of Lewis's literary imagination. It took him by surprise. He had seen Lewis as the 'plain, honest man, with no nonsense about him, usually wearing when out on a walk an old tweed hat and coat, and accompanied by a pipe, a stick and a dog.'[13]

That physical description of Lewis is very close to that of George Sayer, his former pupil at Magdalen College and a close friend for three decades. His biography of Lewis is among the best.[14] Lewis would always take the early train from Oxford so he could say his prayers and enjoy the scenery before arriving in Malvern. What he liked was to walk and talk with friends. He wore a rumpled tweed jacket with leather patches on the elbows, baggy woollen trousers, walking shoes and an old hat. He had a somewhat battered rucksack and left his watch behind in Oxford, so as not to be aware of the time. Sayer, who lived nearby, would walk with him and their friends along the ten-mile Malvern Ridge, from where you can see the Welsh mountains in the distance on one side and the Cotswolds on another.

'Beauty was so important to Jack and so was good conversation. What could be better than putting the two together? . . . One could not have found a better walking companion.'[15] Jill Freud remembers: 'he liked beer, he loved the company of men in pubs, he loved walking. He and Warnie or he and his friends used to go on a walking expedition every year, have a week's walking holiday in the Lake District or something like that. He'd have his maps out. He loved those manly pursuits. He liked the dog which he'd walk every day.'[16]

Though a demanding schedule faced him for much of the time, Lewis was also conscious that in comparison with life in the army, he had an easy time. 'I am almost ashamed to describe my leisurely days to one leading such a gruelling life as you,' he told his brother in a letter of 24 November 1939. A few months later he is again apologetic. 'It seems almost brutal to describe a January walk taken without you,' but describe it he does. Lewis met his friend Cecil Harwood, known as 'Lord of the Walks', who despite his professed knowledge managed to take them to a village called Luccombe without a pub! They were compensated by finding a cottage that provided tea and bread and cheese and jam 'in one of those slippery, oil-clothy, frosty best parlours, with an oil stove that created an intolerable stench and a small library of reference works'. Lewis was particularly amused by the ambitious title of one volume: *Every Man his own Lawyer – Illustrated*. The title suggested this was an invaluable layman's guide to understanding the law with lots of helpful pictures. It wasn't, but it did include many illustrations of law courts and judges.[17]

The Inklings

The main group of friends in Oxford from which Lewis derived strength and inspiration was The Inklings. Edward Tangye Lean had formed this little society in 1930 when he was an undergraduate. Here people came to read out their own writings to their peers. At that time Lewis and Tolkien were meeting regularly and they both joined that group. When Tangye Lean left after taking his degree, they took the name over and that was the real beginning of the formal Inklings. The first weekly Inklings meeting took place on 25 April 1940. They met on Thursday evenings in Lewis's rooms and on Tuesday in the Eagle and Child pub, or as they called it, the Bird and the Baby.

The work would be read aloud, discussed, scrutinised and criticised. Among this group were the Lewis brothers, the writer J.R.R. Tolkien and Lewis's close friend Owen Barfield. Charles Williams also joined the group. In this forum of close friends, mutual self-respect provided a secure environment in which new ideas could be tested. When Warnie was away at war, Lewis would mention The Inklings in his letters. On 11 November 1939, having noted the absence of his brother, The Inklings dined at the Eastgate. However good the food may have been, it could not hope to stand comparison with the literary feast to follow. The fare included a selection of *The Hobbit* from J.R.R. Tolkein, a nativity play from Charles Williams and a chapter of *The Problem of Pain* from Lewis.

The subject matter of the three readings formed almost a logical sequence, and produced a really first-rate evening's talk of the usual wide-ranging kind – 'from grave to gay, from lively to severe'.[18] So The Inklings were the first to enjoy J.R.R. Tolkien reading his early drafts of *Lord of the Rings* and to hear C.S. Lewis test the ideas presented in *The Problem of Pain* and, later in the war years, *The Screwtape Letters*. There is always a risk attached in subjecting work-in-progress to the scrutiny of one's peers. Writers are at their most vulnerable at this stage when ideas are coming together but not necessarily fully-formed. The quality of relationships within The Inklings enabled the creative process to benefit from this additional level of refinement.

The group went most Tuesdays to the Eagle and Child or other Oxford pubs from 1930 until Lewis's death in 1963. Enjoying a relaxing conversation over a pint of beer has contributed much to British academic life and C.S. Lewis and J.R.R. Tolkien were no exception. The Inklings enjoyed a jug of beer in Oxford pubs just as much in the 1940s as Watson and Crick were to do at the Eagle pub in Cambridge decades later when unravelling the genetic code as a double helix. Even in wartime, life in Oxford had more than its share of compensations.

The Socratic Club

For many years Lewis was President of the Socratic Club, where the ideas of philosophy and faith were rigorously examined in a debating format. Although a skilled debater, Lewis did not always come out on top, even in disputation with other Christians. Lewis found his arguments for the existence of God refuted on one occasion by a Roman Catholic, Elizabeth Anscombe. Lewis told Bede Griffiths that her logical positivism had 'demolished' his position. Interestingly, that was not her own recollection of the debate. She thought it more even-handed but Lewis felt he had lost the contest that day.

It did not affect Lewis's personal faith. He may have lost a debate, but it did not shift him from what he saw as the truth. 'We have no abiding city in philosophy' was his view and no attempt to explain in logical terms the mystery of 'the God who is there' would ever be satisfactory. His faith had an in-built resilience because of its firm foundations, worked through over many years in his passage from atheism to theism and finally to Christian conversion.

Despite the war and the challenges it presented to faith, life at Oxford continued for Lewis and the Socratic Club was an important forum in which to test out his ideas. If The Inklings were to provide the security and intimacy of intellectual cut and thrust amongst trusted friends and confidants, at the Socratic Club Lewis's ideas could be sharpened, if at times cruelly exposed, in the rigid format of debate. But he minded not a jot. All of this was grist to the mill. Much of his best-known theological writing dates from these formative years.

In 1940, Lewis first conceived the idea for The Screwtape Letters and The Problem of Pain was published. The first Screwtape letter was published in the Church journal The Guardian on 2 May 1941. He preached The Weight of Glory in June and delivered the first talks on Right and Wrong for the BBC in August the same year.

This was followed up in 1942 with the second series on *What Christians Believe*, during which year the Oxford University Socratic club held its first meeting on 26 January. Later the same year, *The Screwtape Letters* were published and the series of broadcast talks were delivered.[19] More was to follow in the next few years, not least the publication of *The Abolition of Man*, *Perelandra* and *That Hideous Strength*. According to Professor Adrian Hastings, 'the popular religious apologetic of modern Britain was – to exaggerate somewhat – being composed almost at a stroke!'[20]

The private man

The personal characteristic which left the deepest impression on others was more often than not, Lewis's mind, or as Bede Griffiths puts it, his 'sheer intellectual power'. He was capable of being as witty and humorous as anyone in Oxford and was ready to discuss anything, but he never compromised when it came to argument. His criticism of any proposition was always 'rigorous'.[21] There were boundaries within the friendships. Lewis expressed irritation when Griffiths extended the debate they enjoyed in correspondence on matters of faith and practice into areas Lewis found unhelpful. That Griffiths had moved from Anglicanism to become a convinced Roman Catholic was not a problem for Lewis until Griffiths tried to persuade him to do likewise. This is not how Griffiths saw it. But Lewis had drawn a line.

Lewis was a deeply intellectual man but could also become quite emotional. 'The man I knew was highly persuasive, quite comical and very entertaining', his friend and biographer George Sayer recalls.[22] 'Above all, he loved a good argument and he rarely passed up a chance to jump into the thick of things.' Lewis was also capable of being annoyingly pedantic at times, without necessarily being aware of it. Walter Hooper recalls an incident towards the end of Lewis's life . . .

I remember when he was in the hospital that summer, I was in the room when the nurse came in. She said something like 'Professor Lewis your books are delightful and . . .' then she used another word. Whatever it was, Lewis said 'those two words mean something quite different. Did you mean when you used this word . . .'. She said 'Oh Professor Lewis, you need your medicine.' She just wanted to say something to describe her delight. Here was a man who really thought in words – he did not commit what he called 'verbicide', he didn't kill words by use of them.[23]

Nor did he suffer fools gladly. One of his pupils at Magdalen put his finger on it when he said to talk with Lewis was like entering a beauty contest, 'you had to be prepared to be told you're damned ugly'.[24] When Hooper moved into The Kilns as Lewis's secretary, he felt some personal apprehension.

I was a bit worried when I moved into his house. I had seen him in The Inklings group. I thought if I moved there, it would be too much for my brain. It would be overloaded. But he didn't talk all the time. What I found on the first day, when I moved in there, after a while he just picked up a book and asked 'did you bring your book Walter?' Then he was reading, you know. He didn't want to talk all the time any more than you did. I found that you could be in the same room with him, that was as much privacy as he needed and suddenly he was away. What was so great is that when you were talking, it really was talk about something. I don't think you wanted to wander off.[25]

Lewis loved to be surrounded by his friends. He was sociable and gregarious, enjoying their camaraderie and fellowship to the full. Hooper again: 'What meant the most to him was friendship. The many hours spent in the pub – there was nothing he liked more than the sound of adult male laughter.'

When it came to his writing, he would set aside the companionship of his friends to complete the task ahead. Jill Freud recalls one occasion when he was trying to get a piece of work done and he had sinus trouble and was having to work in great pain. 'Then there was a kind of shush in the house and everybody was trying not to disturb him.'

Just as Lewis adopted a disciplined approach to his academic work and his writing, he exercised the same self-discipline in his personal spiritual life. Prayer mattered to him deeply and he studied a wide range of religious literature. He read the *Imitation of Christ* by Thomas à Kempis nearly every day, he told his friend Arthur Greeves in a letter.[26] He added with typical self-deprecation, 'It's rather like creatures without wings reading about the stratosphere'.

One way in which he could ensure his personal spiritual life was maintained was to impose upon himself the discipline of regular confession before his spiritual director. Once a week, he went to see one of the so-called 'Cowley Fathers', members of an Anglican order called the Society of St John the Evangelist, based in Cowley just outside Oxford. Father Walter Adams heard the confession of C.S. Lewis every week from September 1940.[27] As in the relationship between doctor and patient, what takes place between a spiritual director and his charge is entirely private and confidential, so what was said at these meetings we will never know.

The decision to take on a spiritual mentor was apparently one of the hardest he ever had to make, he told his correspondent Sister Penelope. To submit himself to the oversight of another person was not easy for someone so strong-willed. But it was one he did not come to regret.

The discipline that these private times of reflection delivered gave Lewis a structure to his life that enabled him to fit in everything else. Life at The Kilns, his academic responsibilities as a tutor and lecturer, the discussion groups provided by The Inklings and the Socratic Club all kept his mind alert and his intellect satisfied. Into this C.S. Lewis fitted the letter-writing, the reading and preparation of books, the sermons and talks to the RAF and, when he could manage it on top of the rest, his broadcast talks for the BBC. It was a rigorous schedule by any account but the wartime years were among the most productive of Lewis's whole life.

Notes

[1]   7 July 1930, in Clyde S. Kilby and Marjorie Lamp Mead (eds), *Brothers and Friends: The Diaries of Major Warren Hamilton Lewis*, 1982 and quoted in Hooper, Walter, *C.S. Lewis: A Companion & Guide,* Harper Collins, London 1966 p. 767

[2]   Jill Freud was born June Flewett. After living with the Lewis household in Oxford she trained at RADA and became a professional actress. She now runs her own theatre company Jill Freud and Company which in 2000 presented its sixth season of Summer Theatre in Aldeburgh in Suffolk, described by the *Observer* newspaper as 'the Rolls Royce of summer repertory'. She was interviewed on 19 November 1999.

[3]   Interview with Jill Freud, 19 November 1999

[4]   Lewis W.H., *Memoir of CS Lewis* contained in Hooper (ed.), *Letters,* p. 22

[5]   Gilmore, Charles, *To The RAF,* p. 186 ff. in Como, James, *C.S. Lewis At The Breakfast Table and other reminiscences*, A Harvest Book, Harcourt Brace & Company, New York, 1992

[6]   Letter to Sister Penelope C.S.M.V. 15 May 1941 in Hooper (ed.)., *Letters,* p. 359

[7]   Gilmore, op. cit. p. 187

[8]   My source is Walter Hooper, interviewed on 28 October 1999

[9]   23 December 1941: *They Stand Together – The Letters of C.S. Lewis to Arthur Greeves (1914-1963)* edited by Walter Hooper, Collins, London (1979) p. 491

[10] Brewer, Derek, *The Tutor: A Portrait,* in Como, *op. cit.* p.41–67

[11] Ibid.

[12] Como, James T., op. cit. p. 12

[13] Ibid. Griffiths, Alan Bede OSB

[14] Sayer, George, *Jack – A Life of C.S. Lewis*, Hodder & Stoughton, London, 1997

[15] Mattingly, T, *George Sayer talks about C.S. Lewis*, published in the public domain on the Internet 28.11.1998

[16] Interview with Jill Freud, 19 November 1999

[17] 9 January 1940 in Hooper, (ed.), *Letters*, p. 333

[18] Ibid. 11 November 1939, p. 328

[19] Chronology taken from Walter Hooper's *C.S. Lewis – Companion & Guide*, p. 123–124.
[20] Hastings, Adrian, *A History of Christianity 1920-1990*, SCM Press, London, 1991 paperback edition p. 389
[21] Como, op. cit, p. 17
[22] Mattingly, op. cit.
[23] Interview with Walter Hooper on 28 October 1999
[24] Ibid.
[25] Ibid.
[26] 25 May 1941, Lewis,*They Stand Together*, p. 490
[27] Hooper, op. cit. HarperCollins, 1996, p.32

CHAPTER EIGHT

Getting Lewis to Air

∾∾

The domestic environment in which Lewis lived and worked was not ideal for writing for radio. He was a fair distance from those who had commissioned his BBC talks. The religious programmes department was still operating out of a hotel in Bedford. Its staff would regularly come to London, but Lewis relied on correspondence with his producer Eric Fenn for feedback. The task of producing his recordings in the studio was often left to another member of the production team, A.C.F. Beales.

With the question of the title resolved, the next test for Lewis was the script itself. Fenn wrote to Lewis on 31 July inviting him to a script rehearsal and read-through. This had a number of purposes.

Although Fenn and Lewis had become well acquainted by now and built a relationship of trust and mutual respect, there was no escaping the truth that Lewis was a broadcasting novice. The fact that he could write was not in question. His skill as a lecturer was beyond doubt. His abilities as a public speaker, to judge by the ever-increasing demands of the RAF, were highly valued. But there is a world of difference between public speaking and broadcasting. Even in his public address, Lewis did not always enjoy the reception he had grown to expect from his students at Oxford. He had not found it easy at first to adjust to the new audience within the armed forces, so how would he fare as a broadcaster? Would he find broadcasting on radio just as daunting? For his producer a proper rehearsal in front of a microphone with C.S. Lewis was essential 'because of getting the timing fixed and knowing exactly where we are in view of its being considerably short of the allotted time'.[1]

On the day of the broadcast Fenn and Lewis arranged to meet at 6.30 for a meal in the canteen before the rehearsal at 7.10. Eric Fenn had another concern, which he revealed in an internal memo to the Director of Programmes.

> These talks are very short compared with similar manuscripts, but until I rehearse Lewis on Wednesday next, I won't know how quickly he speaks. My impression is that he will take them slowly. It is likely however that he will under-run by a good 2 and a half minutes. I have done something to compensate for this with a longish opening and closing announcements, but I had thought I better warn you.

It was a classic producer's solution. Always have to hand something for the continuity announcer to say in the event that a live broadcast under-runs.

Authorship came easily to C.S. Lewis. Apart from his earlier academic books, his writing was done mostly in the evenings at home. As he put it once to one of his students, Derek Brewer, he wrote at night when he was too tired for serious work. 'He wrote because he could hardly stop himself, running off a few pages on return to his room late at night, just for the fun of it, writing at his table with his steel-nibbed dip-pen.'[2]

Curiously, Lewis did not see his writing as something particularly creative. He saw real creativity as something applicable to God but not really to man. Creation, as it applies to human authorship, seemed to him an entirely misleading term. Writing was to him a process of re-arranging elements that God has provided. For that reason we can never know the whole meaning of what we write and the truest meaning may be something the writer never intended. Lewis concluded that 'if one could *really* create in the strict sense wd one not find we had created a sort of Hell?'[3]

Lewis considered it easy enough to be published but much more difficult to get people to read what you have written. 'Even his religious books,' Brewer observes, 'were in this sense by-products. His primary energy went into tutorial teaching.'[4]

Having seen more of his original manuscripts than probably anybody else, Walter Hooper observes that there is next to no evidence of rewriting or of copious changes. The manuscript of *The Screwtape Letters* is a case in point. There was only the one draft.

> The only changes he might make might be the change of a single word. In *Screwtape,* I remember, he knows that a particular word is misspelled so he strikes it to try again, still can't spell it so he strikes it to use a different word. I have seen the occasional thing, like the opening of *That Hideous Strength*. In one of his notebooks he makes Jane Studdock not a student of English but a biochemist. Then I think he realises he didn't know enough about Biochemistry to fake it and so he thought no I'll have to give her something I really do know about myself. So that was a false start but I don't think it happened to him often. It's him just simply writing a book as he did right up to the end of his life. *Letters to Malcolm* – just a single copy of it you know. You don't have a man revising or anything like that – so it came out almost as it is which you read in print.[5]

Once his mind was applied to the task in hand, Lewis did not find it difficult to put pen to paper. He was not easily distracted. Hooper recalls an incident he witnessed which showed Lewis's ability to concentrate his mind upon something:

> The house-keeper came in to say the meal was ready. Lewis would stop in mid-sentence, put the glass down, go in and

have supper and come back in the room. He'd then pick up mid-sentence where we were before. Nothing was left unfinished. In conversation with him you had to be prepared for this. You couldn't just wander off or leave something by saying 'well whatever . . .', you had to follow to what he called the 'ruddy end'. 'Had we finished with that?' he would say. But if you are going to start something you finish it. If you say you think something is like something else – he might say 'in what way?' So you think, 'I wish I hadn't started that' because you are really forced to go on to the absolute end. But I think it was the method of his thought, nothing was left dangling.[6]

The process for preparing the script was itself an unwelcome complication. Lewis would write it out in neat longhand in blue ink and send it to the BBC. It would then be typed, with the top copy sent back to Lewis and carbon copies left for the producer in London to read through or refer to others for a second opinion. Eric Fenn could also read it aloud in an attempt to mimic Lewis's speed of delivery with a stop-watch running. This would give the producer an approximation of whether or not the script was the right length to fill out fifteen minutes when read out 'live' on air by C.S. Lewis. If it fell short, there was time to contact Lewis to get additional sections added and to make any amendments.

C.S. Lewis's first broadcast: the schedule that day

Wednesday 6 August 1941 was not a particularly auspicious day for C.S. Lewis to make his first broadcast.[7] His slot in the schedule was 7.45 p.m., allowing him time to get into London during the day, to do a run-through if needed, before going live in the early evening.

The broadcasting day began at 7 a.m. as usual with Big Ben followed by the news. Music played until the first religious output of the day, the five-minute talk *Lift up your Hearts!* given by the Rev. Anthony Otter. The breakfast news at 8 a.m. was followed by the usual cookery tips on *The Kitchen Front,* in which Dr Margaret Wright spoke about healthy eating. The BBC Salon Orchestra occupied the next forty minutes with a selection of dance and ballet music, from Evesham. More film scores and organ music from the BBC theatre organ followed. At 9.50 a.m. it was time for the topical magazine programme *At Home Today,* with news commentary for schools from 10.05 till 10.15 a.m. This brought the second religious programme of the day, *The Daily Service.* This came from Bedford. It was very traditional, opening with the hymn *Holy, Holy, Holy* and ending with *My God, How Wonderful Thou Art.* Listeners were encouraged to follow the service at home from their worship books, *New Every Morning.* At 10.30 a.m. there was a live broadcast of the opening ceremony of the National Eisteddfod of Wales, the annual arts and culture festival. *For The Schools* at 11 a.m. was followed by a talk on first aid before another music programme, *Rhythm and Romance.*

Noon meant comedy with an interview by Wilfred Pickles with Albert Burdon, followed by more from the festival in Wales and the next musical entertainment programme *Happy-Go-Round.* At 1 p.m. after the Greenwich Time Signal, came the lunchtime news bulletin, fifteen minutes in duration.

The afternoon schedule had a little more speech than the music-led morning schedule. But it was music that followed the news. The Amponians Dance Band played until 2.30 p.m., when Sidney Harrison presented the second of a series of programmes exploring how different composers had tackled the themes of love and war. This half-hour programme was probably not assisted by its absurdly long title *None But The Brave Deserves The Fair.* From 3 till 3.30 p.m., Jack Leon and his Orchestra played *Music While You Work,* an important programme of upbeat music designed to lift morale and to keep the production lines going.

At 3.30 came the first broadcast talk of the day. R.W Paine was employed from 1925 to 1934 by the government of Fiji as a coconut entomologist, during which time he made visits to Java and other islands in the Pacific. In 1936 he started commercial horticulture on a 24-acre estate in Argyllshire, in Scotland, where his market-garden business was flourishing. His talk was predictably on *A Highland Market-Garden in Wartime*.

The antidote to that was an immediate quarter of an hour of recorder music, then a repeat of *The Happidrome,* a popular variety show starring Walter Widdop, Iris Sadler, Stanelli, Cheerful Charlie Chester and Billy Bennett. Welsh news and features followed.

It was now 5.20 and most schoolchildren would be settling down around the tea-table ready for their supper before bedtime. This was their time and from 5.20 until 6 p.m. the BBC broadcast *Children's Hour*. On this particular day, they heard the first part of a new adaptation for radio of the ever-popular children's book *Anne of Green Gables* by L.M. Montgomery. The play was followed by *Children's Hour* prayers.

At 6 p.m. with the Greenwich Time Signal came the early evening news bulletin followed by National and Regional announcements. At 6.30 p.m. the popular broadcaster Freddie Grisewood presented *The World Goes By*. This was a news magazine programme in which Grisewood 'brings to the microphone people in the news, people talking about the news and interesting visitors to Britain'. On this day they included Colonel Clement Egerton talking about Portugal, Evarts Scudder on America, John Bevan on life in the Home Guard and an anonymous naval sub-lieutenant on sea-faring in wartime. Douglas Hastings ended on a humorous note with 'These things have made me laugh'. By this time C.S. Lewis would probably have been preparing to rehearse his talk in the studio.

At 7 p.m. another thirty-minute magazine programme went out called *Under Your Hat*. This was billed as a weekly radio magazine for those 'who guard the homes of Britain, the Civil Defence Force'. This was another attempt to boost morale with items by Auxiliary Fire Service and police bands, choirs and concert parties from all parts of the country.

It had such improbably named groups as the Berkeley Square Bunkhouse Singers and the Hillbilly Swingers from Dover Auxiliary Fire Service station led by Fireman Marsh with his rendition of 'Home on the Range'.

A regular feature called *Salute to Heroes* gave personal glimpses of the men and woman who had been awarded medals for bravery. Charity Bick described how she won her George Medal. In a sentence of great bravura, the *Radio Times* billing courageously promises that 'amusing and interesting people among your colleagues come to the microphone to entertain you'. If that was not an open invitation to switch off the radio then what followed would be the kiss of death to any lingering hopes Lewis may have had of inheriting a sizeable audience from the programme that preceded his first radio broadcast.

After the home entertainment of fire wardens came another fifteen-minute bulletin of news at 7.30 p.m., this time not in English or even in Welsh but in Norwegian. This could be heard via long wave in Scandinavia and was an important service to the Norwegians who tuned in at that time of day to hear it. It is hard to imagine a more difficult broadcasting debut. Following the news in Norwegian is not the most dramatic entrance in broadcasting. It was not quite a graveyard slot as there was still a sizeable audience, but the listeners he would inherit would be largely Norwegian apart from those who switched on again at 7.30 p.m. after completing their evening meal. The *Radio Times* billing simply reads:

7.30	News in Norwegian
7.45	'RIGHT AND WRONG'
	A clue to the meaning of the universe?
	1. 'Common Decency' by C.S. Lewis, Fellow
	of Magdalen College, Oxford.

It's important to appreciate that for the BBC, this was the first of a series of broadcast talks produced by the religious programmes department. C.S. Lewis was not well-known. With hindsight, it seems extraordinary that this first series of broadcasts, which was to shape Lewis's life and produce a world best-seller, *Mere Christianity*, should begin in such a humdrum way. Humble is barely the word. This would probably not have bothered Lewis one bit. He was not concerned with questions of vanity or drawing attention to himself. This was simply an intriguingly different speaking engagement to a bigger audience than he could hope to reach by any number of public addresses or university lectures.

For the BBC, it solved a scheduling problem. Something thoughtful was needed to insert in the radio schedule between the nightly news in Norwegian and songs from the National Eisteddfod of Wales. It had long been a tradition among Welsh people to entertain themselves in family parties in each other's homes with the recital of impromptu verses and the singing of folk songs and choruses. 'This evening's broadcast takes you for half-an-hour to such a gathering, which has been organised as part of this year's Eisteddfod.'

So the schedule delivered to Lewis an audience of Norwegian speakers and those who turned on as a matter of course once the Norwegian news was over. And those who had been enraptured by the intermittent coverage of Welsh culture from the Eisteddfod throughout the day, would have caught the end of Lewis's talk. After this came a melodrama produced by Val Gielgud called *Under Suspicion* (with characters that included Freya, a celebrated pianist; Gretel her maid; Strenk of the Secret Police; Major Breska of the General Staff and Herr Bormer, the Leader's Deputy) followed by the most important news bulletin of the day.

Music, ranging from the BBC Orchestra playing Wagner, to *Dance Cabaret,* from Gaelic folk tunes to the light classics, continued until the midnight news. Not that C.S. Lewis would have heard the programmes that followed him. He would have been on his way back to Oxford by train from Paddington Station.

The BBC's verdict on talk one

Despite its difficult slot in the schedule, Lewis's first broadcast went well. Eric Fenn was delighted. He wrote to Lewis on 7 August 1941 apologising for having to rush away after the broadcast 'but I did get my train, which was something. I also got a seat, which was more'. Fenn was still worried about the length of the talks. 'I think it would be wise to have a run-through of the script before the broadcast. This gives a clear idea of the timing and enables provision to be made for the gap.'

As the series progressed, the schedule seemed to grow more favourable to Lewis. The third talk – on 'Materialism or Religion?' – Lewis inherited an audience, with Freddie Grisewood's interviews in *The World Goes By* and cabaret beforehand, and *The Marriage of Figaro* conducted by Malcolm Sargent afterwards. The following week was better still. This time Lewis was sandwiched between *Melody Unlimited* and *Operatic Music* from the BBC Theatre Orchestra and Chorus. When it came to the fifth talk in the series, in the week of the second anniversary of the declaration of war, Lewis's final talk answering listeners' questions fell between a comedy show, *Can You Beat It?*, in which listeners tried to be funnier than star comedians, and a special documentary on the second year of the war called *No Longer Alone*.[8] That on its own would have guaranteed Lewis a multi-million audience.

How did it go down with the listener? RAF officer John Lawler was in the officers' mess when someone had ordered a drink. The radio was on and Lewis came on the air as the barman was about to hand the drink back. 'Suddenly everyone just froze listening to this extraordinary voice. And what he had to say. And finally they end up and there was the barman with his arm still up there and the other man still waiting for his drink. And they all forgot it, so riveting was that.'[9] So what was it that gripped the barman?

Content of the first broadcast

The first talk sets out the theme for the whole series. Lewis's very first sentence and what follows is what journalists would call a 'grabber'. It engages you right away.

> Every one has heard people quarrelling. . . . 'That's my seat,
> I was there first' – 'Leave him alone, he isn't doing you any
> harm' – 'Why should you shove me in first?' – 'Give me a
> bit of your orange, I gave you a bit of mine' – 'How'd you
> like it if anyone did the same to you?' – 'Come on, you
> promised.'[10]

The point Lewis makes is that each of us appeals to or falls back upon a standard of behaviour to which we hold others to account. We may call it lots of things, decency or fair-play, or even morality. The point of a quarrel is to prove someone else is wrong and you are right. This makes no sense unless both sides have some agreement of what is right and what is wrong, just as a foul in football, for instance, means nothing unless both sides are playing to the same rules.

The rest of the talk follows in the same vein, probing and clarifying, using plenty of illustrations that would ring true. He underlines the assumption we make that the human idea of decent behaviour is universal. If not, then all that is said about the war is nonsense: 'What is the sense in saying the enemy are in the wrong unless right is a real thing which the Germans at bottom know as well as we do and ought to practise?' This sentence, written at the height of the war, is simply put into the past tense when published in *Mere Christianity*. The ideas that Lewis explores on natural law do not date with the passage of time. One of the keys to Lewis's appeal was his willingness to identify wholly with the listener and to reject any sense of preaching or speaking down to people. He says that none of us succeeds in keeping the law of nature. 'If there are any exceptions among you', he tells the listener, 'I apologise to them. They'd better switch on to another station, for nothing I'm going to say concerns them.' It takes a brave broadcaster to invite listeners to switch off. Lewis could take the risk because he knew that no listeners would consider themselves to be morally perfect, certainly not in August 1941.

Assessing Lewis as a broadcaster

Lewis made the connection with the audience as strongly as he could in this first broadcast. He insists that he is not preaching, and in common failings such as broken promises and excuses for bad behaviour he is no different to anyone else. He ends by saying that we can't shake off the idea that we know how to behave but in practice don't do so. We break the Law of Nature. Realising this is in fact the basis for all clear thinking.

The first talk set the tone for the remainder of the series. Lewis had found a style that suited him and the listener. It was direct, colloquial and intellectually challenging. Only one recording survives of a single talk from Lewis's eventual four series for the BBC. There is a simple explanation for this. Live broadcasts offered a number of critical advantages over pre-recorded talks. First, a live talk has an immediacy and direct conversational approach that a pre-recorded broadcast can seldom match.

Second, once cleared by the censor, a talk could be broadcast without delay. A pre-recorded talk might need to be re-recorded if circumstances had changed between the recording and broadcast.

Third, recording was an expensive process. All recordings were made on twelve-inch metal discs with a coating of cellulose acetate. A steel needle cut the sound track into the disc, producing four minutes of airtime.[11] With metal a costly and scarce resource, recordings were not made of studio broadcasts unless there was a special justification such as historic interest. Reporters in the field had to rely on discs entirely however to record the sounds of war.[12]

At the outbreak of war the use of disc-cutters was widespread. A model called Presto was imported in large numbers from the United States, installed in cars and vehicles and became the mainstay of war correspondents all over Europe. BBC engineers produced a recording device in 1938 which was the most adaptable and portable yet. It consisted of a disc-cutter scarcely bigger than a record deck, with amplifiers and power supplies carried in portable units connected by plugs and sockets. This enabled it to be carried from a car or ship to any location. Power came from the mains, or a battery in the boot of the car. Four hundred yards of microphone cable was provided just in case. This was a breakthrough for the BBC as recordings up to four minutes long could be made from ships at sea, aeroplanes or even on a submarine. One famous recording was made in a Lancaster bomber flying over Germany on a bombing raid.

In Germany, a scientist called Pfleumer had discovered that instead of using steel, as the Marconi-Stille Blattnerphone did for transmitting recorded material, iron oxide (rust) could be used instead. It had better magnetic properties and could be deposited on a paper backing. This was the beginning of reel-to-reel magnetic tape recording. The German company AEG-Telefunken released a highly efficient magnetic tape recorder, called the Magnetophon, to the industry in 1937. Remarkably, it was only when Allied forces liberated Luxembourg in 1944 that the British discovered what the German broadcasters had been using. The quality was so good that live and recorded programmes had been indistinguishable.[13] It also explained why Hitler had appeared to be in so many different locations at once.

At their peak, some 7,000 discs were being cut every week. But the metal was recycled and often diverted into military production. If a broadcast could be transmitted live there was no need for a disc-cutter or pre-recording. Although all of this series of broadcasts by C.S. Lewis was live and therefore no recordings exist, one of his later broadcasts was pre-recorded and has survived. How does Lewis sound as a broadcaster today to the ears of this radio producer?[14]

Lewis had a rich, deep, booming voice. To the modern ear it

undoubtedly sounds rather well-to-do and 'plummy', not unlike that of Trevor Howard in the film *Brief Encounter* but deeper. It is a natural voice that commands your attention but Lewis does not talk down to you or sound patronising, even when he is explaining complex issues. He has the accent and timbre of a man of his age and his time – beautifully-spoken English in a somewhat upper-class voice in the vernacular of the 1940s. There is an elegant turn of phrase, a clarity of thought and logical structure that is always evident.

You cannot escape from the sense that Lewis is a teacher and this is the teacher addressing the pupil but not from a position of ascendancy but as an equal. What comes across as enthusiasm to one listener would seem like hectoring to another. Later on it becomes evident that Lewis divided his audience down the middle – indifference was not an option. There is a slight urgency in his voice, a desire for you to listen which gives it a degree of compulsion. At the first sound of his speech you are curious. But once the arguments are laid out before you and the illustrations creep in, he grips you or drives you away. I found the tone captivating but I can see that some would find it overbearing.

There are no awkward pauses or hesitations. He reads his script with a fluency that suggests he is talking directly to you. As with every good broadcaster, there is a sense of personal contact. He carries you along as a good companion walking down the road. It is like listening to a benevolent uncle trying to explain the laws of cricket to his nephew. Or if you disagree, to a schoolmaster trying to explain the laws of physics while your mind is somewhere else. The voice carries conviction with the utmost clarity. The logic is irresistible. The force of his argument may be a little intimidating but there is no threatening tone or sense of danger.

He leaves you in no doubt that he believes what he is saying with passion. It is not the fervour of a bigot but the enthusiasm of someone who is sharing with you a personal discovery which he believes can withstand the most rigorous examination. He opens up avenues of thought you have not wandered down before, knowing precisely where he is leading you but letting you get to the end at your own pace and with your intellectual faculties fully engaged. He appeals to the mind and to the spirit, and it is not in the least didactic.

The remaining talks in 'Right and Wrong'

With the first talk completed, the production process went into full swing. Once producer Eric Fenn received the scripts, he returned the top copy for the following week to C.S. Lewis, with the news that James Welch was pleased with the talk: 'You will be glad to know that Welch thought last night's talk was excellent and the pace exactly right (so it is a case of "When doctors disagree" -- though my disagreement was small).'[15]

At this stage letters began to pour in. From the start of the second talk, Lewis weaves the observations received into the broadcasts. Although the original correspondence sent in has not, to my knowledge, survived, there are plenty of indications in the talks themselves as to the points raised.

The second talk begins with an attempt to identify this natural law or 'Rule of Decent Behaviour'. Lewis dispels the thesis that it can be defined as the 'herd instinct' with a devastatingly simple example. When someone is in danger we can have an instinct to help, matched by another instinct for self-preservation, followed by a third that tells us it is better to help than to run away. The judgement between them cannot itself be either of the first two impulses. A sheet of music is not itself one of the notes on the piano. 'The moral law is, so to speak, the tune we've got to play: our instincts are merely the keys.'

Lewis develops the argument that the moral law exists outside and beyond our instincts and natural impulses. Again he uses the analogy of the piano to make the point. He argues that there are no such things as good and bad impulses, just as there are not 'right' and 'wrong' notes on a piano – every note is right at one time, and wrong at another. It is the moral law which determines the tune we play by directing our instincts.

Lewis uses other points raised by listeners to start a section of the second talk on social conventions. Some moral ideas are real truths and others – driving on the right or left-hand side of the road – are conventions. Moral progress enters his broadcasting monologue, as one strand leads to another. Again the war looms as an easy way of explaining issues – for if all moral ideas were equal, what sense would there be in preferring Christian morality to Nazi morality?

Towards the end of the second talk, Lewis is confident enough not only to use the listeners' letters as questions to be answered, but also to correct misunderstandings. One writer asked: 'Three hundred years ago people in England were putting witches to death. Was that what you call the Rule of Human Nature or Right Conduct?' Lewis points out that the difference is that nobody believes today that people sell themselves to the devil in return for supernatural powers to kill their neighbours or drive them mad or bring bad weather. There is nothing more moral about not executing witches when you don't believe in them. The advance is not one of morality – simply one of knowledge.[16]

The third talk makes the distinction between natural law as it applies to nature and to people. Natural law as it applies to nature – such as the law of gravity – tells you what will happen when you do something. Applied to human nature, it only tells you what humans ought to do, and don't. Something else comes into play. 'In war, each side may find a traitor on the other side very useful. But though they use him and pay him they regard him as human vermin.' So decent behaviour is not just the behaviour that suits us or that pays.

The moral law is more than a statement of how we should like humanity to behave. Lewis leads the listener to a conclusion, written in such a way that they feel they are following him on a journey of self-discovery. 'It begins to look as if we'll have to admit that there's more than one kind of reality . . . [and] a real law, which none of us made, but which we find pressing on us.'

In his fourth talk, Lewis suddenly changes gear. No more dealing with listeners' letters this fourth week. He has established the ground-rules and moves the debate. The talk begins with a summary of the first three. What we call the law of nature may be just a figure of speech meaning that nature does behave in a certain way. These laws for nature may be no more than we can observe, but the law of human nature or of 'Right and Wrong' is more than the facts of how we behave. A real law is at work which 'we didn't invent and which we know we ought to obey'. He devotes the rest of the talk to considering what this reveals about the universe we inhabit.

First he distinguishes between the materialist view and the religious view. A materialist will say that matter and space exist as a result of a cosmic accident, where some matter came alive, and living creatures developed after a long series of coincidences. Or there is the religious view, that there is a conscious mind behind the universe; a mind with preference and purposes. Interestingly, Lewis is anxious to make the point that he is not attacking science or being unscientific. But the nature of science is to experiment and to make observations. Whether there is anything behind the things that science observes – the 'why' rather than the 'how' – is not a matter of science.

Although Lewis had by now completed four talks for the BBC, he was still having problems writing to time. He was finding again and again that while speaking before an audience allows the possibility of ad-libs, a radio talk following a closely-argued line of thought affords no such freedom.

Making changes

As was becoming the pattern, Lewis sent his draft script for the fifth talk to Eric Fenn for approval and to have it retyped with the correct number of carbon copies for the studio producer, the engineer and for the record. In returning the script for the fifth talk, Fenn is quite clear about the changes required from Lewis.

Lewis received back the annotated script with the marked passage where Fenn thinks a cut can be made – 'you did rather pile up illustrations'.[17] But ever mindful that some writers can be notoriously sensitive, Fenn did end the letter with the reassurance that he had considered the last talk to be 'excellent'.

Lewis responded to Fenn with a brisk hand-written postcard. 'I've done what I think will be sufficient cutting and we must do without the last para. CSL'

Amendments made to first versions of scripts, suggested by the producer, rewritten by Lewis and typed up by the BBC, were not the end of the process. Changes were also made in the studio. This may have been to improve the flow of a sentence. When the rehearsal took place, the presenter might have found himself stumbling on a word or finding a sentence too long and clumsy. Sometimes it is just a matter of changing the punctuation. Sometimes a better choice of word emerges from the read-through. Or the producer may not understand something and ask the presenter to alter it. With a book, if something is not grasped immediately, you can simply turn back to the offending paragraph or sentence and read it again. With radio there is no second chance. If the listener does not grasp the meaning at once, there is no turning back the clock or replaying the tape. You have to be able to understand it the first time around.

Lewis was already a logical thinker who followed his thoughts through to their inevitable conclusion. For him to have a professional extra pair of "ears" listening, in the form of producer Eric Fenn, ensured that nothing would slip through that was not readily comprehensible to the listener. In this we see how working for the BBC helped Lewis with his clarity of expression and his economy of words.

This becomes apparent in the original scripts preserved at the BBC's Written Archives Centre in Caversham. Here you see the last-minute changes made in the studio. For instance, at the beginning of the live broadcast of the third talk in the first series of 'Right and Wrong', Lewis has scribbled in pencil at the top of the script an apology to the listeners for his voice. He says:

> I've managed to catch an absolute snorter of a cold so if
> you hear this talk suddenly interrupted by a loud sound, you
> needn't jump to any rash conclusion, it's probably only me
> sneezing and coughing.

Those are the opening words with which Lewis began that talk –
not preserved on any recording and not included in any transcript
or published version of the address either in *Broadcast Talks* or in
Mere Christianity. In fact there is an even earlier version. Lewis
originally put in a joke but it was deleted, either by Lewis himself
or more probably Eric Fenn. What appears in pencil is *'you needn't
jump to any rash conclusion that we are being bombed, it's probably
only me sneezing and coughing'*. The reference to being bombed
was dropped, no doubt on grounds of taste.

The fifth talk in the series was devoted to answering letters sent
in by listeners and discussing the issues which they have raised.
Lewis decides to focus on the points he considers of the greatest
general interest. One of these is the idea that it is absurd to think
of a huge power in a huge universe being interested in man, let
alone that man could find out about this power. Lewis is frank in
his dismissal – size and quantity mean nothing. The script says:

> The man who thinks a large building is necessarily better
> architecture than a small one is a blockhead and the man
> who thinks a large income makes its possessor a more valu-
> able man is a snob. I don't think my legs more important
> than my brain because they're bigger.

However, many of the original sentences are bracketed in pencil –
potential cuts made for time or to improve the text. As this final
broadcast was not recorded, we cannot be certain which version
was transmitted. It is not impossible that Lewis had second thoughts
about using colourful language which might go down well in the
student lecture hall or the RAF camp but would sound unguarded
when broadcast to a general audience of millions on the BBC.

Evidence that the relationship between Fenn and Lewis remained slightly strained can be seen in Eric Fenn's final letter, which thanks Lewis and credits him with a broadcasting success, despite striking a rather low blow in its description of the second of the talks:

> My dear Lewis,
> I warned you as I bade good-bye that we should make a more formal expression of our gratitude to you by post, and this is meant to be it!
> We should like you to know how extremely grateful we are for these five talks and for your promise of further talks at a later date if we can find a suitable time.
> I do think the talks were really good. The only one that seemed to me to be turgid was the second, which was in many ways the most difficult. Last night's I thought was an excellent finish.[18]

Before the ink was dry on series one Lewis was being asked to consider series two, on *What Christians Believe*, for January 1942. This alone speaks volumes for the high regard with which the BBC was treating this new broadcasting talent. For Lewis, it was a welcome new adventure to fit into a schedule that left him with little time to himself. Yet it was to be one of the most creative periods of his life.

Notes

[1] 31 July 1941
[2] Brewer, Derek, *The Tutor: A Portrait*, in Como, op. cit. p. 12
[3] Letter to Sister Penelope C.S.M.V. 20 February 1934, in Hooper (ed.), *Letters*, p. 371
[4] Brewer, op. cit.
[5] Interview with Walter Hooper, 28 October 1999
[6] Ibid.
[7] All schedule details taken from *Radio Times* issue dated August 1, 1941, Vol. 72 No. 931 covering programmes for August 3–9, 1941.

[8] *Radio Times* Vol. 72 nos. 933-935, 15, 22 and 29 August 1941

[9] Source: Walter Hooper in interview 28 October 1999, referring to John Lawler's story

[10] All the quotations taken from C.S. Lewis's first series of broadcast talks in this chapter are from a combination of the original scripts held in the BBC Written archives Centre in Caversham or from the published edition, *Broadcast Talks*. This was first published in July 1942 by Geoffrey Bless: The Centenary Press, London. The first volume of *Broadcast Talks* reprinted (with some alterations) the scripts of the first two series. This comprised *Right and Wrong: A Clue to the Meaning of the Universe* and *What Christians Believe*, given in 1941 and 1942. They were printed on the wartime economy paper in a slim volume of 62 pages in grey boards. Astonishingly, the author was still able to find these wartime editions on sale in a second-hand bookshop in Eastbourne, East Sussex, as recently as 1994.

[11] David Martin of Cobham, Surrey, handled thousands of such discs and told Peter Hill about the process in a letter to the BBC magazine for retired staff, *Prospero*. This was reproduced in the journal *Tune into Yesterday* Issue 33, journal of the Old-Time Radio-Show Collectors Association (ORCA), who can be found on the internet www.eurekanet.com/~orca/

[12] German propaganda was able to take advantage of more advanced technology, the use of magnetised PVC plastic tape for recording on a Magnetophon. A BBC engineer had seen this before the war but it was not until Radio Luxembourg was captured by the Allies in November 1944 that this technology was seen again. Source: Peter Hill as above.

[13] Harris, Steve, article on the History of Sound Recording part 18, published in *Airwaves* magazine, Vol. 3 No. 6, issue Nov/Dec 2000.

[14] The author, Justin Phillips, joined the BBC in 1979 as a current affairs producer in the BBC World Service before moving on to BBC Radio 4 in 1982 as producer of the *Today* programme. From 1985-89 I was a Foreign Duty Editor and Deputy Foreign News Editor in the BBC's newsgathering operation before being appointed Deputy Editor of *The World Tonight* from 1989-94. During this time as a radio producer, I have produced many distinguished radio broadcasters from Robert McKenzie, Brian Redhead, John Timpson, Sue Macgregor, Richard Kershaw and Robin Lustig to World Service luminaries such as George Steedman, Maurice Latey and Frank Barber, not to mention Alistair Cooke's *Letter From America*.

[15] 21 August 1941

[16] *Radio Times*

[17] 28 August 1941

[18] 4 September 1941

CHAPTER NINE

What Christians Believe

∞

For each talk in his first series, the BBC paid C.S. Lewis a fee of ten guineas plus an allowance to cover the cost of the railway journey from Oxford to London and back. Lewis had no intention of keeping the money for himself, and told his producer, Eric Fenn, that he'd prefer to give the fee to someone else. Fenn promised Lewis to let him know if this was possible,[1] and before too long the BBC Contracts Department wrote to Lewis accordingly: 'We understand from Mr Fenn that you would like us to make the fees for your talks 'Right & Wrong' payable to some person other than yourself. Please let us know to whom you wish these fees be made payable, we will act in accordance with your instructions.'[2]

Lewis's instructions are heeded: 'As you request, we have asked our accounts department to make the cheque for fifty guineas payable to Miss Whitty of 7 Chertsey Road, Bristol 6 and I enclose a copy of the letter sent to her today. The [train] fare will be sent direct to you.'[3] In the accompanying letter to Miss Whitty, the BBC's Contracts Department wrongly assumes that C.S. Lewis must be a clergyman to give a religious talk and simply states that 'the Rev. C.S. Lewis has recently broadcast five talks in our programmes and asked us to make the cheque for his fees payable to you'.

Lewis never kept the fees for himself but always gave them away. When *The Screwtape Letters* was published in the Church

periodical *The Guardian* at £2 per 'letter', he left instructions for
the entire £62 to be paid into a fund for clergy widows. Lewis was
not good with money and was horrified to discover that he owed
the taxman what Walter Hooper, in his *Companion & Guide*,
describes as a 'hefty tax bill'. His friend Owen Barfield, who was
a lawyer, stepped in with a neat solution. A charitable trust was
set up called The Agape Fund, using the Greek word for love.
Until his marriage in 1957, two-thirds of all Lewis's royalties went
into this fund to help those in need – normally under the cover
of anonymity. One of the beneficiaries was the young evacuee who
lived in his household, Jill Freud. His generosity laid the foundation for her future career.

> He paid for me to go through the Royal Academy of Dramatic
> Art. He paid my fees for two years and gave me an allowance
> for two years. He'd done an amazing thing and it wasn't at
> all a thing that a lot of people did in those days, though
> much more common now. He formed a covenant trust and
> all the money from his religious books, all the royalties, went
> into that trust and was used to help people through their
> education. Because there wasn't free university in those days
> and there weren't the grants. He just sent a lot of people
> through university on the proceeds of his religious books. I
> think I benefited from that because it was done through his
> solicitor.[4]

In the last year of Lewis's life, when Walter Hooper was his secretary, he had a conversation with Lewis about the fees.

> When Lewis was ill during the summer of 1963 when I was
> with him – somehow I knew, he must have told me, that
> beginning with the BBC talks (and you see this with the
> correspondence – he never receives any money from them,
> he has the BBC send every fee to some widow or orphan)
> – and he did the same thing at the same time with the

Screwtape Letters which were appearing in the *Guardian*, the church newspaper. He kept this up, he told me, until he married when he thought he ought to be saving the money. He was giving away two-thirds of his income, two-thirds of all he made. I said to him but why so much? And he said 'well I felt that God was so good in having me that the least I could do was to give back what I made in his name'. And I think that would apply not only to the money but to the fact that he would undertake it. I don't think he felt that he was exactly free to refuse, you know.[5]

Lewis's fee included the cost of his train tickets from Oxford to London. The journey to Broadcasting House was to become an increasing irritation for Lewis. It was difficult to work on the train. All trains travelling by night had to comply with the blackout regulations. Railway carriages were fitted with bulbs that gave off only a dim blue hue. As Jill Freud recalls . . .

I can remember him going off to do these broadcast talks. And he had to take terrible train journeys. He did lectures in RAF or Army bases all over the country with terrible train journeys to get to them. And he suffered dreadfully from sinus because he smoked and people didn't know in those days that [this was harmful] . . . he smoked a pipe and he was constantly getting infected sinuses which are unbelievably painful. In those days you only had a couple of aspirin and that was it and he was always going off on these long journeys in tremendous pain. The trains were cold and then they'd stop for half an hour and then start again. All the lights were blue'd so they fulfilled the blackout regulations. He would have hated travelling late at night. Mrs Moore was a great tartar as well. Minto we called her. She would have hated him coming back late. It was a sort of [disaster] if he wasn't there by eleven.

Travelling by road would have been no better. One immediate consequence of the introduction of the blackout regulations was a dramatic increase in road accidents. Thick lines were painted on kerbs. Lamp-posts also gained a wide white stripe to help people see where they were going, but cars continued to crash. Citizens were urged to wear something 'white at night' to improve their visibility to drivers. In the first year of the blackout, 4,000 people died in accidents.[6]

Lewis could have taken advantage of the sleeping accommodation on offer at Broadcasting House but declined for good reason. The Concert Hall on the lower ground floor, today called the Radio Theatre, was converted into makeshift sleeping quarters overnight. Those with too dangerous a journey to contemplate or needing a break between shifts in the newsroom could sleep during the night in the hall. A curtain was suspended to separate the men's sleeping quarters at the front from the women's under the balcony at the rear of the hall.

In reality, a good night's sleep was very difficult to obtain with many BBC staff getting up to start a new shift while others tried to sleep. So the facility was used mainly by those who had no choice in the matter. It was principally the newsreaders, the subeditors and the announcers who tended to sleep overnight in Broadcasting House ready for any developments. Outside contributors like C.S. Lewis went home to sleep in their own beds if they possibly could.

Much in demand

The success of the first series *Right and Wrong: A Clue to the Meaning of the Universe* convinced the BBC's Religious programmes department that C.S. Lewis was far too good a find not to exploit to the full and without delay. So within a week of the final broadcast on 27 August, Eric Fenn wrote to Lewis, not only suggesting dates but also the title for his next series of talks. The commissioning proposal comes in the same letter in which Eric Fenn agrees with Lewis to pass on his request for his fees to be given away:

> . . . In the meantime, the dates I should like to suggest for a series of talks on 'What Christians Believe' are January 11th, 18th, February 1st, 8th and 15th – all Sundays, 4.45 – 5.00 p.m. If these dates aren't possible we could manage any series of Sundays except that the fourth Sunday in each month is ear-marked for a talk on books by the Dean of Lichfield. Do let me know what you can manage.[7]

Writing from Magdalen College, Lewis replies by return with a brief note to say 'I'll take the job'. He also thanks Fenn for moving ahead on his request for the distribution of his fees, which are to be processed by a Mr Boswell. Is he, he asks jokingly, worthy to carry the same name as Dr Johnson's esteemed biographer?[8] So within two weeks of the first series being completed on air, the BBC and C.S. Lewis have agreed details of the second series, confirmed in writing by the BBC.[9]

As well as considering the needs of the Home Service, James Welch had to provide religious output to the Forces Programme. There was still a heavy dependence on 'men of the cloth' to deliver the goods. Ordained clergymen were the most obvious ones to fill the religious slots and could be guaranteed not to overstep the mark and enter areas of controversy, which the Ministry of Information wished to avoid. One of the most prominent speakers was the Rev. Ronald Selby Wright. He was seconded by the Army to become the BBC's 'Radio Padre' in April 1942.

Coding the clergy

Wright's talks were typical of what was wanted, concentrating on prayer and worship or on theological or ecclesiastical questions.

Many went out on Wednesday evenings in the Forces Programme after the nine o'clock news. The setting up of the Political Warfare Executive by the government led to a greatly improved propaganda effort. Much of this was outside the BBC, jamming enemy broadcasts and transmitting 'black propaganda' from inside Britain but apparently coming from France or Germany. The BBC was involved in such methods at times, sending messages in code to underground Resistance fighters, well disguised. These messages were hidden, using carefully pre-determined coded phrases, in talks given by the Radio Padre. They also appeared as personal messages in the French Service.[10] They might sound nonsensical to most listeners, but to members of the Resistance they would be detailed signals of parachute drops, subversive activity and sabotage instructions. As an Army officer as well as an Anglican clergyman, Selby Wright provided the perfect channel for such covert propaganda. There was never any suggestion of using C.S. Lewis in the same way, but Welch was keen to get Lewis onto the Forces Programme.

A week after the exchange of correspondence with Lewis on proposals for a second series, something bizarre takes place that suggests either a breakdown of communications within the BBC or a complete misunderstanding of the potential availability of C.S. Lewis. Despite the fact that Eric Fenn has only just confirmed a second series of talks on the topic of *What Christians Believe*, to go on air the following January, Fenn's head of department, James Welch, then invites Lewis to write a different series of ten-minute talks for the Forces Programme. Written from the wartime base of religious broadcasting, the Kingsley Hotel in Bushmead Avenue, Bedford, Welch's letter to Lewis is long and persuasive.

> We wonder whether you would consider helping us by giving a series of talks in our Sunday Programme for the Forces. These talks are broadcast every Sunday from 2.50 to 3.00 p.m. In the past, we have run them as fairly prolonged courses. At the moment, for example, we are just getting to the end

of a series of twenty-four talks, by various speakers, on the Creed. Our idea now is that speakers should be given a month each and should be quite free to develop any subject on which they feel keenly. If you could manage this for us, would you be prepared to undertake the five Sundays in May (i.e. 3rd, 10th, 17th, 24th and 31st May)? If you do undertake this, perhaps you could be so kind as to let us have a rough indication of your general line as soon as possible. We're planning for the first two quarters of 1942, and so of course we shall have to avoid the danger of overlapping.

There are one or two guiding principles which are important. The first is the question of time. Allowing for the opening and closing announcements and for the thirty seconds run out at the end, each talk should be devised to last about eight and a half minutes. We aim, as far as possible, to reach the simple listener, and your material would be at about the right intellectual level if you imagined that you were explaining what you want to a gardener, a docker or a bus conductor. Since all our scripts have to be submitted in good time for Security Censorship, we should have to ask you to let us have each one at least three weeks before the date of the broadcast. We much hope that you will be able to manage this for us.[11]

It takes Lewis a fortnight to reply, suggesting that he may have given the request serious thought. After all, it was James Welch who had first contacted him and introduced him to broadcasting, so the least he could do was to consider seriously the latest invitation before him. But of all people, Lewis understood the difference between what was desirable and what was feasible. His reply to James Welch was hand-written, polite but final.

I'm afraid in view of my other commitments I shd be 'overtalked' if I accepted the job you kindly suggest for me . . . The gramophone will wear out if I don't take care![12]

It is a disappointment to Welch. But he is careful to leave the
door that Lewis has firmly closed, open. 'We are sorry that you
will not be able to undertake these talks to the Forces, but we
quite understand that you are already doing more than enough.
Perhaps we shall be able to ask you again later on, when things
are a little easier.'[13]

If Lewis thought the worst of the pressure was over, it was in
reality only just beginning. Inevitably, many of the letters that came
in following the first series included requests for copies of the
scripts and queries about whether or not *Right and Wrong* might
become available in book form. Fenn wrote to Lewis in October:
'I know the SCM Press showed some interest in them. Could you
let me know what the decision now is?'[14] In fact, Lewis had already
been in talks with the publisher Geoffrey Bles. He had agreed
with them that they would publish the original talks and the five
new ones.[15] In the event, Kathleen Downham, assistant editor of
SCM (Student Christian Movement) Press Limited wrote to Eric
Fenn on 20 October 1941, returning the scripts, and soon heard
that Geoffrey Bles would definitely have the claim to their publication.

Fenn left Lewis alone for the next few weeks, no doubt aware
that the new academic year was taking its toll on Lewis as he
started teaching a new intake of undergraduates. By the middle of
November he has still heard nothing from Lewis about the second
series to be broadcast in January. He decided that it might be no
bad thing to jog Lewis's memory: 'You won't forget that you have
promised . . .' In the same letter, Fenn repeated the mistake that
James Welch had made two months earlier. Not content with
Lewis's commitment to a second series of five talks, he floated the
idea of another series altogether to be broadcast the following
March:

> We are starting in March a series of 12 talks on Worship . . .
> this includes three talks on the Book of Common Prayer,
> one of which is concerned with language. We would very

much like you to give this particular talk. What we are after is not the usual hymn of praise to beauties of Elizabethan English but rather a talk which helps to resolve some of the plain man's mystification by much of the language of the collects and prayers – hence the description of the talk as concerned with 'difficulties'. I think this ought to be done by a layman and by somebody who is an English specialist, and who fits the category better than yourself? Anyway, do think this over and let me know how it strikes you. I do hope you may be able to do it for us.

Yours ever

Eric Fenn

PS Tell me, in which of Trollope's novels does Dr Thorne get married to the heiress? It doesn't happen in Dr Thorne and I have only found back references to it in other of his works.[16]

Again he gets a warm but firm reply from C.S. Lewis who wastes no words or paper.

My dear Fenn,

I'm plugging away at the 5 talks and have nearly finished. I'm thinking of sending copies to 3 theologians (C of E, RC and dissenting) to see if there's any disagreement. Let us at least be ecumenical. Sorry I couldn't do anything on worship. It's in the church of Michael Robarts that Dr Thorne marries Miss D – either Framley Parsonage or The Small House[17].

Yours

CS Lewis

This was to become a familiar pattern over the coming years and one that would eventually lead to Lewis's disenchantment with the BBC. The Corporation always wanted more from Lewis than he was able or willing to deliver. Lewis also learned the hard way that schedule changes could come from nowhere and alter plans at the last minute. Broadcasters live in a world of constant change. Fluid scheduling and flexible response go with the territory. For an academic who knew his lecture times months in advance, such a disruptive culture was not always easy to accommodate.

Notes

[1] 4 September 1941
[2] Programme Contracts Director dept. to C.S. Lewis, 5 September 1941
[3] 17 September 1941
[4] Interview with Jill Freud, 19 November 1999
[5] Interview with Walter Hooper, 28 October 1999
[6] Charman, Terry, contributor to *Yesterday's Britain*, *Reader's Digest*, London, 1998, p.123
[7] 4 September 1941
[8] 7 September 1941
[9] Fenn replies confirming booking 10 September 1941. 'We will book you definitely then for a series of talks on "What Christians Believe" to be given . . .' (repeats dates/time)
[10] Cain, John, *The BBC: 70 years of broadcasting*, BBC, London, 1992, p.55
[11] 17 September 1941
[12] 30 September 1941
[13] September 1941
[14] 17 October 1941
[15] 22 October 1941
[16] 11 November 1941
[17] 14 November 1941

CHAPTER TEN

Communicating Core Beliefs

A little over a month before Lewis's talks were due to be broadcast, the BBC moved the Sunday afternoon time slot from 4.40 p.m. to 4.55 p.m. for two of the programmes.[1] There is another change a few weeks later. The Sunday talk of 11 January to be given by C.S. Lewis was rescheduled to run from 4.45 till 5.00 p.m. because the Dorothy Sayers play in *Children's Hour* that day had been cancelled. The reason for the cancellation will become clear later.[2]

On 5 December, Eric Fenn sent Lewis his first response to the scripts. He is bountiful in his praise.

> I have at last had time today to read your scripts. I think they are quite first class – indeed I don't know when I have read anything in the same class at all. There is a clarity and inexorableness about them, which made me positively gasp! I am handing them round my colleagues and I will send along any suggestions our corporate wisdom, or foolishness, dictate next week. The one thing that I do feel is that they are again on the short side – but there are one or two places where some slight expansion suggests itself. Anyway, this is just to thank you for sending them in such good time and to let you know how very much I like them.[3]

So what was it that made such an impression on the not easily impressed churchman and producer Eric Fenn? What he is referring to are the five radio talks which set out *What Christians Believe*. Such a title is in itself presumptuous as it assumes that Lewis is able to position himself as spokesperson for the Christian faith. Yet as a layman, this was also to open himself to criticism from every quarter. On what basis could he, a university lecturer in English, presume to explain the belief system of a faith in which he held no recognised position, no ordained priesthood or even expertise as a lecturer in theology? Lewis was sensitive to the possible criticism he might receive. The danger he anticipated was that he would be seen as presenting 'common Christianity' as something unique to the Church of England.

To protect himself, Lewis sent the original script to four clergymen in the Anglican, Methodist, Presbyterian and Roman Catholic Churches for their critique. All made some comments – the Methodist wanted more on faith and the Catholic thought Lewis had gone too far in stressing the 'comparative unimportance' of atonement theories. Otherwise, all were agreed.[4] The four were Dom. Bede Griffiths (Roman Catholic), Rev. Joseph Dowell (RAF Padre and Methodist), Rev. Eric Fenn his producer, a Presbyterian. The Anglican was probably the chaplain of Trinity College Oxford, Lewis's friend Austin Farrer.[5]

The last-minute changes were made. Lewis asked for a fair copy of the whole revised text as soon as possible, to practise on.

The first talk

The first talk in *What Christians Believe* dealt with alternative belief systems, with atheism and with pantheism. This was broadcast on 11 January 1942. When eventually published in the collected talks, better known as *Mere Christianity*, this first script was entitled *The Rival Conceptions of God*.

Lewis begins by telling the listener one thing that Christians do not have to believe. They don't have to believe that all other religions are entirely wrong. All can contain 'a hint of truth'. Atheists, on the other hand, have to believe that every religion has at its heart a massive mistake. Drawing on his own experience as someone who moved from atheism to theism and then to Christian conviction, Lewis admits that as a Christian he can be more liberal towards other religions than he could as an atheist. Although Christians maintain that what they believe is right and others are wrong, they can acknowledge that some answers, even wrong ones, can be closer to the right one than others. That's why those who believe in God are in a majority – atheism is harder than belief. And Lewis goes on to say that the one argument that most convinced him is the ability to think. If there is no creative intelligence behind the universe then his brain was not designed for thinking. If this was just a cosmic accident, he argues, using a brilliant illustration, 'it's like upsetting a milk jug and hoping that the way the splash arranges itself will give you a map of London'. How can one trust one's own thinking to be true?, he ponders. Lewis concludes: 'Unless I believe in God, I can't believe in thought: so I can never use thought to disbelieve in God.'

After this argument of powerful logic Lewis spends the remainder of the talk exploring concepts of God and explaining the difference between pantheism and the Christian idea of God. He focuses on the distinction between good and bad and his belief that for such concepts to have meaning, God must be separate from the world. Consequently there will be things within it contrary to his will. Where the pantheist could argue that this is also God, the Christian would reply 'Don't talk damned nonsense'. Lewis was making a serious point here but it provoked a complaint from one listener who found his use of the word damned offensive and criticised Lewis for introducing frivolous swearing into the talk. In a footnote in the published edition of *Broadcast Talks*, Lewis explained that his use of the word damned was intentional and precise. Damned means under God's curse – and except for grace – nonsense can lead those who believe it to eternal death.

He goes on to say that God insists very loudly on our putting right again the many things that have gone wrong with the world. He describes Christianity as a fighting religion. We should not forget that Lewis was giving this talk during one of the bloodiest global conflicts in the history of mankind. That there were serious things wrong with the world was not in question. The power of evil was transparent and evident in every news bulletin, which in these first few weeks of 1942 would report such living nightmares as the siege of Leningrad, claiming the lives of up to 3,000 people a day through starvation and disease.[6] Therefore it was impossible for Lewis to evade the biggest question of all – the existence of a loving God in a universe that seemed so cruel and unjust. But he argues that even to ask that question assumes that the universe has meaning and that justice has a reality and a significance. Atheism, Lewis concludes at the end of the first talk, is just too simple: 'If the whole universe has no meaning, we should never have found out that it has no meaning'.

The second talk

The context of the war and the influence it had upon Lewis's writing and choice of illustrations becomes paramount in the second talk, broadcast on 18 January. In *Mere Christianity*, it is entitled 'The Invasion'. Having dealt with atheism as too simple, he says the same about what he calls the 'Christianity and water' approach, a dilution of true Christianity which leaves God in his heaven and the world fundamentally all right. This is religion for boys, not for men, he argues. Real things are not that simple but incredibly complex, and you cannot second-guess them. Difficulties must be confronted and accommodated. Lewis speaks from the heart when he reveals that this is one of the reasons why he believes in Christianity. 'It's a religion you couldn't have guessed . . . it has just that queer twist about it that real things have.'

Facing the problem of evil and suffering head-on, you can take the dualist position of good and evil in conflict as equal powers, or you can take the Christian view, where wickedness, on closer examination, is the pursuit of God in the wrong way. There must be good impulses that were originally good in order for a bad power to be able to pervert them. Lewis holds that, according to Christianity, all that was created was good, but some of it went wrong. Therefore the war between good and evil is in fact a civil war. 'Enemy-occupied territory – that's what this world is.' Every listener will have understood that concept well enough – with Britain still feeling the threat of invasion from Nazi Germany's occupation of France and the Low Countries, and the continuing daily battles for territory in North Africa.

Christianity, Lewis says, is the story of how a rightful King has landed as if in disguise, where we are all part of his campaign of sabotage. In Lewis's analogy, going to church becomes an opportunity to listen in 'to the secret wireless from our friends' – just as so many in the occupied countries of Europe relied on listening to the BBC to discover the full picture.

Between the second and third talks, the BBC tried yet again to persuade Lewis to extend his burgeoning broadcasting career by appearing on another programme. A Bristol-based producer called Howard Thomas had come up with a new format for 'easily assimilated knowledge and information'.[7] This was *The Brains Trust*, precursor to the ever-popular *Any Questions?* which is a mainstay of BBC Radio 4's output to this day. A panel of experts answered questions put to them by listeners or by a studio audience. The first broadcast of *The Brains Trust* in January 1941 boasted a panel of scientist Julian Huxley, philosopher Professor C.E.M. Joad and military expert Commander Campbell. Within a few months, Professor Joad had upset the sensitivities of many listeners by a throw-away remark. In answer to a question about whether the panel would design human beings as they are now or could they have improved upon the design, Joad said: If I had to make human beings . . . as I think I could have done . . .' he'd have made them capable of improvement. This was seen as impertinence bordering on blasphemy by many listeners.

This kind of controversy helped to make *The Brains Trust* become a legend in the BBC for its outspoken but popular intellectualism. It was only a matter of time before the BBC asked C.S. Lewis to take part. The invitation, on 16 February 1942, asked him to come to Broadcasting House in London for *Any Questions*, 'popularly known as the Brains Trust programme'.[8] It consisted of 'spontaneous answers to questions sent in by listeners'. Lewis would join the resident experts, namely 'Commander Campbell, Professor Joad with Mr McCullough as Question Master. The fee is twenty guineas'. It would be recorded on Tuesday 17 February. Lewis gives the briefest reply, that Monday is impossible.[9]

He did take part later in the spring, however, when listeners were asking practical questions about compulsory church parades and religious teaching. The discussion did not go well for C.S. Lewis. According to James Welch, Julian Huxley 'won the day' and Lewis was 'eaten alive'.[10] He proved less effective in this format than in the more considered broadcast talk. The BBC Governors were growing more uncomfortable with the way in which religion was stirring up controversy in what was not seen as the right context for the debate of religious issues. In June 1942, the BBC Governors decided that *The Brains Trust* was 'not the appropriate setting for the discussion of religious matters'. Archbishop William Temple was deeply unhappy about the decision. 'The Christian view should have an even chance with others in answering questions put up by the general public and not only those . . . specially interested in religion.'[11]

Had Lewis been in a position to make regular appearances on *The Brains Trust*, he may very well have achieved the kind of fame and popularity that would have introduced him to a far wider audience than his Sunday afternoon talks were to achieve. On the other hand, it might equally have trapped him into becoming the kind of regular celebrity guest panellist and pundit that could have undermined his credibility as an academic or distracted him from the other assignments he faced. Being a radio regular might have pointed him in altogether new directions and even have prevented him from writing the *Screwtape* series. We will never know. The fact is that Lewis could have taken part as a regular panellist in one of the BBC's most popular wartime programmes, but in term-time, it simply could not be done. So having said no, he was free to focus on his third talk in *What Christians Believe*, to be given two days later. Just as well. It was the best so far.

Third talk

In *Mere Christianity*, the third talk in *What Christians Believe* is entitled 'The Shocking Alternative'. First broadcast on 1 February 1942, it is probably this talk above all others which established Lewis's reputation as a Christian apologist of the first rank. No radio broadcast, before or since, has laid out so clearly the heart of the Christian gospel. Lewis manages to do this with language that is fresh and compelling. It is totally free of Christian jargon. He achieves that rare feat of explaining Christian truth in plain English that does not rely on any of the imagery or in-house language that almost imperceptibly creeps into so much of Christian apologetics.

The talk begins with the point Lewis had reached in the first two programmes, that Christians believe 'an evil power has made himself Prince of the World'. This happened because 'God created things free to be bad as well as to be good'. It is free will that makes evil possible. The alternative, a world of automata, is unthinkable. God thought that allowing us to use our freedom in the wrong way was worth the risk. Free will means that when things turn out right, they will be all the better – enabling humankind to experience the happiness of being united with God and the ecstasy of love and delight. However, the worse it will be when things go awry. We want to put our 'self' first – in other words, we want it to be God. This was the sin of Satan, taught by him to the human race. From this attempt to create happiness apart from God have come the hallmarks of human history: money, poverty, ambition, war, prostitution, classes, empires and slavery.

In this way Lewis describes the outcome of sin without using the word, making its meaning and consequence clear enough.

Lewis uses an outstandingly simple illustration to explain why when seeking our own happiness outside of God we can never ultimately succeed. Once again, in the context of wartime and of fuel rationing, it has even more powerful connotations. Some people tried to run their cars on alternatives to petrol – using alcohol – and inevitably failed. Just as a car will only run properly on petrol, God designed humans to run on him, with himself as the fuel. He is 'the food our spirits were designed to feed on. There isn't any other.'

The logical conclusion Lewis draws is that we cannot gain real happiness and peace apart from God. He argues that even when we direct our energies and create great civilisations, some fatal flaw creeps in, the selfish and cruel rise to the top and it all slides: 'the machine conks'. God's solution was to give us a conscience and an innate sense of right and wrong. He sent stories about a god who dies and rises to life again. He selected the Jewish people, who were told again and again the sort of God he was. The real shock comes when a man turns up talking as if He is God.

The final paragraph of this talk is one of the finest written by Lewis. He anticipates how the listener will react and deals with it head-on. To those who say they are ready to accept Jesus as a great moral teacher but not his claim to be God, Lewis is dismissive:

A man who was merely a man and said the sort of things Jesus said wouldn't be a great moral teacher. He'd either be a lunatic – on a level with the man who says he's a poached egg – or else he'd be the Devil of Hell.

The original script reveals another sentence – deleted from the published version – in response to the theory that the disciples invented what Jesus said:

The theory only saddles you with twelve inexplicable lunatics instead of one. [*Mere Christianity* picks up here . . .] You must make your choice. Either this man was, and is, the Son of God: or else a madman or something worse. You can shut Him up for a fool, you can spit at Him and kill Him as a demon; or you can fall at His feet and call Him Lord and God. But don't let us come with any patronising non-sense about His being a great human teacher. He hasn't left that open to us. He didn't intend to.

This reflects much of Lewis's own experience from his long spir-itual journey from handed-down belief towards atheism, theism and then conversion. He had personally explored the option of rejecting God. Christianity had already been dismissed by him as a myth to set alongside other ancient mythology. Yet his search for truth had brought him back to faith, to a biblical Christianity. In the preface to *Mere Christianity* he stated that no mystery sur-rounded his own position. He described himself as an ordinary layman of the Church of England who was not especially high or low or anything else. It was this talk which prompted Eric Fenn to write to Lewis on the Tuesday following Sunday's broadcast in what for a BBC producer are the most effusive terms: . . .

Many thanks for last Sunday's talk. I was again bottled up with other arrangements and unable to listen myself, but my colleagues were ecstatic about it. Welch felt that it was the best of the series so far and quite admirable both in content and manner. Here is next Sunday's with all our best wishes.[12]

The fourth talk

On 8 February, Lewis delivered the next talk in the series, which in *Mere Christianity* is called 'The Perfect Penitent'. This again starts where the previous talk ended, reminding the listener of the frightening alternatives of Jesus as the Son of God, a lunatic or something worse. If we rule out that Jesus was mad or a fiend, then all that is left is the possibility that he was God, 'landed on this enemy-occupied world in human form'.

The talk goes on to explore the purpose of it all. That Jesus came not just to teach but to suffer and be killed and to come back to life again. Lewis puts the emphasis firmly on the significance of *what* took place and warns the listener not to worry about *how* this happened – to ask 'how' is to ask for an explanation, not the real thing. Although he admits he is only a layman, Lewis sets out his view that Jesus' death represents a point at which something from the outside is showing through into our world. We just can't imagine or understand everything about it – just as pictures of atoms help us understand, but represent something far more complex; or just as a man can eat without understanding the mechanics of why it is good for him. We can accept what has been done without knowing how it works.

When he has to summarise what Christianity is in a sentence, Lewis does introduce the word 'sin'. But even so, he manages to describe the impact upon death itself in a quite new way.

We are told that Christ was killed for us, that His death has washed out our sins, and that by dying He disabled death itself. That's the formula. That's Christianity. That's what has to be believed.

Theories to explain how this all happened are quite secondary. That said, Lewis explores one or two 'atonement theories' without using that phrase. He speaks of Christ paying the penalty for us in the sense of standing the bill. When a person gets into a hole, it often falls on a kind friend to get them out of that hole. The sort of 'hole' that man had got into was to behave as if he belonged to himself, rather than to God. The way out is to change – what Christians call repentance, which Lewis admits is no fun at all. What enables us to do this is the help of God himself. God could surrender his will, suffer and die as a man – and do it perfectly because he was also God. With characteristic self-effacement Lewis urges listeners to drop any illustrations they don't find helpful. The way he finds it useful to see things is just one more picture – it is not the thing itself.

So in just four talks Lewis has moved from the arguments against atheism and pantheism and schoolboy religion to the inescapable reality of God and of good and evil. He confronts the listener with the stark choice of coming to terms with who Jesus is – a lunatic, a fiend, or what he claims, God himself. And he has explained the significance of Christ's death and our proper response of repentance and faith.

With one talk left to complete the series on *What Christians Believe*, Lewis wrote to Eric Fenn at the BBC with his usual request for his fees to be donated to others. They go, in descending proportion, to a Miss Webb of Gloucester, to the clergy widows' fund, Miss Buron of Twyford, and to the Society of St John the Evangelist.[13]

The fifth talk

The fifth and final talk was broadcast on 15 February. In *Mere Christianity* it can be found under the chapter heading 'The Practical Conclusion'. The conclusion is that if we share the humility and suffering of Christ, we shall also share in his defeat of death and so discover a perfect, happy life after we have died. People often ask, Lewis suggests, when the next step in evolution will happen. Lewis says it has happened already. In Christ a new kind of man has appeared – and his new kind of life is to be in us.

This enables Lewis to talk about the three means of grace, that is the three areas that bring Christ's life to us. They are baptism, belief, and the mysterious Holy Communion – or Mass, of the Lord's Supper. Again by his careful use of language Lewis succeeds in remaining inclusive and presenting as the Christian faith the points which different Churches and denominations hold in common. He never allows himself to slip into the trap of sectarianism. Here the advice of those to whom he wrote and tested his manuscript upon was hugely helpful.

Lewis states that Jesus' authority is all we need to believe. After all, most of what we believe is on the authority of those we trust. Why treat Christ any differently? He uses the example of his friends telling him about New York. He has never been there, but believes that there is such a place because reliable people have told him so.

Lewis deals with other objections head-on. To those who find it 'frightfully unfair' that some who have not heard of Christ cannot participate in his life, he points out that we don't know what the scope of God's saving capacity is. But by our own efforts we can help everyone to know about him. Similarly, he remembers the objections present even when Jesus was alive, that perhaps God should land in force, rather than starting what seems to be a 'secret society'. For this, Lewis draws directly upon the occupation of much of Europe by Nazi Germany to illustrate the point – the wartime context once more giving his argument compelling weight. God is delaying to give us the chance of joining forces with him freely.

> I don't suppose you would think much of a Frenchman who waited till the Allies were marching into Berlin and then announced he was on our side. God will invade . . . when that happens, it's the end of the world . . . It will be too late then to *choose* your side.

Lewis warns that at this time we will be faced with 'God *without* disguise; something so overwhelming that it will strike either irresistible love or irresistible horror into every creature'. This is not the point at which we decide – this is the point we discover which side we are already on. Lewis ends this fifth talk and the whole series by throwing down another challenge. He uses the classic approach of the evangelist.

> *Now* is our chance to choose the right side. God is holding back to give us that chance. It won't last for ever. We must take it or leave it.

This series, which appears in the published edition of *Mere Christianity* as Book II, is Lewis at his most accessible. Where the first series dealt with natural law and morality, it is this second series of talks which most closely fulfils James Welch's original vision as Director of Religion of the BBC to make the gospel relevant to a people at war. It speaks of the core doctrines of Christianity and explains them in plain English to the general listener. It assumes no prior understanding and starts from first principles. This ability to start from where people are rather than where one might prefer them to be is a key to Lewis's success as a Christian communicator.

How did the series go down with the BBC? Eric Fenn's letter to Lewis written on the Wednesday after the concluding talk speaks for itself. This time, he tries to cajole Lewis into another series as a way of expressing his thanks.

My dear Lewis,

I won't attempt to 'gild the lily' by trying to thank you for these last five broadcast talks of yours. You know what we all feel about them and I don't think they could have been improved. However, we do owe you an immense debt for them and should like you to know that we are grateful. To show this gratitude, may I ask you whether you would consider doing a longish series of talks in the Forces Programme, say sometime in the Autumn? We have a short ten-minute talk, at present fixed at 2.50 p.m. on Sundays, designated for the troops but listened to also by a fair number of ordinary home listeners. You have been seeing something of the air force and will have ideas about what needs to be said. If you would like to consider this – we very much hope you will – we might meet a bit later on and talk it over. If possible we should like to give you a run of a couple of months or so – September and October or thereabouts.

Yours ever,

Eric Fenn[14]

This was how the BBC came to commission the third of C.S. Lewis's Broadcast Talks for radio. This was how the series on *Christian Behaviour* began, but not before some frank exchanges between C.S. Lewis and the BBC over what was rapidly becoming a point of contention between the parties. Lewis was beginning to drown in letters from listeners.

Notes

[1] 3 December 1941
[2] Memo 3rd Jan Geoffrey Sieveking (RB Executive Bedford) to P.O. (H) London & Studio execs. Sunday talk on 11th January to be given by CS Lewis now timed 4.45 till 5.00 because the Dorothy Sayers play in children's Hour that day has been cancelled.
[3] 4 December 1941
[4] Lewis, C.S., *Mere Christianity*, preface page v111, Special Centenary Edition, HarperCollins Religious, London, 1997
[5] So thinks Walter Hooper – see *Companion and Guide*, p. 307
[6] Leningrad was under siege for over 2 years, claiming the lives of over a million citizens, mainly through starvation.
[7] Wolfe, Kenneth M., *The Churches and the British Broadcasting Corporation 1922-1956*, SCM Press Ltd, London, pp. 205–208
[8] 28 January 1942
[9] 29 January 1942
[10] Wolfe, op. cit. p. 206
[11] Wolfe, op. cit. p. 208
[12] 3 February 1942
[13] 9 February 1942
[14] 18 February 1942

CHAPTER ELEVEN

Attracting Attention

∽⚭∾

The success of *What Christians Believe* had a knock-on effect on Lewis's life which was not altogether welcome. A mountain of correspondence descended upon the BBC and upon him. Much of it was routine – letters of appreciation, requests for copies of the scripts or details of when they might be published. Others brought detailed critiques of the broadcasts needing a more measured response. Lewis treated all correspondence with equal seriousness. Each person who wrote would receive a personal and appropriate reply. Even though Lewis was a prolific correspondent himself, even by his standards it was all becoming a bit too much to cope with. It also took him by surprise.

Lewis was not prepared for the extraordinary variety of letters he received from all walks of life. He remarks on the demands this made on him after the earlier series. Writing in December 1941 to his life-long friend Arthur Greeves, he explained why it was a burden. Lewis had been made Vice-President of the college when the President fell ill. He found himself with additional academic responsibilities coupled with having to take on all the administrative duties of the President. Lewis admitted to his friend that office work was not his line. He may have become a dab hand at dictating letters to a secretary in the office but there were still a great many that had to be answered by hand. They were from a huge variety of people:

... some from lunatics who sign themselves 'Jehovah' or
begin 'Dear Mr Lewis, I was married at the age of 20 to a
man I didn't love' – but many from serious inquirers whom
it was a duty to answer fully. So letter writing has loomed
pretty large![1]

There were some letters that Lewis frankly would happily not have
received. One, apparently lost to us, came from another academic
who had dipped his toes into broadcasting but without the success of C.S. Lewis. Perhaps his letter was motivated more by envy
than by curiosity. What has survived is the covering letter from
Eric Fenn sent from the Kingsley Hotel, Bushmead Avenue,
Bedford.

> My dear Lewis,
> I am sending you herewith a letter from Dr David Yellowlees,
> who is probably the brightest and best psychotherapist in
> Scotland, in somewhat venomous comment on your talks.
> Yellowlees is an absolute first-rate person, whom I have
> known on and off for some ten years. He came, on occa-
> sion, to the Swanwick Conference of the student movement
> and was extremely useful as a speaker and still used as a
> consultant about the place. He did a series, as he says, of
> 'Lift up your hearts!' efforts in the early stages of that pro-
> gramme – though these were not outstanding.
> I add this to his letter in case you don't know him at all
> and in order to indicate he is worth taking seriously, even
> though in disagreement.
> Yours ever
> Eric Fenn[2]

Lewis's growing exasperation with the BBC is clear from his
response to Fenn. He points out that if the BBC had included
the scripts of the talks in its weekly journal *The Listener*, then
everyone could easily obtain a copy of the script. Moreover most

of the correspondence would be dealt with by the magazine which would publish an edited selection in its letters pages. However, as *The Listener* did not carry the talks, all the correspondence arising from the series was re-directed to Lewis at Oxford. The backlog built up and by 25 February, ten days after the last talk had been broadcast, he found himself, as he described it, 'hostage' to them.

Fenn's excuse as far as getting the scripts into *The Listener* was concerned was that they would only carry one religious article a week.

He goes on to say . . .

I am sorry you are being so plagued with correspondence. In the circumstances it is good of you to be willing to do another series in the autumn. I'm very glad to hear it.[3]

Jill Freud recalls how much C.S. Lewis relied on his brother Warnie to provide secretarial support. Warnie did a tremendous amount.

He did all his typing and dealt with all his correspondence which was considerable – so huge it was becoming a problem. There was so much of it from the books and then the broadcast talks. And he was so meticulous about it. Jack wrote to everybody and answered every letter. He was wonderful.[4]

After the evacuation of Dunkirk, Warnie had been sent first to Wales but then home to Oxford in August 1940. During most of his time in France he had been ill and hospitalised, yet returned to England promoted to the rank of major. He continued to serve in the Oxford Home Guard. The marriage of Maureen, Mrs Moore's daughter, to a music teacher in Nottingham, enabled him to take over her vacant bedroom at The Kilns and to create a study in one of the rooms in the extension.

With his father's desk and the aid of a portable Royal typewriter, he attacked the piles of correspondence with military precision.

Warnie's letters are business-like and to the point. Those penned by C.S. Lewis can be just as short but are often adorned with wry humour and liberal use of exclamation marks, never knowingly used by Warnie. Walter Hooper had discovered a calculation made by Warnie in 1967, described in his diary some four years after Jack's death, that by the time the typewriter finally packed up Warnie must have written at least 12,000 letters on it on his brother's behalf.[5] C.S. Lewis had learned to type but often preferred to reply in his own hand. If Warnie was around it made life so much easier. Hooper recalls that . . .

> Warnie was so skilled. That little typewriter and two fingers could produce an enormous amount of letters on that. And of course he and Lewis cut the piece of paper so you just received a strip of paper with the letter on it. They wouldn't send a whole sheet.[6]

This is evident from Lewis's replies to Eric Fenn which were by now arriving on smaller and smaller off-cuts and scraps of paper. One such reply measures 4 inches by 3 inches – Lewis apologised for it: 'Excuse paper economy!'[7]

Another sign of the pressure building up on Lewis from the mass of correspondence generated by the series appears in a letter from Eric Fenn to him a few months later. It was now the last week of June and there was no sign of any synopsis of Lewis's next series to be broadcast in September. Fenn asked Lewis to send him a synopsis of the talks 'fairly rapidly'. He then apologised for failing to arrange a meeting between Lewis and the young scientists 'who were peculiarly unhappy about your last series, but it proved much more difficult to arrange than I had thought'. Fenn continued . . .

> I think, however, that you will have got enough material from your contact with the RAF to know where your particular shoe is apt to pinch, and it is more important that the talks should be related to questions in the minds of

people in the forces than to things which bother other people. I think, therefore, that the thing for you to do, is to think first of what you would want today in a series of short talks of this kind to such people in the RAF as might come to hear you, and let us have the result.

Whether Lewis was running out of paper or just under pressure of time, his response consists of a curt one-line reply on a post-card from Magdalen College on 26 June 1942. It reads: 'Thank you. Yes, I prefer to talk from London.'. Fenn's letter had the desired effect though in galvanising Lewis into action and putting some-thing on paper about the third series. Three days later on 29 June, he sent Fenn a provisional set of topics for the proposed series on *Christian Behaviour*. They were . . .

1. Ordinary ethics – Fair play
2. How Christianity makes a difference
3. Christianity & pleasure
4. Chastity
5. Humility
6. Charity
7. Hope and Faith as Virtues
8. The Problem of Faith and Works

By 15 August, Lewis was discussing the overall title for the series with the BBC. Lewis's preference was to call the series *Christian Ethics*. He was not sure what this would be in the vernacular. To save space, he abbreviated 'Christian' to 'Xtian'.

Xtian Morals? Xn Morality? Xtian Moral Standards? Xtian Behaviour? I think the last would be the best, myself. All the other words have been more or less spoiled; I think if Aristotle were writing now he'd call the Ethics 'Behaviour'. Or wd they like *The Xtian Technique of Living?*

James Welch had the last word on the title and agreed to go along with Lewis's suggestion of *Christian Behaviour*. The BBC confirmed a fee of eight guineas and two railway vouchers (Oxford/London return).[8]

Accidents will happen

All seemed set for the series, and C.S. Lewis spent a week in Cornwall, talking to members of the RAF. He was contactable via Rev. Padre Scutt, No 9, ITW Newquay in Cornwall 'in case you have anything urgent to say. What is the hour of my talk?'.[9] The first talk was to be carried on the Forces Network of the BBC on the Sunday afternoon of 20 September between 2.50 and 3 p.m.

This is when the best-laid plans begin to unravel. The BBC woke up to the fact that the draft scripts arriving from Lewis to be typed up with the correct number of copies looked far too long. What had happened was that Lewis had written scripts of the same length as the first two series – each talk lasting fifteen minutes. But in this series, the talks are five minutes shorter. So they had to be quickly cut down. These cuts were restored in the published edition of 1943 with a few further revisions for *Mere Christianity*.

First three talks

The first three talks in this eight-part series set out the various alternative options for how we behave and so prepare the ground for the more explicitly Christian content to follow. The first talk looked at what Lewis calls the three parts of morality and the cardinal virtues. The second talk dealt with social morality and the third with morality and psychoanalysis.

The opening programme began with the story of the schoolboy who was asked what God was like: God was the kind of person who is always 'snooping around to see if anyone is enjoying himself and then trying to stop it'. Lewis says that to many people this is their idea of what morality is like, something that interferes and gets in the way of fun. Lewis proposes another definition – that moral rules are instructions for smooth operation of the human machine. When humans drift apart or are in collision, the machine goes wrong – like a musical instrument playing a bad tune.

Morality, he argued, is concerned with three things. First, with fair play and harmony between individuals. Second, with 'tidying up' or harmonising things inside each individual. Third, with the purpose of life as a whole, what humanity is made for. He accuses modern man of focusing on the first two at the expense of the third. By 'Christian standards' people really mean fair play in our social relationships. Stick to this and there is little disagreement. But it is self-deception unless we are prepared to do something about ourselves. Rules for good social behaviour fall apart if our selfish natures get in the way.

Different beliefs lead to different moralities – particularly beliefs that say we live forever. Are we landlords or just tenants of our minds and bodies? A bad temper might be manageable in a lifetime but in a million years might be hell. And if Christianity is true then hell is the correct technical term. So if Christianity is true, the individual is far more important than the life of a state or civilisation.

In the published edition of these talks, Lewis added another section on the four cardinal virtues of prudence, temperance, justice and fortitude. However, the restriction of the length of the broadcasts meant this strand was excluded from the radio talks.

The second address stated boldly that Christ did not come to preach any brand-new morality. Rather the reverse. It is the old morality – do as you would be done by – that still applies. When Christianity tells you to feed the hungry it doesn't give you lessons in cookery. When it tells you to read the scriptures it doesn't give you instructions in Hebrew and Greek. Morality is primarily for living by, not a programme of political action. Clear hints in the New Testament show how this might work in a Christian society. It would be a community where everybody works to eat, and to produce what is good, rather than superfluous luxuries. There would be no putting on airs. It would be what in the 1940s was termed Leftist, a curious mixture of socialist in its economic view but old-fashioned in its family life and manners. It would be respectful and cheerful. In short, a society which Lewis concludes might be 'more than we can take'. We'd all enjoy bits of it but few would like the whole thing.

That is how people approach Christianity too – some aspects attract them and others do not. Lewis ends by saying that Christian morality compels us to be people who give away more than we can spare. He knew his talk would make some listeners angry if they had not switched off already – but maintains that a Christian society cannot be created unless most people really want it, and we won't until we become fully Christian. So we cannot do as we would be done by – in other words love our neighbour as ourselves – until we learn to love God and obey him.

The third talk explored morality and psychoanalysis. Christian morality claims to be a technique for putting the human machine right. Psychoanalysis makes the same claim. Lewis is forthright on the subject. While he respects Freud when he talks about curing neurotics, when he speaks on general philosophy Lewis regards him as an amateur. Lewis argues that psychoanalysis itself is not in the least contradictory to Christianity. There are overlaps. Moral choices arise from impulses that may be due to things that have gone wrong in the subconscious, such as an irrational fear of cats or flies. Bad psychological material is not a sin but a disease – it needs a cure, not repentance. At the heart of Lewis's argument is the importance of moral choices. Every time we make a choice we are changing the position of our central part. The twist in the central man can be straightened out again, when one turns to God. Making the right moral choices, heading in the right direction, leads not only to peace but to knowledge – it is sometimes only when we are getting better that we see the evil we have come from: 'Good people know about good *and* evil: bad people don't know about either'.

Sex and marriage

In talk four the issue of sex raises its head. In its first sighting of the scripts before any of the talks had been broadcast, the BBC was concerned that Lewis might be sailing a bit close to the wind with his references to the Christian teaching on sexual morality. Eric Fenn sought some changes to the script only five days before the first transmission. The exchange is preserved on the surviving copy on pink-coloured paper.

My dear Lewis,

Thanks for your note. I was greatly relieved to extricate the talks from what promised to be a rather serious difficulty. I am returning herewith the typescript of Talk 4 because there are four small points which we should like you to look at. They are these:

1. At the bottom of page 1 we think it would be better to leave out the figures. Not that the illustration is not apt, but the quoting of figures would probably make the listener pause to make certain obvious calculations and therefore cause him to miss his way in your argument. It does not seem to me that the figures are necessary and some general phrase like 'Father of an incredible number of children' would cover the point you are making.

2. On page 2 it has been pointed out to me that eating earth is not necessarily a sign of disease in children! One of my superiors had a brother who made quite a practice of it when young but was, in fact, a model of physical health. I confess that this phenomenon is outside my own experience, but I wonder whether some small alteration of the passage marked might not be called for.

3. On page 3 towards the top, you assert that 'Our sex instinct is in quite a different position from our other instincts . . .' but previously, and again later on, you com-

pare it directly and without qualification with other instincts, such as hunger. Aren't you likely to lay yourself open to the charge of contradiction unless you safe-guard the position in some way?

4. On the same page, a bit lower down, '. . . the devil's propaganda . . .': it is none the less true, surely, that at certain times – and possibly always among certain groups in the church – the view of sex has been unhealthily negative. Would you consider inserting an admission to this effect, while maintaining your central statement that the main line of Christian teaching has been characterised by an approval of the body? We should like this inserted if you agree, and I personally think it would strengthen the main point that you are making rather than weakening it.

These, I think, are all the suggestions we should like to make. Would you consider them and let me have the script back with such alterations as you are inclined to make as soon as possible.

The time of the talks is 2.50–3.00 p.m. each Sunday, beginning on September 20th. We attach herewith the official copy of your first script which has the time on it, in case it slips your memory.

Which reminds me that I am a little worried about the length of the scripts and I wondered whether you appreciated the fact that the talks are ten minutes and not fifteen. We may find we have to cut in order to avoid undue hurry and, in any case, if you could possibly arrive in Broadcasting House on Sunday next at 2.00 p.m., it would be a relief as we could then have adequate time to test the length and make any adjustments necessary. I am afraid I shall not be able to be there myself, but my colleague A.C.F. Beales will meet you and look after you.

With kind regards,

Yours ever,

Eric Fenn[10]

Every one of the suggestions presented by Eric Fenn, Lewis accepted. The numbers are deleted; the 'eating earth' analogy is replaced; the sex instinct reference is modified and there is no mention of 'the devil' as propaganda. This is a fine example of the producer's guidance improving and strengthening the broadcast talk, more mindful of audience sensitivities than his contributor might be.

Though Lewis must be credited with his unique skill in articulating doctrine and ideas in such an accessible way, the BBC deserves huge credit too. The attention given to Lewis's scripts by his producers in religious broadcasting made him a better writer. The analogies and examples which gave his talks so much of their life were not always his own. This is perfectly normal. It is the producer's job to improve a script by removing the superfluous, eradicating replication of ideas and making a talk flow from one point to the next. Being one step removed and the intermediaries between the writer and his audience, the BBC's producers, Eric Fenn in particular, helped Lewis to become the outstanding broadcaster we see emerging in this third series of talks.

The changes suggested by the BBC did not reduce the impact of the programme. Lewis did not pull his punches. Far from it. As the talk deals with core Christian principles, it remains highly relevant sixty years later. What gives Lewis's thesis its power is its honesty. For example, he is under no illusions as to the popularity of chastity. The Christian rule gives only two options: faithful marriage, or total abstinence. Of course this goes against our instincts. But then which is wrong – Christianity or our sexual instincts as they now are? Lewis makes no pretence of his verdict – that it is the instincts that have gone wrong.

Drawing comparisons with our appetite for food and the perils of excess, Lewis remarks that where perversions of the food appetite are rare, perversions of the sex instinct are 'numerous, hard to cure and frightful'. He says he is sorry to have to go into such details but he must, since we have been fed only with lies about sex for twenty years.

> We've been told, till one's sick of hearing it, that sexual desire is in the same state as any of our other natural desires and that if only we give up the silly old Victorian idea of hushing it up, everything in the garden will be lovely. It's just not true.

Sex has not been hushed up – and is still in a mess. The fault does not lie with seeing sex as a pleasure. A pleasure is what it should be. Lewis knows that 'some muddle-headed Christians' speak as if sex or the body or pleasure are bad in themselves. They are wrong. Christianity thoroughly approves of the body and has glorified marriage more than any other religion. And, a point that would mean much to Lewis, all the greatest love poetry in the world has been produced by Christians.

Lewis asserts that propaganda against chastity has made things harder, saying that there are people who would keep a sex instinct inflamed to make money out of it. Again, it comes down in the end to moral choices. It is a matter of returning to the Christian rule – to abstain or to marry and stay faithful – and, most importantly, persevering in it. We may fail, but if a man can pick himself up and start again, he'll be on the right track. It is such a combination of human realism and stark principles that makes Lewis so compelling.

The talk ends with a thorough dismissal of any idea that Christians are sexually repressed. Repression is not to resist a conscious desire. It is to be 'so frightened of an impulse that you don't let it become conscious at all'. On the other hand, he corrects the extremes of those who see unchastity as the worst of all vices – it isn't. The sins of power or hatred – the sins of the 'diabolical self' are worse than those of the 'animal self'.

> That is why a cold, self-righteous prig who goes regularly to Church may be far nearer to hell than a prostitute. But, of course, it is better to be neither.

Fenn's concerns over the fourth script proved to be well-judged. The *Daily Mirror* published the broadcast on sexual morality without the permission of Lewis or the BBC on 13 October. The paper printed the script of the talk under the mischievous and sarcastic headline *This Was a Very Frank Talk Which We Think Everyone Should Read*. Lewis is unaware of all of this until tipped off by Eric Fenn. Now confining himself to a strip of paper just an inch and half high, Lewis's response is characteristically blunt. 'Thanks for letting me know about the "Daily Mirror" – damn their impudence'.

The fifth talk

Even more unpopular than chastity is the virtue of forgiveness, suggested C.S. Lewis in his fifth talk. 'Every one says forgiveness is a lovely idea, until they have something to forgive, as we have in wartime.' Even to raise the subject opens one to howls of anger. How does a Jew forgive the Gestapo? And yet right there in the middle of Christianity we find the prayer 'Forgive our sins as we forgive those that sin against us'.

If the last talk on sex was all the more powerful for its frankness and honesty, then this next on forgiveness is even more impressive. If we want to start to forgive, Lewis says, we'd better begin with something easier than the Gestapo; with those nearest to us – spouses, children, family. Then try to understand what loving our neighbour as ourselves means. This is not about fondness or niceness. We can dislike our own bad qualities, our conceit or greed or cowardice, and yet love ourselves. We can hate the sin but not the sinner.

Loving your enemy does not mean remitting his punishment. Lewis states candidly that it is, in his opinion, perfectly right for a Christian judge to sentence a man to death, or for a Christian soldier to kill an enemy. He bases this view on the distinction in Greek and Hebrew between to kill and to murder – Jesus used the Greek word for murder, rather than the word that means to kill. Therefore killing is not the same as murder, just as sex is not adultery. It is the desire for revenge that must be killed. We must try day by day to love our enemy, wishing for what is good for him, rather than attempting to be fond of him, whether he is loveable or not. God loves us as we are – creatures like us 'who actually find hatred such a pleasure that to give it up is like giving up beer or tobacco'.

The sixth talk deals with the great sin of pride or self-conceit – the opposite of the Christian virtue of humility. Pride caused the devil to fall: it is the zenith of an anti-God state. Pride takes pleasure in having more than the next person – that is what makes us proud. The proud man with more than he needs will still want added wealth just to assert his power, and yet pride remains the chief cause of misery at all times and in all places.

But how do we know when we are proud? Lewis strikes at the heart of religious complacency by describing how pride smuggles itself into the most virtuous of appearances. Pride is there when we feel our religion is making us better than the next person – and it is the work of the devil, not of God. Even in the knowledge of God's love for mankind Lewis goes as far as to say that '. . . the real test of being in the presence of God is that you either forget about yourself altogether or see yourself as a small, dirty object.'

Pride is like a spiritual cancer that eats up the possibility of love. In comparison, taking on humility is liberating – it releases us from 'a lot of silly, ugly, fancy-dress' in which we 'strut about like the little idiots we are'. Lewis concludes the talk by urging us to recognise our pride – recognition is the first step to dealing with it.

Before this sixth talk was broadcast, there was an on-air mistake. The introduction was inadvertently chopped. As he had tried so often in the past, Eric Fenn slips yet another invitation to broadcast into his apology to Lewis, this time directed to his new Master at Magdalen College.

My dear Lewis,

I am sorry about last Sunday afternoon and the lack of an opening announcement. It *would* happen just when neither Beales nor I could be there to look after you. I hope it didn't put you off your stroke. There were certainly no signs of that in the broadcast.

And now, do you know whether Sir H.T. Tizard, your new Master, is a Christian or not, and would he be in the least interested in chairing a series of talks we are planning on Religion and Politics?

Briefly, in view of the archbishops and the Albert Hall we want to run a series of four talks on Religion and Politics, the speakers being drawn from the three main political parties and an independent chairman running right through and giving the fourth talk as a summing up. He must be outside the political and ecclesiastical arena – either a prominent academic person or a judge. Tizard would do admirably if he has sufficient sympathy with the religion end of the discussion and that I don't know.

Lewis is unable to help with Tizard: 'He doesn't turn up at weekday chapels, and it's not very easy to ask him a direct question. But I'll keep my eyes and ears open.'[11]

Talks seven and eight

The final talks are in effect a pair, dealing with hope and faith. Looking towards heaven with an eye on the eternal, the true Christian hope, Lewis argues, is very different from escapism. He quotes historical precedent to argue that the Christians who did most for the present existing world were those who thought most about the next. He cites as examples the apostles, the 'great men' who built up the Middle Ages and the evangelicals of the William Wilberforce era who abolished slavery. Lewis's thesis is deliciously simple: 'Aim at Heaven and you will get earth "thrown in": aim at earth and you will get neither'.

It is not easy to aim at heaven; and it is made harder by our misguided efforts towards it. The self-blaming fool continually seeks new relationships and experiences in a vain search for something he cannot find. The disillusioned 'sensible' man decides that the whole thing is 'moonshine' and settles for less. It tends to make him a prig but on the whole he feels comfortable with it.

In comparison to both of these, the Christian way is neither to lose hope of another world, nor to mistake earthly blessings for something else of which they are an echo or mirage. Instead we must keep alive a desire for a true country, a home, which can only be found after death. But can we desire an eternity of harp-playing? Lewis anticipates the objection, and patiently points out that the harps, crowns and gold, are just a symbolical attempt to express what is ultimately inexpressible.

Faith

Faith is more than just belief. Lewis knows that we can believe something at a time, and not carry on as if we believed it. We can know that anaesthetics work, but still get nervous before the operation. No, it is, he says, a battle between on the one side faith and reason, and on the other, emotion and imagination.

From this starting point, Lewis looks at faith from the point of view of the senses. It is a helpful way of explaining it – as the art of holding onto things accepted by reason, in spite of changing moods. Whether Christian or atheist, there are moments when a mood rises up against faith. Faith, then, needs to be reinforced in the mind and will every day, whether it be through daily prayers, religious reading or churchgoing. All these are necessary parts of Christian life if only for that reason. It is a question of giving ourselves a continual reminder of what we believe. More often than not, Lewis suggests, those who lose their faith don't go through some crisis of belief; they just drift away.

To practise the Christian virtues, we will learn that we fail. Using a wartime analogy again Lewis suggests that it is only by fighting against the German army that you know how strong they are – not by giving in. The same principle applies with temptation. There is no bargain with God or exam to be passed. This idea God has 'blown to bits' – another wartime image. All we have is given by God. Like a child going to his father asking for sixpence to buy his father a birthday present, we all know the sixpence comes from God.[12] There comes a point of discovery, of bankruptcy, when we understand that Christ has offered us everything, even though we have nothing to offer in return. The test is sometimes just to accept that offer. The new Christian will not understand it all at once. Some things just have to be left and will come to make sense later. Although Christianity seems at first to be all about morality, duties and rules, it leads on beyond that. Lewis is talking about heaven – and his wonder at the thought shines through his imagery. He describes it as a country where the issues we struggle with on earth are not talked about because everyone there is full of goodness, 'as a mirror is filled with light'. Concentration is on the source of this light. Heaven is where 'the road passes over the rim of our world'. He closes the series with a sentence of great humility. 'No one's eyes can see very far beyond that: though lots of people's eyes can see further than mine.'

On the same day on which he delivered the eighth and final talk of the series on *Christian Behaviour*, Lewis made the usual arrangement for his fees, asking for the cheque to be paid to Mrs Boshell, c/o Mrs Moore, The Kilns, Headington Quarry, Oxford.[13] In fact there was a delay in making this payment. The BBC system then (and still today) required the artist to sign the contract before the fee could be paid. The BBC had not received Lewis's signed contract so Eric Fenn asks Lewis to 'have a look round and see if you have mislaid it'. He had, and apologises for being such a nuisance. Two days after the last talk went out on air Fenn wrote his letter of thanks to Lewis on behalf of the BBC.

Just a note to convey our thanks to you for the eight talks just completed. They really were, as usual, admirable and I have had very appreciative comments from people inside the Corporation about them; and to have risen to the level of a *cause célèbre* in the columns of the 'Free Thinker', to say nothing of the Daily Mirror, must give you a peculiar satisfaction!

Anyway, we are grateful and not unmindful of the amount of time and labour they have involved. If I can short-circuit the cheque as instructed I will, but it may already have gone to you.

Yours ever,

Eric Fenn

PS I will make gentle enquiries about the Daily Mirror episode.[14]

Notes

[1] 23 December 1941 in Hooper (ed.), *They Stand Together*, p. 492
[2] 24 February 1942
[3] 27 February 1942
[4] Interview with Jill Freud, 19 November 1999
[5] Hooper, *A Companion & Guide*, p. 33
[6] Interview with Walter Hooper, 28 October 1999
[7] 2 March 1942
[8] BBC confirmation letter of 5 September 1942
[9] 11 September 1942
[10] 15 September 1942
[11] 31 October 1942
[12] Lewis, *Christian Behaviour*, Geoffrey Bles, p.59. It has been suggested that this sixpenny parable in miniature has allegedly influenced the naming of the music group 'Sixpence none the richer'.
[13] 8 November 1942
[14] 10 November 1942

CHAPTER TWELVE

The Joys of Domesticity

✒︎✒︎

Life was never dull at The Kilns. C.S. Lewis went ahead with his preparation of university lectures, marking of student work, writing of broadcast talks, groundwork for sermons and talks to the RAF in a busy household coping with all the exigencies of a country at war. The household was run by Mrs Jane Moore, known within the house as 'Minto' and sometimes referred to in the correspondence of C.S. Lewis simply as Jane.

Minto was Irish and received some help in the kitchen from Vera, a professional cook who worked at one of the grander hotels in Oxford.[1] She would come up twice a week to prepare dinner that night and do odd jobs around the house, including giving the teenage resident Jill Freud some cookery lessons. Every household had to cope with the restrictions of food rationing.

From January 1940 supplies of bacon, ham, butter and sugar were restricted. Over the next two years, the rationing was extended to cooking fat, meat, tea, cheese, jam, eggs and sweets. An additional sixteen points were available each month which could be spent how you liked. Some food could be purchased for a certain number of points. This included biscuits and cereals, fish and tinned fruit. The number of points required was related to the food's scarcity. Salmon was rated at sixteen points at the close of 1941 but within three months had doubled in cost.

Non-essential goods like tobacco and alcohol fell outside the scope of rationing. They became scarce and costly, sometimes available only on the black market. Most pubs managed to stay open even though beer went up in price from sixpence a pint before the war to one shilling and threepence during the war, an increase of 150 per cent. Those landlords who went dry had to pin a 'no beer' notice on their door.

One person's ration for an average week in 1941 was . . .

> Bacon & Ham 4 oz
> Sugar 8 oz
> Butter 2 oz
> Cooking Fat (Lard) 8 oz
> Meat (by price) 1 shilling
> Tea 2 oz
> Cheese 2 oz
> Jam 2 oz

Some of this was supplemented. Corned beef would be added when fresh meat was scarce.[2]

There were no supermarkets or shopping malls in those days, so each shop-keeper would have their 'regulars' – customers who came in nearly every day and were well-known to them. Items in short supply were hidden under the counter. Biscuits, for example, were set aside and saved for their favourite customers with small children and hidden among the other shopping in the basket so that no one else could see. 'Under the counter' became a well-known phrase for any commodity in short supply, such as nylons. Biscuits made of charcoal, apparently good for digestion, were not rationed but as they were black and without flavour, few people risked eating them. They were said to be very good. Little tartlet cases filled with pastry and a tiny amount of jam at the bottom, topped off with a mound of mashed potato flavoured with almond essence, made delicious Bakewell tarts.[3]

The rationing was extended to clothes as well from June 1941.

In announcing the new restrictions, the President of the Board of Trade responsible for the measures, Oliver Lyttelton, said: 'I know all the women will look smart, but we men may look shabby. If we do we must not be ashamed. In war the term "battle-stained" is an honourable one.' The annual allowance amounted to just sixty-six coupons per person. A three-piece suit was twenty-six coupons and dresses were eleven coupons each. By 1942, 'utility clothing' was officially encouraged, thereby dictating fashions. Ladies' skirts and men's trousers had to lose their pleats, and hems had to be higher to save material. Government-dictated fashion has never proved popular, but this era of drab dull clothing was to survive in Britain until well after the end of the war.

The clothing restrictions would not have hit the Lewis household too hard. C.S. Lewis and his brother Warnie were well supplied with tweed jackets and corduroy trousers. Food rationing was another matter. Minto did most of the cooking which was very basic. She made porridge every night on the Aga stove. Jill Freud remembers . . .

Everything Minto did was a kind of ritual – everything had to be done exactly the same every day. The hens had to have their doors closed 15 minutes after dusk and they had to have them opened in the morning 15 minutes before sunrise. So when it was my responsibility, I had to get up at half past five in the morning in the summer in order to open them up – as if it mattered. And she hoarded. She got her ration of butter, for instance, which for the whole family would be something like half a pound maybe for the week. She would date it and put it in the fridge, and every now and then we'd have to pull all the butter out of the fridge and put the later ones to the back and put the older ones to the front. But they never got eaten, they never got any less. She never got any benefit from all this hoarding because it was always the same amount in the fridge. It was always *full* of butter. She had these big jars of flour which inevitably always got [infested with] weevil. But everything was done by ritual including the porridge – it was put into the cool oven in the Aga and then in the morning she'd come and stir it.

This was solid, wholesome food. Fish pie, heavily reliant on potatoes, was a favourite. Jill was used to her mother's 'wonderful' fish pie and so offered to make it one week to her mother's recipe. The memory burns strongly nearly sixty years later.

> Of course it failed, it wasn't any good. But goodness, the disapproval! It was just awful. It was this 16/17-year-old girl who had actually been trying, but no quarter was given because I hadn't done it the way I was told to do it. And I hadn't – I'd been disobedient.

Having discovered from seeing the whole lot of his books on a shelf that the Jack known to the family was the writer C.S. Lewis, Jill Freud realised with whom she had become the resident evacuee, except by now she was an invited family guest and not, technically, an evacuee. She acknowledges that she developed a typical teenage infatuation with C.S. Lewis.

> Here was this man whom I'd been chatting away to quite freely and I suddenly realised that he was somebody who could see into my inner soul and what an awful person I was. So that was very devastating. But of course I fell madly in love with him. It was a tremendous crush. I was 16. And I would have lain down and he could have walked all over me for the next two years. I'm afraid everybody must have been aware of this. I don't think there was much disguising it really. Unfortunately, I'm sure I made a complete idiot of myself. He was a very honourable man – he wouldn't have taken any sort of advantage of it.

The relationship was probably closer to that of a benevolent uncle or godfather than anything else. From Jill Freud's vantage point of a teenager, it is hard to tell:

> Every smile, every kind word was like daylight, like the summer. I just took the crumbs that I was offered. He took a lot of trouble with me. He'd lend me a book and then talk to me about it as if my idiot childish opinions were of any interest. Minto once told me he thought I was very intelligent. I think he regarded me in a very benevolent way as a very young student. He would coach me in that sort of sense. He was also – if you've read anything he's written about me – totally over the top about what a wonderful thing I'd done for them [with the household help] and how they couldn't manage without me.

This is not an exaggeration. The arrival of this enthusiastic hardworking 16-year-old solved a problem. With her ailing health, Minto was finding it harder to keep on top of her routines. Jill's arrival would release C.S. Lewis from many of the domestic duties Minto pressed on him. Now there was somebody else to clean out the hens, help in the kitchen and save Lewis from the constant interruptions to his work.

Minto

Many thousands of words and chapters in numerous biographies have been devoted to C.S. Lewis's relationship with the woman who fulfilled almost the role of surrogate mother in his life. Born in 1872, oldest of five children of a Northern Irish clergyman, Minto married a clergyman herself, Courtenay Moore. The marriage was not a success and she separated from her husband and moved to Bristol with her two children, a son Paddy and a daughter Maureen. In 1917 they moved again to Keble College Oxford, where Paddy joined the Officers' Training Corps. It was here that she and Lewis met for the first time. Lewis liked her 'immensely' and began to spend more time with her than with his father, with whom relations were strained. Paddy Moore and C.S. Lewis made a pact and promised one another that if either were not to survive the First World War and the other did, then the survivor would look after Paddy's mother and Lewis's father.[4] It was the last time the two young men were to meet.

Lewis was wounded in April 1918 when on service with the Somerset Light Infantry fighting in France. Paddy was with the Rifle Brigade trying to resist a major German offensive around Pargny. He fought bravely but was reported missing on 24 March. He was confirmed dead in April and awarded the Military Cross for bravery in December 1918. Albert Lewis, father of Jack (C.S. Lewis) wrote a letter of sympathy. Minto expressed the depth of her grief: 'I just lived all my life for my son, and it's hard now to go on . . . Jack has been so good to me. My poor son asked him to look after me if he did not come back.'[5]

C.S. Lewis returned to Oxford in 1919. Minto took a place to be near him and they, and for most of that period Lewis's brother, Warnie, were to share a house for the rest of her life until her death in 1951. They were to become joint owners of The Kilns in 1930. Her surviving child, her daughter Maureen also lived with them until her marriage in 1940 to the Director of Music at Worksop College, Leonard Blake. *The Problem of Pain* was dedicated to them.

It is clear the relationship was certainly a highly complex one of mutual need and of deep affection. One of the most helpful descriptions of it comes in the *Memoir of C.S. Lewis* written by his brother.[6] Warnie sees the failure of his father to come and visit his wounded son Jack as a pivotal moment in their difficult relationship. For C.S. Lewis, to be neglected by his father at such a time was beyond excuse. 'Feeling himself to have been rebuffed by his father,' Warnie records, 'he turned to Mrs Moore as to a mother, seeking there the affection which was apparently denied him at home.' So we find a mother whose son had been killed and a son who felt abandoned by his father, forming a joint household with Maureen Moore and Warnie Lewis. The relationship developed much more strongly and 'he may have felt also some sense of responsibility, a duty perhaps of keeping some war-time promise made to Paddy Moore'.

In Warnie's *Memoir*, he portrays Minto as a difficult autocratic woman. She would tell visitors that his brother Jack was 'as good as an extra maid in the house'. For more than three decades, his brother lived under her regime. It was an autocracy 'that developed into stifling tyranny'. Warnie describes her as the kind of person who thrives on chaos. A minor domestic problem would quickly be upgraded into a potential disaster. Minto 'every day had to have some kind of domestic scene or upheaval, commonly involving the maid', he recalls. It was upon Jack that the stresses and emotional angst were firmly dumped.

Minto had a controlling influence on the entire household but she was not without charm and a sense of humour. But these were less in evidence as she grew older and more infirm. She was sixty-seven when the war broke out and during the next few years, her health began to deteriorate.

There are frequent references in Lewis's correspondence to her declining health and the demands she made upon all who lived with her, himself especially. He turned to Sister Penelope for support, asking her if she has room for an extra prayer for Minto.

> She is the old lady I call my mother and live with – an unbeliever, ill, old, frightened, full of charity in the sense of alms, but full of uncharity in several other senses. And I can do little for her.[7]

The relationship of Lewis to Minto has received much scrutiny by his various biographers. Lewis's residency with her in his undergraduate years has prompted speculation about the nature of the relationship. Whatever the situation prior to Lewis's conversion, afterwards he was strictly celibate. Jill Freud was aware of his devoted care of her:

> I realised that the relationship between him and Minto, even in my very naïve and innocent state, was unlike any other mother-son relationship I had ever seen. It was so devoted. He was so caring and wonderful with her and she doted on him. She lived for him, absolutely. Everything she did was for him. Everything about how the house was run was all for him. And he was the idol of her life.

Although her motivation was to protect his time, in reality she had the opposite effect. One of Lewis's biographers has correlated the state of Minto's health with Lewis's productivity.[8] Although she sincerely believed she was helping Lewis by providing him with a stable home background and some privacy for his work, in practice it did not always work out that way. Although she might prevent others from interrupting him, she did not impose the same restraint on herself. Minto did not hesitate to summon Lewis if she needed his help in some domestic task or other, however trivial. But once her aching legs and rheumatism restricted her, he got a lot more writing done.

He looked after her as if she was his own mother with tender loving care. Each night he went to her bedroom to get it ready, turning down the sheets, putting on the lights and helping her into bed. He would then sit with her or read to her for about half an hour before leaving her to sleep. This ritual was one of the reasons he was so reluctant to be away from The Kilns for any longer than necessary. It explains why he was so anxious that his broadcast talks would enable him to return to Oxford the same evening and not stay in London overnight. It also curbed his freedom of movement. Hooper remembers:

> He had a letter from Lord Salisbury asking him if he could possibly come and join them on a panel that the Lordship had got together to discuss the Church of England and what could be done to help it. He said in his reply that he had to do all these things – Mrs Moore was not well he could

Broadcasting House: Damage by enemy action

C. S. Lewis at Magdalen College, Oxford, 1947

TALKS BOOKING REQUISITION

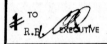

TO R.B. EXECUTIVE

FROM Assistant Director of Religious Broadcasting

DATE OF APPLICATION: 31.8.42

Please book the following for........Forces........transmission

in the........English........language.   PHONE No..........................

NAME AND ADDRESS........C.S. Lewis Esq., Magdalen College, Oxford.

SERIES ....CHRISTIAN BEHAVIOUR........

TITLE OR SUBJECT........A series of eight talks........

SCRIPT AND READING/READING ONLY (Please cross out whichever does not apply)

PRE-RECORDING DATE(S) ....

TIME..........................   PLACE..........................

FIRST BROADCAST DATE(S) Sundays, Sept. 20, 27, Oct. 4, 11, 18, 25, Nov. 1 and 8,
TIME 2.50 – 3.00 p.m.   PLACE London   1942.

REMARKS ....Excellent broadcaster: high top fee.

FROM R.B. EXECUTIVE

2 TO TALKS BOOKING MANAGER

DATE OF APPLICATION Sept. 1st 1942

Please book above, fee not to exceed 8 guineas + Vouchers (enter)

REMARKS Has been getting 10 guineas for 15 min. talks.

DIARY ✓   INDEXED 4/9/42.   Pierce? EXECUTIVE

FROM TALKS BOOKING MANAGER

3 TO R.B. EXECUTIVE

DATE 12.12.42.

Please note booking as above, fee £8.8. and - rly. vouchers

REMARKS (Oxford/London) return.

TALKS BOOKING MANAGER

P/81/P. 20M K. 200 Pads. 24.2.42.

Talks Requisition Form booking Lewis for a series of eight radio talks.

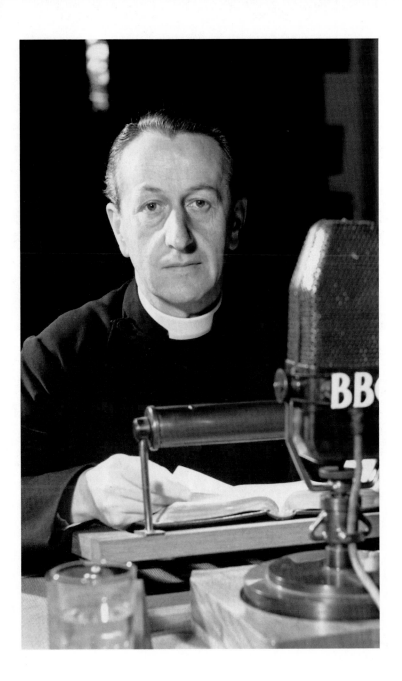

The Rev Prebendary J. W. Welch

TOP J. B. Priestley

BOTTOM *The Man Born to Be King*: Dorothy L Sayers, who wrote the play, with Robert Speight, who played the part of Christ, and Val Gielgud, the producer.

Magdalen   Feb. 10ᵗʰ 44.

Dear Fenn

              Pox on your "powers"! Who the
devil is going to listen to anything at
10.20? If it is possible (but I suppose you'd
have anticipated my suggestion if it were)
cancel the whole thing for this spring and
put it on later in the year. If not — I
can't spend any Tuesday nights in town,
so a talk at 10.20 means catching the
midnight train and getting to bed about
3 o'clock. Well, I'll give three under
those conditions. The rest you'll have to
record. I don't mind which.
    If you know the address of any reliable
firm of assassins, nose-slitters, garotters and
poisoners I should be grateful to have it.
    I shall write a book about the BBC —
you'll see if I don't! gr-r-r-r!!,

                              yours

                              C. S. Lewis

'If you know the address of any reliable firm of assassins…': A letter showing
Lewis's response to the BBC's suggested timing of his radio talks.

C. S. Lewis in 1955

never stay away overnight and he would try to fit it in if he could. But Lewis was a very stretched man you know. All that teaching, all these commitments. Home. And Warnie drinking a lot at that period.

In a revealing letter to his confidante Sister Penelope, on whom he could rely for the utmost discretion and devoted prayer, Lewis paints a sorry picture. Some of the domestic difficulties were becoming too much to bear. He tells her that he would like to spend a few days staying at the convent in Wantage but things are so bad at The Kilns that he is even having to cancel several pre-agreed RAF arrangements.

> Pray for me, Sister, and for my poor Jane (*very* bad with her varicose ulcer) and for Muriel (a kind of lady gardener & 'help' who is putting off an operation she ought to have, out of funk, and getting hysterical and going into rages, and losing her faith) and for poor dear Margaret (certified 'mental deficient' maid, at times the humblest, most affectionate, quaintest little person you can imagine, but subject to fits of inexplicable anger and misery).[9]

By Christmas 1943, all the domestic help had left. Minto was lying up with a very nasty varicose ulcer and had been told not to walk and there was nobody to do anything. Jill Freud wrote to the Royal Academy of Dramatic Art asking if she could postpone her entrance until the following term. With no improvement in Minto's health, Jill kept writing to the Royal Academy and putting it off and putting it off. Eventually after nearly two years they said they wouldn't keep her place any longer, she would need to re-apply and take the entrance exam all over again. This she did successfully. Encouraged by her father, she ended up going two years later when she was older but had benefited from the intellectual stimulation of living in the Lewis household for those years. It was to provide her with a foundation for the future.[10]

Minto and Warnie

It may be the case that Minto seemed to live in orbit around C.S. Lewis, but her affection did not seem to extend to his brother Warnie. The reverse in fact. Jill Freud feels that Minto resented Warnie.

> She wasn't terribly nice to Warnie. I didn't understand that at the time – I do realise now that there were problems [Warnie's excessive drinking]. I never saw Warnie in anything except in a completely sober state. I never saw him the worse for drink in any way. When he binged, he went away. Occasionally somebody would ring up and say Warnie's not coming back. The boys, we called them the boys – Warnie must have been nearly 50 and Jack 44 or 45 – but they were always referred to as 'the boys' and they always walked back every evening.

Because C.S. Lewis was the hub around which Minto and Warnie revolved, anyone who might show affection to him was quickly excluded. Jill, as a mere teenager, was easily tolerated as she contributed so much to the running of the household. A lady called Muriel Morris became the gardener at The Kilns for a while, but that did not work because she developed an infatuation with Jack. There was a great upset about her and she eventually left.

What made the domestic crisis even worse was that there was never a moment when all the women in the house were in a good temper at the same time, according to one of Lewis's letters. Anger and moods were as much part of the domestic furniture as desk and chair. To Lewis's credit, and surely a sign of grace, the emotional turmoil in his household did not dampen his sense of inner peace, even if it might prompt the occasional outburst. 'From praying anxiously for a little of God's peace to communicate to *them*, I have been given more of it myself than I ever think I had before.'[11] Lewis took this as evidence that when you seek something for yourself, you don't get it, but when you seek it for others, then God grants it to you. With all this distraction, it is amazing that Lewis got any work done at all. Yet this was one of the most fruitful periods of his life.

There is a curious juxtaposition here. Lewis was writing his broadcast talks in the midst of quite a domestic maelstrom, often highly emotionally charged. He was surrounded by the adoring but over-attentive, demanding, dominating mother figure, the hormonal admiration of a teenager acting as unpaid domestic help and a brother to whom he was devoted but who had a drinking problem. All this helped to 'earth' Lewis's writings in the real world. It gave his theology a grounding that enabled him to be more empathetic to his listeners and readers. It took him out of the seclusion of the Oxford don trapped in his ivory tower and gave him a real home life more like that of his listeners than many of his professional colleagues.

Although C.S. Lewis was able to drive a car, he chose not to. He once told Walter Hooper why. Lewis had bought a car in the Thirties after they acquired The Kilns. Driving down Headington Hill one day, which is quite steep in places, his foot hit the accelerator instead of the brake in a scene reminiscent of Mr Toad in *Wind in the Willows*. A gentle meander downhill became a charge towards oblivion. How he managed to stop the car before they crashed remains a mystery. The accident was averted but Lewis lost his nerve. After that, it was agreed by one and all that it was in everybody's interests that he refrain from getting behind the wheel again.[12]

Before the war, the task of looking after the eight acres of ground around The Kilns had fallen to Fred Paxford, a gardener who lived in a bungalow within the grounds. He had to give up the garden duties when he was seconded by the motor car factory in Cowley to assist with war work there. He still provided household help by acting as chauffeur. Lewis left all the driving now to him and went everywhere on foot, going into Oxford most days and walking home again. Paxford would drive him to the station sometimes if he was available but, with petrol rationed, opportunities to do this were restricted. 'Not driving was not out of the ordinary. It wasn't anything to be remarked upon at that time if the car wasn't used.'

C.S. Lewis would listen to the radio sometimes, the news in particular and also to music, but much of his spare time was spent in the study at the end of the house. Jill recalls that in this room 'Warnie had an old-fashioned gramophone with a huge wooden horn and all these old LPs of classical music and they used to sit down regularly and listen to a whole symphony or whatever it was'. The only radio listening was to news bulletins or to background music. Lewis preferred to work in his study than listen to the radio.

It was not just the broadcast talks that generated the huge volume of correspondence that came through the letter-box each day. Lewis was a prolific letter-writer himself. There were some people with whom he corresponded all his life, such as Arthur Greeves, a friend since childhood.

The letters of C.S. Lewis to Arthur Greeves fill a volume in their own right of nearly 600 pages.[13] It was in a letter to Arthur on 18 October 1931 that Lewis explained his struggle with Christianity and his difficulties with believing before his conversion – his puzzles over the doctrine of redemption, and his bewilderment that someone who died two thousand years ago could be more than just an example.[14]

Conversations with two friends and fellow-members of The Inklings changed his thinking. One was a lecturer and tutor in English at Reading University, Hugo Dyson, and the other was J.R.R. Tolkien, Professor of Anglo-Saxon at Oxford. The pair helped Lewis understand the difference between Christianity and the idea of sacrifice that he could follow well enough in pagan literature. The pagan myths could be profound and suggest meanings beyond his grasp. The story of Christ was different. It was, as Lewis described it to Greeves, a true myth, 'a myth working on us in the same way as the others, but with this tremendous difference that it *really happened*.'

So from the first days of his conversion to Christianity, Lewis was able to define it as God expressing himself through things that are real. Therefore it is true, not in the sense of being a 'description' of God (that no finite mind could take in) but in the sense of being the way God chooses to appear to us.[15] Even in this first letter to a close friend concerning his conversion, Lewis reveals his gift for finding new ways to express the Christian faith. The fact that he could accept that 'it really happened' was to underpin his Christian apologetics.

One of the first to detect within his writing the strong spiritual themes Lewis wanted to convey was Sister Penelope. In 1912 she had entered the Convent of the Community of St Mary the Virgin at Wantage, not far from Oxford, an Anglican religious order. She began to correspond regularly with C.S. Lewis after reading his first science fiction novel, *Out of the Silent Planet*. It had given her 'a joy and delight quite impossible to put into words'. It had inspired her. 'Wherever it is most delightfully suggestive one senses the most profound scriptural basis . . . There are bits . . . which are more lovely and more satisfying than anything I have met before.'[16] The correspondence between them was to continue for the rest of Lewis's life. She was to become a prolific writer of theological works and, thanks to her passion for Greek and Latin, a translator of the writings of the Church Fathers.

Lewis was surprisingly open with her from his very first letter. He told her what had led him to write the novel and his motivation. He had discovered that one of his pupils took the dream of the colonisation of other planets in the solar system so seriously, that it made Lewis understand that there could be thousands like him who really believed that humanity's future might lie in living on other planets. Perhaps this might be the key to improving human life? In other words, Lewis realised that a scientific solution to the problem of death could be a real rival to Christianity. He revealed to Sister Penelope that only two of the sixty reviews of the book had spotted the spiritual basis. 'Any amount of theology can now be smuggled into people's minds under the cover of romance without them knowing it.'[17]

A bond of trust developed between them. Walter Hooper credits Sister Penelope with having a major influence on his thinking. 'She more than anyone helped him to appreciate the Catholic side of Anglicanism.' She sent him a photograph of the Turin Shroud, which grew upon him 'wonderfully' as a reminder that Jesus was really a man (even a dead one). Lewis kept the photograph on the wall of his bedroom for the rest of his life.[18]

Two months after the correspondence began, Lewis was explaining to Sister Penelope his failure to identify himself with a distinction between high and low church. To him there was another more pressing distinction: 'real supernaturalism and salvationism on the one hand and all watered-down and modernist versions on the other'.[19] This informed his writing. Lewis rejected being labelled. He strove always to find the common ground. He had no truck with liberal theology or modernisers. At times this made Lewis feel like a dinosaur in a modern world: 'I don't understand its economics, or its politics, or any dam'thing about it – even its theology.'[20]

One of the most interesting paradoxes about Lewis is that this rather crusty old bachelor, set in his ways, enjoying the company of his peers and identifying with values he saw disappearing, saw himself almost as a species in danger of extinction. Yet at the same time, he was able to tap into the mindset of the ordinary listeners and into popular culture with confidence and with ease. Although he rejected what was fashionable, he was able to transcend it. From an old-fashioned dinosaur came contemporary ideas that were vibrant and relevant. Of such paradoxes is great writing born.

There was no protection from what he saw as the 'ferocity and grimness' of modern thought even amongst the Christian community. Lewis saw himself as a staunch upholder of the old stern doctrines against modern 'quasi-Christian slush'. He had no time at all for Karl Barth, who he considered to be 'dreadful'. The view that we are all 'under judgement', Lewis considered a denial of the value of human conscience and reason.

Lewis's churchmanship was a topic regularly raised by those who wrote to him or who met him. He was blunt in his correspondence, making clear that discussing such matters would only

emphasise difference and 'endanger charity'.[21] C.S. Lewis was traditional in his Anglicanism and conservative in theology, his belief
rooted in the conviction that Christianity was a supernatural faith
and that it was based on historic truth. He was a biblical Christian,
Anglican by temperament and practice, but also ecumenical. He
never claimed to be a theological expert at all. Some things could
never easily be grasped. A long discussion within The Inklings on
'the most distressing text in the Bible' that 'narrow is the way . . .
and few there be that find it', provoked a heated debate. The general sense of the meeting took the view that, as Lewis recounted
to his brother,[22] 'Our Lord's replies are never straight answers and
never gratify curiosity, and that whatever this one meant its purpose was certainly not statistical . . .'

The relationship with Sister Penelope moved from correspondence to visits, when she invited him to speak to her Anglican
nuns at the convent, which Lewis found highly amusing.[23] And
the more his broadcast talks were heard, the more people with
unanswered questions on matters of faith would write to him for
help. A former pupil at Magdalen elicited a long response from
Lewis on a whole range of issues. He asked Lewis for his opinion
on psychoanalysis. Lewis feels bound to warn him of his 'patho-
logical hostility to what is fashionable', but is content to have no
quarrel with anything that 'remains a science and doesn't set up
to be a philosophy.'

In the same letter, Lewis unpacks his own somewhat depressing
experience of first reading the gospels. He had been told he would
not be able to help loving the figure of Jesus Christ. He could
help it. He had been told he would find moral perfection, but
Lewis felt there were too few everyday situations on which to base
a judgement. In fact, some of Christ's behaviour he found per-
plexing and seemingly open to criticism.

He cites as an example Christ accepting an invitation from a
member of the Pharisees to join him for a meal and then heaping
abuse upon him. So if, at first reading, the person of Jesus Christ
had not fulfilled his expectations, what did Lewis discover? That

the divergence between his anticipation and his discovery lay not with Christ himself but with the layer of nineteenth-century scepticism laid upon him by those who found his divinity unacceptable but wanted to hang on to a sweet-natured Jesus. Once you strip away that layer of cultural accretion, the pearl remains intact within the gospel. This is not a Christ upon whom we pass judgement. He is the one who will judge, and we are the ones to receive that judgement.

Lewis adds a curious observation, asking his correspondent if he has ever noticed that one's imagination can hardly be forced to picture Jesus Christ as shorter in height than oneself. The letter ends with Lewis's recommended reading list for a new student of the Gospels. He asks the writer to come to see him when he is feeling better.[24] The length of Lewis's reply and the time he has taken to write such a detailed letter was typical of the man. Nothing was done in a hurry or in a slipshod way.

Home Guard

The war was disruptive to Lewis's work. An early discovery, which reminded Lewis of the last war, was that some information always comes too late to prevent you from doing something unnecessary. In Lewis's case, there was a strong expectation that one of the buildings within Magdalen College would be taken over by the Government. In anticipation of this, Lewis had packed away many of his books and moved them to another part of the college. Within a week of the outbreak of war, this contingency plan had been cancelled. So instead of picturing himself either never seeing those books again or unearthing them after the war with Warnie's help, Lewis had to haul them all back from their wartime store on his own.

Like so many of those not called up into active service or simply too old for it, C.S. Lewis volunteered to join the Local Defence Volunteers, who were renamed soon after as the Home Guard.

Their role was to mobilise local support and provide another, maybe final, line of defence in the event of invasion or parachute land-ings by enemy troops. In reality much of their time was spent on guard duty or in supporting the auxiliary fire services when there were bombing raids. They would wait for something to happen, hope they would be in the right place if it did, but also that it wouldn't happen at all. The reality of his first night with the Local Defence Volunteers was not untypical. He started at one-thirty in the early hours of a Saturday morning, going straight to the ren-dezvous from a meeting of The Inklings. He was put with two other much younger men 'neither too talkative nor too silent'.[25] They were allowed to smoke on duty and the three-hour night-watch did not drag. Apart from the irksome task of lugging a file, he concludes that 'pleasure distinctly predominated'. At 4.30 a.m. Lewis enjoyed a really beautiful walk home and was in bed by 5 a.m.

There were some gains from wartime. His close friend, the writer Charles Williams, was evacuated with other colleagues of the Oxford University Press from London back to Oxford. He quickly joined Lewis, Dyson, Tolkien and others in the twice-weekly gatherings of The Inklings. For Lewis this was 'one pure gift' to set against the loss of his brother to army service. But even the absence of Warnie did not last for long. The Army had finally decided that Warnie's health was taking far too long to recover for him to be considered for active duty. He was retired and trans-ferred to the Army's list of reserves.

Notes

[1] Interview with Jill Freud, 19 November 1999. Excerpts used through this chapter.
[2] Interview with Vera Phillips
[3] Ibid.
[4] I commend the mini-biography of Mrs Moore in *C.S. Lewis – A Companion & Guide*, by Walter Hooper, HarperCollins, London 1996, p. 712 ff.
[5] Ibid.
[6] This memoir is published in Hooper, Walter (ed.), *Letters of C.S. Lewis*

[7] Letter to Sister Penelope C.S.V.M., 9 November 1941, in Hooper (ed.), *Letters*, p. 361
[8] Wilson, A.N., *C.S. Lewis – A Biography*, Flamingo, imprint of HarperCollins, London, 1991, p.92
[9] Letter to Sister Penelope C.S.V.M., 10 August 1943, in *Letters*
[10] Jill Freud never lost her love of the stage and today runs her own theatre company
[11] Letter to Sister Penelope, in *Letters*
[12] Interview with Walter Hooper, 28 October 1999
[13] *They Stand Together – The Letters of C.S. Lewis to Arthur Greeves* (1914–1963), Collins, London, 1979
[14] Hooper (ed.), *Letters* p. 288
[15] Ibid.
[16] Hooper, *A Companion and Guide*, p. 719; Hooper (ed.), *Letters*, p. 322
[17] Hooper, *Companion and Guide*, p. 717
[18] Letter to Sister Penelope, 8 November 1939, ibid. p. 327
[19] Letter to W.H. Lewis, 18 February 1940, ibid. p. 339
[20] Letter to Mrs Halmbacher, March 1951, *Letters of C.S. Lewis*, ibid. p. 406
[21] Letter to W.H. Lewis, 18 September 1939, ibid. p. 326
[22] Letter to Sister Penelope C.S.M.V., 10 April 1941
[23] Letter to former pupil, 26 March 1940, ibid. p. 343-5
[24] Letter to W.H. Lewis, 11 August 1940, ibid. p. 356

CHAPTER THIRTEEN

Radio Drama

∾

James Welch, as well as commissioning C.S. Lewis, became intimately embroiled in the production of another milestone in Christian broadcasting – the radio play *A Man Born to be King*, written by Lewis's friend Dorothy L. Sayers. This was commissioned by Val Gielgud's BBC drama department, which worked alongside the religious department to push the boundaries of broadcasting during the war years. In order to appreciate how fully the war provided a catalyst for change in broadcasting, one needs to consider radio drama, where another quiet revolution was taking place that was to have a significant effect on religious programming.

Drama came of age under the inspired leadership of Val Gielgud. Although he was not a Christian believer himself but firmly agnostic, Gielgud was responsible for propelling religious drama into a new era. New forms had been emerging in radio drama, with closer collaboration than ever before with writers and playwrights. Audiences were rising. Innovation became the norm. This period included the first broadcast of Rudyard Kipling's *Just So Stories*, adding hugely to their popularity. They have scarcely left the public consciousness since, immortalised in Disney's film version of *The Jungle Book* decades later. One wonders if they would have survived so long in the public psyche without Val Gielgud's pioneering work.

Origins

Val Gielgud came from a family with the theatre in their genes. His brother was the actor, John Gielgud. Their great-aunt was the famous actress Dame Ellen Terry. Val joined the BBC on 28 May 1928 as assistant to the editor of the listings magazine, *Radio Times*. The BBC was at that time based at Savoy Hill in the Strand. John Reith was Director General and his personality dominated the Corporation. Gielgud found him austere and Calvinistic in theology but meticulous about standards. If any members of staff were known to be having an extra-marital affair or to be homosexually inclined, their careers were cut short. There was not a single person in the BBC at that time, Gielgud said, whose heart did not beat faster when the telephone rang and they found John Reith on the other end.

Gielgud then worked for the larger-than-life personality Eric Maschwitz, a workaholic. In Gielgud's elegant phrase, 'his disinclination to delegate work approached a disease'. It was inevitable that someone of Maschwitz's energy and vision would find John Reith's BBC too restrictive. Radio alone could not satisfy his ambition and he went on to become an esteemed writer and producer of the hit musical *Goodnight Vienna*. He wrote the screenplay of *Goodbye Mr Chips* for MGM.

Gielgud, now in the Drama Department, had a fortunate break. He was asked to produce a cast of amateurs in *Tilly of Bloomsbury* at the Rudolph Steiner Hall. The cast included Sir John Reith (as the broker's man) and his second-in-command Admiral Carpendale. Reith was sceptical of the value of drama and disapproved of Gielgud's agnosticism. He saw the broadcasting of plays as a necessary evil. Reith once dismissed the whole business of dramatic production as 'telling a few actors what to do'.[1] However, he did enjoy this brief experience on the boards and Gielgud's career never looked back.

Although now well established, Gielgud never felt entirely at ease with Reith. There were restrictions. One Reithian rule was that the theme of the 'eternal triangle' should not be explored in drama, in case it encouraged adultery. This was impossible to enforce. Gielgud sensed that Reith liked to be feared but that those who feared him earned his contempt. So his tactic was to stand up to Reith's dictates. Disagreements were frequent but Val Gielgud usually got his way in the end. Within a year of joining the BBC he had become Director of Productions in charge of both Drama and Variety, a rapid rise indeed.

Early days

The radio play took a long time to develop as a successful format.

In the early days of broadcasting the microphone was seen as a device to eavesdrop upon conversation or to convey information. Few people dreamed it could become a precise medium of artistic expression. Radio drama had to do more than replicate what was heard in the theatre.

Attempts to place microphones around West End theatres to record plays for radio proved a dismal failure. They produced poor quality sound and no sense of drama.

The key was the microphone and the producer's control panel. Radio began to provide its own interpretations of the great works. Coupled with all the techniques of radio production, the microphone could bring a play alive and stir the imagination of the listener. Radio could paint pictures in the mind to rival any film or theatrical design. Imagination was the key. Sound effects were developed and fascinated the public. Potatoes were rolled on a drum to simulate an avalanche. Matchboxes were crumpled to represent an iceberg splintering. A tin bath and roller skate brought trains in and out of stations. Crackling paper simulated fire.

When Drama moved to the purpose-built Broadcasting House in 1932, it gained the use of seven specially-constructed studios. This meant it was possible to have proper rehearsals and the use of the control panel designed for recording drama. The Thirties saw the radio play come of age. One of the most ambitious productions was that of Compton Mackenzie's *Carnival!* The writer involved himself fully in the production alongside Val Gielgud. One particular oyster bar got used to the sight and sound of Mackenzie, Gielgud and Maschwitz interrupting what Gielgud called 'the solemnity of oysters and stout' as one of them would burst into song with a favourite melody or Edwardian song.[2] No longer could the broadcasting play be confined to a handful of voices.

This demonstration of mastery over radio drama encouraged the BBC to broaden its ambition. The bigger the dramatic canvas, the better. Gielgud provoked controversy by suggesting that Shakespeare could be more successfully interpreted through the broadcasting medium than on stage. It brought the wrath of the theatrical establishment down upon him but the storm passed. The undoubted quality of performance on BBC radio deflected much of the criticism. Of course, having John Gielgud as his brother gave him a trump card to silence any critic. John's portrayal of Iago on radio received much critical acclaim. Other memorable performers included Marius Goring and Fay Compton as *Romeo and Juliet* and the formidable trio of Leslie French, Ralph Richardson and John Gielgud as Ariel, Caliban and Prospero respectively in *The Tempest*.

Original radio plays captured the public imagination. *Danger*, the first of these dramas, written by Richard Hughes, was set at the bottom of a coal mine. In the United States, Orson Welles's adaptation of H.G. Wells' *War of the Worlds* on CBS broke new ground in convincing many of its listeners that Martians had indeed landed on Earth. Millions of Americans had heard the spoof production and taken it seriously, despite repeated broadcast disclaimers on the night it went out, 31 October 1938. Reportedly, one terrified resident of Grovers Mill, site of a Martian landing in the radio play, committed suicide and others fled their homes with whatever they could toss into their cars. The Federal Communications Commission investigated the broadcast.

With all the newspaper coverage this attracted, it is not surprising that radio drama on this side of the Atlantic seemed mild by comparison.

The BBC was open to criticism for being too timid. A production of Ibsen's *A Doll's House* was banned because it might be seen as an attack on the basis of domestic morality. Reith's guiding principle, enhanced by his strong personal convictions, was that to base British broadcasting on anything but the trust and affectionate goodwill of the average British home would be to build upon sand. Respect for its audience has been a core principle of the BBC throughout its history. However, when the BBC has demonstrated courage in believing public taste to be higher than is generally assumed and relied on the common sense and intelligence of its audience, the listener has usually justified that trust and rallied to the BBC's support. Taking risks is fundamental to creative pioneering programme-making. Some efforts will fail and bring the ceiling down. The successes stay in the public imagination for a generation.

The move to Evesham

The onset of the war brought huge difficulties for radio drama. During the phoney war it was more or less taken off the air for three months and reduced to simple readings. The department was evacuated to Evesham and this only added to the problems. Instead of having access to rehearsal facilities and Broadcasting House's seven purpose-built drama studios, the department had to improvise with what they could find. The pressure on space in London meant that the drama studios in Broadcasting House were being increasingly reassigned to service speech output.

It was not a happy time. In Evesham, the local population seemed to resent the arrival of the BBC Drama Department. They could not understand the hours involved in producing drama. According to Gielgud, they were quick to assume that the keeping of irregular hours had less to do with working conditions and was more connected with what some saw as the home of original sin, the theatre. 'They made no attempt to admit us to their hearts,' he felt. Given that Gielgud was turned away from his first billet on the grounds that his Siamese cat was 'a wild animal', it's easy to understand why his view may be a little jaundiced.

For Val Gielgud to have been compelled to watch the German occupation of Poland in 1939 from what seemed to him such a safe distance, in an environment so peaceful with next to nothing to do, ranked as 'probably the most disagreeable experience' he could remember.

A number of factors contributed to the frustration. Working conditions were very difficult for drama: typewriters on cold parquet floors, stables and billiard rooms converted into recording studios often with accompanying acoustic nightmares. They had to introduce nightly patrols to protect the makeshift studios, in case anyone should try to sabotage the place. Scripts frequently went astray. Actors found themselves playing leading parts in two productions on the same night. Plays went from first reading to microphone recording in a single day. Accommodation arrangements varied hugely. One drama producer found himself sent to a bird farm with wallabies at large in the garden. Another hit the jackpot and shared a house with a French chef.

The demand for radio drama increased hugely as listeners wanted their minds elevated beyond the restrictions and risks of a country at war to be absorbed in great literature and entertainment. The BBC Repertory Company began to show its huge range and quality. Gielgud borrowed St George's Hall to put the first wartime Shakespeare on the air with stirring sequences of Henry V's speech at Agincourt, the Forum scene from *Julius Caesar* and the final act of *Othello*. The Features Department led by Laurence Gilliam made *The Spirit of Poland* and *The Empire Answers* to wide acclaim. The rise of Nazi power was portrayed in *The Shadow of the Swastika*. Gielgud spent what he describes as a hideous afternoon in a listening room auditioning actors for the role of Hitler and selecting actual Hitler speeches. In the end Marius Goring played the part with ability, stamina and success.

At the end of the year the Drama Department moved away from Evesham and joined BBC colleagues at the office and studio accommodation in Manchester. Working conditions were far better with access to purpose-built studios instead of converted stables. The demand for broadcast drama continued to grow. The need for blackout, in which all windows and doors and lighting had to be invisible to enemy aircraft, made it dangerous and difficult for people to go to theatres. An air-raid warning could end a live stage play at any moment. Transport was difficult. All of which worked in favour of listeners discovering the benefits of 'fireside' theatre, listening to the wireless at home.

Listening at home may have been safer than venturing out to the theatre, but for the programme-makers, there were risks to face wherever they were based. On Christmas Eve 1941, Val Gielgud was in Manchester in the BBC office on Home Guard duty when an incendiary bomb hit and burned out four great ware-house blocks immediately facing the BBC's North Regional Offices in Manchester's Piccadilly. The heat was so intense, those viewing helplessly across the square felt their faces almost scorched. It was the most frightening air-raid he ever experienced.

Innovation flourished in these extraordinary circumstances. The danger of death from the skies was no impediment to the creative energy of programme-makers or writers. One of the most distin-guished contributions to radio drama in 1941 was the series *The Saviours*. These seven plays on a single theme, with specially com-posed music, dealt with great English heroes. They were written by Clemence Dane, with whom Val Gielgud became close friends. The series focused on those who had come to help the English, tracing the recurrence of this theme through British history. It began with the legendary tales of Merlin coming to the aid of King Arthur and the passing of Camelot and carried on through Robin Hood's heroic stand for the oppressed of Nottingham to the his-toric and heroic figures of Elizabeth the Great, Essex, Nelson and finally to the Burial of the Unknown Soldier in Westminster Abbey at the close of the First World War. The plays were deeply moving and appropriate at such a time. Harking back to heroic leaders in times of danger boosted morale and drew parallels with Winston

Churchill. Although intended as uplifting drama and not explicit propaganda, the popularity of the series demonstrated the power and effectiveness of radio drama to a population needing all the encouragement it could get.

Two of the stars of the film *Gone With The Wind* offered their services to the BBC. Leslie Howard shared a microphone with J.B. Priestley. Vivien Leigh portrayed Lady Teazle in the BBC's production of Sheridan's comedy *School for Scandal*. It was her first opportunity to play this part. The programme was arranged by actor Robert Speaight. He was to win the leading role in the most controversial cycle of plays ever undertaken by Val Gielgud and his drama team. This was the series based on the life of Christ called *The Man Born to be King*. Speaight played Jesus Christ and, for the first time, this was to be a flesh and blood portrayal written in everyday English by the queen of the detective novel, Dorothy L. Sayers.

Notes

[1] Gielgud, Val, *Years of the Locust*, Nicholson & Watson, London, 1945, p. 70 ff.
[2] Ibid. p. 91

CHAPTER 14

The Man Born to be King

∽∾∾

Dorothy Sayers was more than just a writer of detective novels. C.S. Lewis, as we shall see, found in her an unexpected equal. Val Gielgud, too, found that she defied all his expectations. In Gielgud's own words:

> I had expected to meet . . . something of an intellectual and academic snob, with an exotic taste in wine and cigarettes. I confess to having felt a mingling of shock and disappointment when I came face to face with a square-shouldered, tweed-clad, evidently practical woman in pince-nez with something of the air of an amiable bull-terrier. On her side, as she told me later, she had anticipated the worst between the beard that I then wore and my gossip-paragraph reputation.[1]

What he encountered was the professional of the professionals who could 'tolerate anything but the sloppy or the slapdash'. After the initial shock, they began to discover how much they had in common. Both loved Oxford and were refreshingly outspoken and opinionated. Both 'hated humbug, waste of time, and bad cooking'.[2]

Lewis and Sayers became acquainted by post before they met in person, but then they lived in an era when the best way to build up and maintain a friendship was by writing a letter. If ever mutual regard was founded on shared respect and nurtured by correspondence, there are few examples as convincing as the friendship between Lewis and Sayers.

Lewis to Sayers

Lewis had been well aware of Sayers' work before they made contact. In a letter to his friend Arthur Greeves, he talks about his summer reading. Dorothy Sayers' *The Mind of the Maker* he thought was 'good on the whole: good enough to induce me to try one of her novels – Gaudy Night – wh. I didn't like at all. But then, as you know, detective stories aren't my taste.'

Soon their correspondence became something in the nature of a mutual admiration society. With so much in common, they took pleasure in discussing areas of interest, such as the art of writing. In thanking her for one 'intensely interesting letter' Lewis agreed that the integrity of the author and their work is paramount. There can be no justification ever for dishonest work. She seems to take as the criterion for honest work the itch to write, the desire. Lewis does not agree, comparing it to 'making "being in love" the only reason for going on with a marriage'. He sees no correlation between the desire to write and the value of what is written. What makes him uneasy is the fact that apologetic work carries its own dangers to one's faith: 'A doctrine never seems dimmer to me than when I have just successfully defended it'.[3] But defend he did, not least in his sparring correspondences with Dorothy Sayers. Lewis considered Sayers to be a greater letter-writer than himself, a tribute indeed.[4]

Sayers to Lewis

Like Lewis, Sayers showed extraordinary patience with her correspondents, however hostile. The exchange of letters with one particular non-believer went on for well over a year. According to Barbara Reynolds, Sayers' biographer, she even allowed the man to call on her twice. She asked Lewis for advice on how to deal with him, describing the atheist in the most unflattering terms as 'this relic of the Darwinian age, who is wasting my time, sapping my energies and destroying my soul'.

She had sent the man copies of Lewis's *Broadcast Talks* and *The Problem of Pain*. 'I only hope they will rouse him to fury,' she writes to Lewis with characteristic bluntness, 'then I shall hand him on to you.'

It may be that Dorothy Sayers planted in Lewis's mind an idea that was to bear fruit later. She laments the lack of any up-to-date book about miracles and the fact that people have stopped arguing about them. She cannot understand why. 'Has Physics sold the pass? Or is it merely that everybody is thinking in terms of Sociology and international ethics?' It was a topic that Lewis had addressed in sermons and articles but not in a book. He told Sayers in his reply that he was starting a book on miracles, eventually published four years later in 1947.

But they did not by any means always agree with one another. The ordination of women was an issue where their positions differed. Lewis wrote to her in July 1948 with the news that had just reached him of a 'movement (starting, I believe, from Chinese Anglicans) to demand that women should be allowed Priests' Orders. I am guessing that, like me, you disapprove of something that would cut us off so sharply from the rest of Christendom . . . Write at least an article (or at the very least a letter) to something – and swear at me as much as you please while doing it.'

Sayers' response was ambivalent. Yes, she agreed with Lewis that 'nothing could be more silly and inexpedient than to erect a new and totally unnecessary barrier between us and the rest of Catholic Christendom.' But no, 'I fear you would find me an uneasy ally. I can never find any logical or strictly theological reason against it ... if I were cornered and asked point-blank whether Christ Himself is the representative of male humanity or all humanity, I should be obliged to answer "of all humanity"; and to cite the authority of St Augustine for saying that woman is also made in the image of God ...'[5]

Their first contact was probably a letter from Sayers to Lewis. She had read *The Screwtape Letters*,[6] and writes to Lewis with a letter that cleverly imitated the style of the book. In this letter – in which Sayers takes the role of a Tempter – there is reference to the one other key area that Lewis and Sayers had in common: the BBC.

> God is behaving with His usual outrageous lack of scruple. The man [a persistent Atheist correspondent] keeps on bothering me about Miracles; he ... objects violently to the doctrine of Sin, the idea of Perfect Man without any sex-life, and the ecclesiastical tyranny of the BBC.[7]

This phrase 'the ecclesiastical tyranny of the BBC' gives us an important clue to how the BBC was perceived and experienced by leading lay Christians of that era. Religious broadcasting was seen as dominated and staffed by men in dog-collars, even by those who were being commissioned by the BBC to change that perception.

One of these commissions was to Dorothy Sayers herself, for her play *The Man Born to be King*. She was not a woman to leave 'ecclesiastical tyranny' unchallenged.

The commission

It is hard to believe that such a deeply controversial project as *The Man Born to be King* should have had such a prosaic start. James Welch and Eric Fenn wanted to use drama as another means of expressing the Christian faith. Welch had been impressed by the success of a nativity play written by Sayers before the war, and thought she might well rise to the challenge of dramatising a complete gospel in the format of a series of plays based upon the life of Jesus, as an interesting addition to Sunday's *Children's Hour*. It was a simple enough commission: a series of half-hour plays for 7–14-year-olds, probably using direct speech. The original idea for these plays and the invitation to write them came from the BBC. Little did Welch know what he had started.

It would be a massive undertaking for any dramatist, however prolific. It would also push out the boundaries of radio drama.

Dorothy Sayers found Welch's suggestion tempting, and already was anticipating some of the issues she would have to encounter in following it.

> If I did do it, I should make it a condition that I was allowed to introduce the character of Our Lord Himself, and to present the play with the same kind of realism that I used in the Nativity play *He That Should Come*. I feel very strongly that the prohibition against presenting Our Lord directly on stage or in films (however necessary from certain points of view) tends to produce a sense of unreality which is very damaging to the ordinary man's conception of Christianity. The device of indicating Christ's presence by a 'voice off', or by a shaft of light, or a shadow, or what not, tends to suggest to people that He never was a real person at all, and this impression of unreality extends to all other people in the drama, with the result that 'Bible characters' are felt to be quite different from ordinary human beings.[8]

The central issue

Dorothy Sayers insisted that she should be able to include Jesus Christ as a living, breathing, main character within the plays. The implication of this was that it would not just be fleshing out his character but giving him a voice. And getting this voice 'right' would be the most difficult task. On the one hand she would need to be faithful to the New Testament account and was not free to invent speeches of Christ or teaching that did not appear in the scriptures. On the other hand, if she confined herself to the language of the King James Bible, it would make dreadful radio. If the other characters 'talk Bible' the realism would be lost. Dialogue using antiquated language full of thee and thou was not likely to go down a treat with children. If they speak in modern English, the result could be what she called a 'patchwork effect'.

> However, the difficulty is not really insuperable; it is just a
> question of choosing language which is neither slangy on
> the one hand, nor Wardour Street[9] on the other.

So Welch was faced with an acceptance of the commission carrying three provisos: Christ must be a central character; be portrayed by an actor; and speak in contemporary vernacular English. Welch replied that her three conditions were not just acceptable but 'exactly what we wanted and had hoped for'. Sayers greatly valued his support and thanked him for 'the courageous spirit which, in order to get the reality of the Gospel across, is prepared even to "give slight offence to some adult listeners"!'[10]

During 1940 and 1941 Dorothy Sayers worked on the plays. It turned out to be a far more formidable task than she had anticipated. She reflected on some of those difficulties in a short introduction to the first published edition of the cycle of plays *The Man Born to be King*.[11] To begin with, the project was unprecedented. There were no guidelines for the dramatist to follow or to prepare the audience and critics for the shock of hearing an everyday Christ. Then there was the law. This banned the representation on stage of any member of the Holy Trinity – God the Father, the Son or the Holy Spirit. This had, in Sayers' view, helped to 'foster the notion that all such representations were intrinsically wicked'. Of course, such restrictions to the stage did not apply to radio, where the Lord Chamberlain had no jurisdiction.

The uniqueness of the raw material to be handled by the dramatist, not to mention the theology, presented other problems. Although aimed initially at *Children's Hour*, it would not just be children who would be listening. Many parents would sit round the radio at Sunday teatime and listen with their children. So the audience would be divided between those who were not only familiar with the gospels in part or whole, but also held the Authorised Version of King James to be sacrosanct, and at the other end of the spectrum those for whom this was all altogether new territory . . .

> . . . a large and most youthful public to whom the whole story of Jesus is *terra incognita* – children who do not know the meaning of Christmas, men and women to whom the name of Christ is only a swear-word – besides a considerable body of agnostics and semi-Christians who accept some incidents of the story and firmly disbelieve the rest . . .

Welch was hugely impressed by the seriousness with which she approached the task. He paid tribute to 'the immense pains' she took over the study and handling of her sources. She was an expert in her own right in her theological understanding by the time she put pen to paper. In a letter attached to the script of her last play, she told Welch that she had 'worn out' one Greek Testament and 'amassed a considerable theological library'. Her attention to details of historical accuracy and theology in the text is staggering, all set as it is within a dramatic conception.

Sayers pulls out

Welch's intention in his commission was that these plays should be produced by his Religious Department but transmitted as part of the *Children's Hour* slot. This was a decision that had been referred to the BBC's Governors. They agreed, recalled Eric Fenn,[12] 'that we should go ahead on condition that it was broadcast only in *Children's Hour* where they were accustomed to using drama and they hoped that it would not cause much trouble.' There remained the question of who was to produce the plays. Fenn remembers Sayers' response:

> . . . she said, 'Anybody other than a parson.' . . . I looked a bit queer and she said, 'Well you see, they will sentimentalise it and this is drama and it must be done objectively and with professional qualifications, and I want Val Gielgud'.

Sayers asked for the proven and successful collaboration with Val Gielgud to continue as producer on the basis that 'he and I understand each other's way of working'.[13]

Welch said no. Responsibility for the plays had been delegated to the Children's Department. The producer would therefore be its head, Derek McCulloch, known to millions of children as 'Uncle Mac'. Welch asked Sayers to visit the Children's team in Bristol but, with the pressure she was under, she refused. She hated talking about work in progress. There is a hint here too that she was circumspect about any external interference in her work at this sensitive stage.

As the summer turned to autumn, all seemed to be going well. Welch liked the first play and sent it on to McCulloch with a warm commendation. Only one copy had been sent – the others were kept apart to prevent an air-raid destroying the lot in one hit. McCulloch told Sayers that 'my staff tore it from me to read in relays, but judging from their excited remarks the general opinion seems to be "favourable" . . .' There was also an extra quarter of an hour allowed for in each broadcast. Sayers was pleased, saying it would save her from having to 'cramp the Bethlehem scene' so much.

The next decision was over who would play Christ. Sayers had made her views on this point clear.

The one kind of Christ I absolutely refuse to have at any price whatsoever, is a dull Christ; we have far too many of these in stained-glass windows.[14]

All seemed to be going well. The most important ingredient of any relationship between an author and a commissioner is that of trust, and Sayers at this stage trusted James Welch and now Derek McCulloch too. But she did not yet trust the BBC. McCulloch, who hadn't actually read the play in full, asked his assistant director May Jenkin to fill in for him when he had to go to Scotland on BBC business. Unfortunately, in comparison with the thorough-bred diplomatic skills of James Welch, May Jenkin was a BBC executive of the old school. She wrote to Sayers with the response of the BBC Children's Department to the first play in McCulloch's absence. At this point, everything began to unravel with terrifying speed.

A single letter did all the damage. It started on the right note.

We have now all read it and let me say at once that we are quite delighted with it. It seems to be admirably dramatic, and both profound and beautiful.

Then May Jenkin dropped the bombshell – a catalogue of short-comings she had detected. First, she thought it would be over the heads of children. Second, she was unhappy with the modern idiom of the language. Third, she asked for Sayers' permission to 'edit the text judiciously'. This was dynamite. The tone of the letter made things worse. May Jenkin comes across in cold print as a prim headmistress pressed for time:

We wonder if you will allow us discreetly to edit? If you would prefer to make these small alterations yourself, I will send you the play back, but we are anxious not to delay having the copies duplicated and the posts are so slow at the moment.[15]

Dorothy Sayers was incandescent. She was always sensitive to any suggestion that her work was being judged by a committee, but May Jenkin had struck at the heart of the whole enterprise. Sayers wrote a robust response, starting with Jenkin's fears that the script might go over the heads of the children.

> Pay no attention. You are supposed to be playing to children – the only audience, perhaps, in the country whose minds are still open and sensitive to the spell of poetic speech . . . But you are not children. The thing they react to is not logical argument, but the mystery and queer beauty of melodious words.

Sayers deeply resented this interference in what she felt to be the writer's creative domain. For the BBC, the issue was one of editorial control. The two strong-willed ladies were on a collision course. Sayers is explicit in laying down the boundaries from her point of view.

> It is my business to know how my real audience will react; and yours to trust me to know it.

And there lies the rub. Sayers felt that she was not being trusted to get it right. At issue was who knew best what was right for the audience. The playwright or the *Children's Hour* production executive?

Derek McCulloch got back to London to discover what had happened. He was unlikely to be in the best of moods anyway after a nightmare nineteen-hour train journey from Glasgow. In the true BBC tradition, the management closed ranks. He read Dorothy Sayers' reply to May Jenkin but supported all his assistant's comments. He invited Sayers to Bristol in the hope that by meeting one another, all the obstacles might soon be swept away. The olive branch was not well received. Sayers responded:

> Oh, no, you don't, my poppet! You won't get me to do three
> days of exhausting travel to Bristol in order to argue about
> my plays with a Committee. What goes into the play, and
> the language in which it is written is the author's business.
> If the Management don't like it, they reject the play, and
> there is an end of the contract . . .[16]

On the same day, she wrote a parallel letter to James Welch
with none of the hostility that appears in her letter to Derek
McCulloch. She explains how she was riled by Miss Jenkin's
'excessively tactless' letter, and felt that McCulloch had over-
stepped the line.

> In his own sphere the producer is God – but he is not God
> in the author's sphere. The author is God there; and the
> producer's business is to produce the play.

Welch was distressed by all this. An exciting and ambitious commission was going horribly wrong because of one insensitive letter.
He was appalled that the Children's Department were handling
it so badly. Welch was a hardened warrior when it came to political battles within the BBC and attempted with a conciliatory
letter to pull the project back on track. However, May Jenkin got
sight of the correspondence and decided she would defend herself with vigour and remind Dorothy Sayers just who was in
charge.

> We cannot delegate to any author, however distinguished,
> the right to say what shall or shall not be broadcast in a
> *Children's Hour* play.

For May Jenkin, at stake was the principle of the BBC's editorial
control. For Dorothy Sayers, the line had been crossed. Her reply
was brutally short.

Under the circumstances you outline, I have no option but to cancel the contract. Kindly return all scripts of Kings in Judaea [the first play in *A Man Born to be King*] immediately. My agents will communicate with you. Yours faithfully,

Dorothy L. Sayers

Barbara Reynold's biography of Sayers reports that the author had enclosed her copy of the contract. It had been ripped up into minute fragments.

When the letter from the agent came it was even more withering in its treatment of May Jenkin and the BBC. Margery Vosper wrote on behalf of Sayers' agent Dorothy Allen in Shaftesbury Avenue to the BBC's Administration Department.

I know very well that there are few authors with artistic integrity – Miss Sayers is one of the few who are prepared to sacrifice everything to the good of her work. She rightly resents being treated as a tuppence-a-line hack and does not feel that she can continue with her work which involves quibbling over non-essentials.[17]

Internal BBC politics was seldom allowed to get in the way of a truly brilliant programme idea, then or now. Talent is paramount. Dorothy Sayers' was too important a talent for the BBC to drive away if there was a simple solution to hand. There was. It was Val Gielgud. Once again it was James Welch who saved the day. In his autobiography Gielgud described Welch as a man of 'courage, persistence and diplomatic abilities'.[18] Sayers' biographer Barbara Reynolds sees him in a similar light as a man of 'vision, courage and diplomacy'. Welch was also driven by a sense of old-fashioned Christian zeal. He was passionate to see radio used to transform lives by giving the listener a proper understanding of the nature and work of Jesus Christ.

Welch used the simple expedient of withdrawing the commission from the BBC's Children's Department and transferring it to the Drama Department. Its head Val Gielgud agreed to be the producer. In BBC terms, this was par for the course. If one department cannot deliver a programme project, a commissioner will think nothing of transferring it to another.

Sayers was calming down and they were back to square one – but with Gielgud as producer, Welch responsible for the contract and May Jenkin and Derek McCulloch excluded.

The production nightmare

Dorothy Sayers was correct to insist on Val Gielgud for such an ambitious production. Not one of the plays was made with a cast of fewer than 35 actors. And not one of them could be allowed more than two days from first rehearsal to production. In these conditions, it takes very little to throw the whole schedule into chaos. From Gielgud's perspective, it all lay 'hideously at the mercy of the single stupid or lazy individual' – and more than once he suspected he may have bitten off more than he could chew.

Gielgud also had to take account of Sayers' insistence on being 'on hand' at each rehearsal. He needed her at his elbow interfering with the production like a mouse needs a cat. The analogy is not unkind to Sayers either – she was a punctilious woman with an eye for detail and utterly perfectionist in her approach, as he realised.

> . . . She was exemplary in her realisation of where the line should be drawn between the spheres of action of author and producer. She had ideas about acting. She had ideas about production. But they were always expressed to the producer, never to the actors. On the other hand she demanded to be convinced with good reason before she would alter a line, and she was resolutely opposed to the changing of lines by actors just because words or phrases were unfamiliar, or

because they seemed difficult to speak. She was always patient. She appeared continuously interested. She was lavish of praise to the cast. Criticism she confined to the producer. This made an ideal working arrangement. Both of us minded our own business. When disputes arose, as of course they did, they were settled privately between us.[19]

When giving Val Gielgud his due in her own published introduction to the plays, and indeed dedicating them to him, Dorothy Sayers gives a broad hint that she fully appreciated his patience with her.

Of the producer, I will only say that he is of that kind which knows our necessities before we ask, that he patiently endured many trials (myself not least), that before the highest and thorniest fence he was never known to refuse, and that – if playwrights know anything about the matter – of such is the Kingdom of Heaven.

Any apprehension Gielgud felt was dispelled by what he describes as the 'very singular atmosphere' which the plays in rehearsal seemed to generate. The impact on the actors of rehearsals and recording was profound. All the emotions of the project came to the forefront when it came to the scenes of Christ's crucifixion. Eric Fenn recalled how deeply the cast were affected by it all – it was 'quite astonishing'.

They were completely reduced to silence afterwards. They just sat there where they were and Bobby Speaight who played the Christ just put on his coat and walked out with tears running down his face. It was most moving. [20]

Letting the cat out of the bag

It is traditional for the BBC to give early notice of its Christmas broadcasts so that it can get some much-valued advance publicity. Nowadays, the launch of the Christmas schedules takes place well ahead of December, allowing plenty of time for the *Radio Times* listing magazine to prepare publication. In 1941, Welch decided that ten days was ample notice to draw attention to his new play for children on the Home Service of BBC Radio. A press conference was arranged and Dorothy Sayers was present to talk about some of the difficulties she had faced as a dramatist telling the story of Christ in contemporary language. Some members of the press, intrigued by the prospect of Christ and the disciples speaking in vernacular English, asked her to read out a sample portion of dialogue. This she did. The next day the storm broke.

The storm

Sayers read an excerpt in which Matthew the tax collector and Andrew reprimand Philip for being cheated of six drachmas.

> Matthew: Fact is, Philip my boy, you've been had for a sucker. Let him ring the changes on you proper. You ought to keep your eyes skinned, you did really. If I was to tell you the dodges these fellows have up their sleeves, you'd be surprised.

Religious programming was rarely scandalous or controversial, apart from the *Daily Mirror's* excitement over C.S. Lewis's frank remarks on sex. In the case of Sayers' plays, one or two spotted in advance the news value of the BBC breaking one of the great taboos of broadcasting – the portrayal of Christ and the disciples in voice and character.

The *Daily Mail* carried a headline, BBC 'LIFE OF CHRIST' PLAY IN U.S. SLANG. The plays were condemned – without having been read, broadcast or heard in any capacity – as 'irreverent', as 'blasphemous' and 'vulgar'. A joint campaign was launched by the Lord's Day Observance Society and the Protestant Truth Society, funded by over one thousand pounds, to bring pressure on the BBC to stop what they considered to be 'irreverence bordering on the blasphemous'.

The shock of the new

The outcry came as a surprise to the BBC. As Welch noted with a glorious touch of British irony, 'it was not an encouraging reception for a great evangelistic enterprise'. What angered him was the opposition from those, in Welch's view, 'whose minds seemed incapable of giving a hearing to the Gospel when preached in an unfamiliar way.' Their chief objection was to hearing an actor portray Christ. In their mind it amounted to impersonation, a cardinal sin.

The abandonment of the English of the King James Authorised Version was also offensive to some. This goes back to a misunderstanding or to be more precise, an ignorance, of how the New Testament came to be written, as common in 1940 as it is today. The original New Testament was written in the conversational Greek of its day, with some Aramaic, the everyday language of first-century Palestine, permeating from time to time. Every Bible translator returns to the original Greek – including Dorothy Sayers, who used the Greek to reach her own vernacular dramatic presentation. Hers is a contemporary interpretation, but based on the same Greek texts. It was the shock of hearing the familiar story in the language that is used every day which gave the plays their full dramatic impact. In Welch's phrase, 'the coverings and the antiquity were removed, and Our Lord, for many of us, was alive as never before'.

Robert Speaight, the actor chosen to portray Jesus, was accused of blasphemy by claiming to be God himself. Others said that the broadcasts were indirectly responsible for the fall of Singapore and pleaded that they be taken off the air before the Japanese Army seize Australia as well! Letters of protest poured in from listeners and the furore even prompted a question in the House of Commons.

Welch's support was resolute and the hard treatment that Sayers and the BBC were receiving from the popular press enraged him. But, being the consummate politician that every head of religious broadcasting is required to be, he took the only action any senior BBC manager under fire would take. He referred it up. Scripts were sent to the CRAC, the Central Religious Advisory Committee, which comprised an Anglican bishop, dean and vicar, a Baptist, a Congregationalist, a Methodist, a Presbyterian and a Roman Catholic – all advisors to the BBC and representatives of the main Christian Churches in Britain. If they came down against the plays, it would have been the equivalent of 'pistols at dawn' for Welch.

The comments from the committee members poured in by post, telegram and telephone. Only one member of CRAC expressed misgivings and he changed his mind soon after. Others were enthusiastic supporters. A prominent evangelical described the plays as 'magnificent', and went on, 'praise God and go ahead – my overwhelming approval anyway'. A Jesuit priest was equally supportive: 'The plays are excellent: go ahead'. Welch was overwhelmed. He was aware of the popular perception that church leaders must be over sixty years old, reactionary, and 'afraid of popular clamour'. He knew many found it 'useless to look to the dignitaries and leaders of the Churches for boldness and imagination'. This, in his mind, was a meeting of minds that should 'go down in the annals of Christian co-operation'. They may have had an average age of sixty but there was nothing reactionary about this group of clerics. As Welch puts it: 'the Corporation felt justified in broadcasting the first play'.

What confirmed the BBC ultimately in its decision to broadcast *The Man Born to be King* was not listener reaction but the support of the official leaders and representatives of the Churches.

Gielgud and Sayers

In his personal memoir written just after the war, the play's producer Val Gielgud gives his own insight into the dispute. Though not a Christian himself, he was fully aware of the difficulties. With classic understatement, he recalls . . .

> The issue was clearly a ticklish one. Religious feelings . . . remain of all human feelings the most unreasoning, the most easily aroused. Every possible attempt was made by prejudice, by sensational paragraphs in the newspapers, even by advertisement, to damn the project in the eyes of the public. One headline condemned Broadcasting House 'A Temple of Blasphemy'. Yet, when the BBC stuck to its guns and produced the plays, the reception . . . provided an unchallengeable response to the outcry of the Lord's Day Observance Society and the gnashing of Mr Martin's teeth [its spokesman].[21]

The public response

A great volume of approval was quickly forthcoming from the listeners once the broadcasts began. Hundreds of letters were sent to Broadcasting House. A vicar noted how many would arrive at his Evensong 'breathless' having stayed at their wireless sets until the play's very last word, and then rushed to church. A mother commended the BBC for 'tearing down the barriers' to her children's understanding of religion caused by the usual archaic English. A factory foreman gave his thanks that 'many working folk' who 'think organised religion has lost its usefulness' would 'listen and learn from these plays who would never desire to listen to a set church service on the wireless'. A teacher wrote of how her pupils deluged her with questions after each broadcast with Bibles in hand. One correspondent wrote:

The whole thing can do nothing but good: what the disap-
provers can't stand is that it makes the thing seem real to
them: the uncomfortable sensations which result make them
call it irreverent.

What was offensive to them was to hear Jesus laughing, or getting angry or even saying 'good morning'. To portray Christ as fully
divine and barely human is to misrepresent him. To portray Christ
as fully human and far from divine is also to misrepresent the
gospel account. But even for those who hold that Christ is both
fully man and fully God, the reality of the 'Word made Flesh' could
offend.

Welch himself admitted how he had been affected by the plays.

I must humbly confess that these plays revealed the poverty
and incompleteness of my own belief in the Incarnation.
Again and again when the figure of Christ in these plays
faced one with a direct challenge one's reaction was 'No!
not that, anything but that!' The Christ in these plays is, for
any who are prepared to read them and think, a veritable
Hound of Heaven. The eleventh play on the Crucifixion,
though it only hinted at the physical horror we were spared,
was almost unbearable because of the stupidity and bru-
tality of the ordinary man and woman in the crowd con-
victed us. We don't want to believe that the Crucifixion was
like that.[22]

Lewis was another who considered the plays 'excellent, indeed
most moving'. In a letter of 1 June 1943 to Arthur Greeves he
compares the objections to them to those directed at a stage play
of 1930 written in black Afro-American dialect – both objections
'silly'.[23] His admiration for Sayers' play-cycle is then evident in
much of Lewis's correspondence. He frequently recommended in
his letters to strangers that they read the published edition. In
response to a query about humour in the New Testament, he cites

a number of examples, including the Parable of the Unjust Steward. 'Its comic element', he tells Mr Lucas, 'is well brought out in Dorothy Sayers' excellent *The Man Born to be King*.[24]

The plays were first broadcast at monthly intervals from December 1941 to October 1942. They were repeated at much shorter intervals during Lent and Holy Week of 1943. Later they went out on the BBC's overseas services to win new admirers the world over. Sayers herself acknowledged the debt for unparalleled publicity given to *The Man Born to be King* by the Lord's Day Observance Society.

Lewis and Sayers remained close. Lewis read *The Man Born to be King* every Lent and 'never failed to be moved'. Their correspondence continued, and it is a measure of their friendship that he wrote to her with his most intimate feelings after his marriage to Joy Davidman: 'My heart is breaking and I was never so happy before: at any rate there is more in life than I knew about'.[25] This letter was written in June 1957 by a man whose wife was dying, to a friend in robust health. Yet Dorothy Sayers was dead herself within six months. It happened suddenly and unexpectedly after a busy weekend. She'd attended a baptism on the Friday in Cambridge when she became a godmother. The following Sunday she received at her home a visit from Val Gielgud. He found her as always to be 'brisk, vital, amusing, almost exuberant self, full of plans for the future . . .' On the Tuesday, a day's Christmas shopping left her exhausted. As Barbara Reynolds describes in her biography: 'she went upstairs, threw her hat and coat on the bed and went down to feed her hungry cats. She fell dead at the foot of the stairs, where she was found the next morning'.[26] It was Tuesday 17 December 1957.

C.S. Lewis, by now Professor of Medieval Literature in the University of Cambridge, was too ill himself to attend the funeral, but he did write a Panegyric to be read out at her memorial service.[27] In five pages of closely typed text, Lewis paid tribute to the assorted works of Dorothy Sayers. He argued that there was no divide between the detective fiction and her other works. She treated writing as a trade that demanded respect from her and others. Sayers was both 'a popular entertainer and a conscientious craftsman . . . with a very few exceptions, it is only such writers who matter much in the long run'. When her writing moved away from detective fiction towards religious plays 'she never sank the artist and the entertainer in the evangelist'. Her aim was to tell the Christian story to the best of her ability within the medium of which she was most in command, to make as good a work of art as she was able. Though distinct, art and evangelism 'turned out to demand one another'. Lewis concluded the tribute: 'For all she did and was, for delight and instruction, for her militant loyalty as a friend, for courage and honesty, for richly feminine qualities which showed through a port and manner superficially masculine and even gleefully ogreish – let us thank the Author who invented her.'

Notes

[1] Gielgud, Val, *Years of the Locust*, Nicholson & Watson, London, 1947, p. 177 ff.
[2] Gielgud, Val, *Years in a Mirror*, The Bodley Head, London, 1965, p. 93
[3] 2 August 1946, Hooper, W., *Letters*, p. 382
[4] 10 December 1945, Ibid. p. 380
[5] Reynolds, Barbara, *Dorothy L.Sayers – Her Life and Soul*, US edition, St. Martin's Griffin, New York, 1997, p. 358 ff.
[6] 13 May 1943, Reynolds, Barbara, (ed.), *The Letters of Dorothy L. Sayers, Volume Two 1937-1943 From novelist to playwright*, St. Martin's Press, New York, US edition 1998, p. 409 ff.
[7] Ibid.
[8] Ibid., p. 145 ff.
[9] Wardour Street is in Soho in London's West End and a magnet for artists, film-makers and the creative community then as now.
[10] 4 March 1940
[11] Sayers, Dorothy, *The Man Born to be King*, Victor Gollancz, London, May 1943. Such was the continuing interest that over the next ten years the 340-page volume was reprinted eighteen times.
[12] Interview with Frank Gillard for BBC Oral History, 4 July 1986
[13] Reynolds, *Life and Soul*, p. 301. In this biography Reynolds quotes Sayers:

'It is my experience that to talk over any work which one is doing has the curious effect of destroying one's interest in the work itself'. Reynolds says she loved to discuss books-in-progress with close friends, however.

14 25 October 1940, *Letters*, p. 186
15 Ibid. p. 195 ff.
16 Ibid. p. 201 ff.
17 BBC Written Archives, letter dated 15 January 1941, Vosper to Miss Candler
18 Gielgud, Val, *Years in a Mirror*, p. 93
19 Ibid. p. 94
20 Interview with Frank Gillard for BBC Oral History, 4 July 1986
21 Gielgud, *Locust,* p. 110
22 Welch, James, Foreword to *The Man Born to be King*. Other quotations are taken from the three essays in this book, first published 1943. I have used the 1953 impression. The foreword is on pages 9–17, author's introduction by Dorothy L. Sayers p.17–41 and production note by Val Gielgud p.41.
23 9 May 1961 in Hooper (ed.), *Letters* p. 497
24 Ibid. 6 December 1956, p. 460
25 Ibid. 25 June 1957, p. 466
26 Reynolds, *Life and Soul* p. 364
27 I am grateful to Christopher Dean, Chairman of the Dorothy L. Sayers Society, based in West Sussex, for sending me a photo-copy of the original typed manuscript of the panegyric written by C.S. Lewis, which has been published elsewhere.

CHAPTER FIFTEEN

'Not my pigeon, I think'

⌘

While *The Man Born to be King* was being broadcast, the concept of the religious radio talk was taking on a momentum of its own.

No sooner had C.S. Lewis finished one series of talks for the BBC than the Corporation was planning another. The idea of using a layman to deliver popular theology that spoke to the 'common man' in language that was easily understood had worked superbly. Lewis was a hot property and could easily have done twice as much broadcasting if the BBC had had anything to do with it. However, it was eating heavily into his time and creating some waves at his college.

Oxford gave its dons considerable latitude in what they were free to do. A don would be given rooms, a certain amount of students and be required to take tutorials. There might well be an obligation to deliver an agreed number of lectures on top of the one-to-one tutorials. The university would have expected some academic research and original work to be going on. It was also wartime, so student numbers were far lower than in peacetime. That said, delivering talks on the BBC on a topic outside your specialist subject area and writing popular books at the same time, would not be well received.

In some circles at Oxford, broadcasting was not altogether a respectable activity. Walter Hooper recalls a conversation with J.R.R. Tolkien, author of *Lord of the Rings,* about this.

> He explained it in this way. In Oxford you are forgiven for writing only two kinds of books. You can write books on your subject – say literature, history, whatever it is because this is what is expected of you. And you can write detective fiction because all dons at some point get the flu and have to have something to read in bed. But what you are not forgiven is writing popular works of theology. And he says Lewis knew this when he accepted the invitation from the BBC and he said the reason he did it, he was driven to do it by his conscience.[1]

Jill Freud confirms that Lewis's activities did not always meet with the approval of the college.

> They didn't like the religious side of things of course. They wouldn't like that. I'm sure you are absolutely aware that for an academic to publish a book which is a bestseller is almost a mortal sin. You absolutely mustn't do that. It means you are a popular writer and that's what you mustn't be. And so he never got the recognition at Oxford that he should have done. He never got the promotion to professorship or whatever. He was looked down on for having written children's books, for having written religious books, for having written bestsellers and therefore he was not a serious academic.[2]

The Jordans Conference

Between the second and third series of Lewis's broadcast talks – in May 1942 – the BBC's Director of Religion, James Welch, asked Lewis to do something quite different. He invited him to attend a staff conference of the Religious Broadcasting Department to help them map out the future. The conference was to take place at Jordans, the old Quaker centre in Buckinghamshire.[3] Welch had also invited the author Rose Macaulay.[4] Coming from opposite ends of the ecclesiastical candle, the meeting of the two writers would have produced a fascinating conference.

Rose Macaulay was suspicious of C.S. Lewis. Although she had read very little of his writings, she admitted to being a 'little prejudiced' against him in a letter to a friend. When she did eventually get round to reading *The Problem of Pain*, she considered it to be somewhat 'slapdash perhaps but vivid and impressive with some good images'.[5] So the conference promised to be lively and engaging.

Regrettably, this encounter of literary and theological minds didn't happen. Lewis pulled out. College duties – and fear of a reputation for absence – had clearly won over the temptation to be involved. He did not withdraw to show disapproval of Rose Macaulay. He imagines what he would have ended up saying to her:

> . . . there can be no compromise (as there may be mutual respect) between those who regard 'religion as a desirable element in a culture' (*emollit mores* and all that) and those who believe Christianity to be objectively true. It's the difference between a man who thinks a lecture on navigation might interest the boys on a Saturday afternoon entertainment and a man who thinks the ship is sinking.

It was many years before the two writers did meet. Rose Macaulay then revised her opinion of Lewis. She described him to a friend as 'very good, quick and witty in public speech'. She had enjoyed listening to him speak.[6]

Although Lewis was missing, the Jordans Conference did attract a number of James Welch's inner circle of advisors. This group agreed with the BBC Governors' verdict that religious issues were not appropriate fare for the highbrow team of *The Brains Trust*. This left religious questions sent in by listeners in large numbers unanswered. The newspapers had caught on to this and wanted religion included more often. The Governors were over-protective of religious broadcasting, sensitive to charges from Parliament that the BBC was undermining the faith of the nation and the work of the clergy,[7] and were wary of stirring controversy that could distract from the war effort. So the conference agreed to proceed with the development of a new programme to accommodate religious issues with a similar panel format called *The Anvil*.

Paradise remains lost

Lewis's letter had expressed his concerns not to stray too far beyond the bounds of what Oxford considered acceptable behaviour by its dons. This might explain why Eric Fenn exercised unusual restraint before following up the third series – which ended in November 1942 – by inviting Lewis to prepare a fourth series of talks. In the past, the commissioning letter inviting Lewis to do another series went out within a few days of the final broadcast of the previous series. But after the end of *Christian Behaviour*, it was five months before Fenn contacted Lewis, on 10 March 1943.

> At the end of your last series of talks for us, you mentioned that you might be willing to do a further series in the summer or autumn of this year. We were discussing the other day the possibility of a series of talks in the Forces Programme (Sunday afternoons 2.50–3.00) on 'Misconceptions of Christianity' and we wonder whether you would consider doing this? Content we could leave for discussion between us, perhaps. We should like to begin such a series on July 11th and carry on until the end of August. Could you think this over and let me know what you feel.[8]

A postscript from Fenn offers a postponement until later in the year if these plans do not fit in with some unidentified 'particular theological concern that we discussed'. Whatever the reason, on a white strip of paper just two inches high, Lewis says no, as he is too fully occupied, but suggests a later date. Even though Lewis has left the BBC in no doubt that he is too busy to take on any more broadcasting that year, Fenn has another go.

> Behold me back again to disturb your peace – this time to ask whether you would be willing to give one of the talks in a series we hope to start on 'Why I believe in God'. These would be 15-minute talks on the Home Service on Tuesdays 10.15–10.30 p.m. and the date should I think for you be August 17th. What we are after is a simple and personal state-ment from each person concerned of the main grounds on which they have come to believe in God – in other words, an attempt to get an abstract argument in more personal terms. We should be very glad indeed of your help in this, but you alone will know if it is either possible or to your taste.[9]

Lewis sent his reply to the BBC four days later in a hand-written note on a post-card.

> Not my pigeon, I think. Not that *personal* 'testifying' isn't most important, but it isn't my gift.[10]

You would think that at this stage the BBC would have got the message and been content to pin him down on a date for series four and to leave it at that. But no. What happened next was that the BBC stepped up the pressure on Lewis to do more.

Within six weeks of Lewis's firm rejection of Eric Fenn's pro-posal, a letter arrived from Fenn's line manager James Welch. Writing in his capacity as Director of Religion, Welch made his own attempt to breach Lewis's defences. His letter was friendly, subtle and enticing. It began by acknowledging Lewis's difficulties and even offered a half-baked apology for bothering him again. The bait is a new programme, a religious version of *The Brains Trust* to be called *The Anvil*. The fact that Welch persisted with seeking to get Lewis on the air tells us a great deal about the respect in which the BBC held Lewis and their desperation to find speakers of his quality.

> We come to you pretty often to help and you are good enough to help us when you think you have a contribution to make. So I am writing, and I must admit rather hopefully, to ask whether you would help us with a recording or two of *The Anvil*. The programme is starting up again with Captain Quintin Hogg in the chair – he is an admirable chairman – with some members of the old team and with one or two new-comers. The procedure is that we send the questions to you beforehand so that you can prepare the answers in your mind and look up any facts if you want to: though you can put one or two things down on paper, we like the discussion at the microphone to be as spontaneous and unscripted as possible. It will involve three hours from 6.30–9.30 p.m. on Monday – and we would pay all expenses and a fee of twelve guineas for every successful recording (half of it if not). Do, please, come over and help us.[11]

Astonishingly, Welch's letter appears to do the trick. The reply is typed and sent by Warnie, Jack's brother. Those typed by Warnie follow a strict format.

> Dear Mr Welch,
> I am replying to your 03/R/JWW dated 23rd April on behalf of my brother, who is laid up with flu. He asks me to say that he will be very pleased to help, and adds that it would of course be easier for him if the selected Monday fell in the Vac rather than in term time.
> Yours faithfully,
> W.H. Lewis[12]

Having secured the victory and persuaded Lewis to take part, Welch pressed home the advantage.

> Thanks for the note your sister kindly sent us [it was his brother]. I hope you are now better from flu'. We should like to use you in this present session, since the future of *The Anvil* is not assured beyond the end of July and we like to record a week or two beforehand. Indeed we have already four recordings ready to go on the air, and we like to work at least three weeks ahead in case we have one or two consecutive failures. Would there be any possibility of getting you for any Monday evening or evenings in June? If not, which is the earliest Monday in July we can hope to see you? It would mean being at Broadcasting House, London, from about 6 p.m. to 9 p.m. If you would let me know the earliest date possible after the end of May we can fix it at once.[13]

Lewis tells him that although June is out of the question, he could perhaps manage to come in on July 19 or 26 to take part in *The Anvil*, 'but, as I shall be examining, it is not easy to be certain. You would be safer in putting me on the next session if there is one'.

Spurred on by this half-acceptance of another booking, Fenn launched a new assault on Lewis's diary.

> I return to the attack. You don't tell us why you believe in God, but will you give a talk on Sunday August 1st 4.45 – 5.00 p.m. in the Home Service on *Paradise Lost*? This is one of a series of talks we are beginning in July, dealing with certain great Christian books, and we should very much like to include *Paradise Lost*, and, if you could possibly take it on, we should rejoice . . .
>
> I know that it is a fantastic proposition in the time but I also know that all one can do is to whet people's appetites

and cause them to go back and read Milton again. I do hope this may be possible . . .[14]

Fenn would have known that Lewis had prepared a Preface to *Paradise Lost* (the Ballard Matthew Memorial Lecture 1941), which was later published in 1942. So he would have thought his request perfectly reasonable. Surely, Lewis could dust off his previous work and prepare a radio version? On a tiny strip of paper again just two inches high, Lewis is dismissive. A talk on Paradise Lost would be 'an absolute waste of time. What's the good of telling them they'll enjoy it, when we both know they won't?'[15]

The reluctant broadcaster

There remained the unresolved issue of whether or not any progress was possible on Lewis's fourth series of broadcast talks. Eric Fenn writes to Lewis again from his hotel base in Bedford.

My dear Lewis,
Two matters:-
1. Have you thought any further about the series of more theological talks you were inclined to when I last saw you? We have been considering lately a suggestion made at a informal conference on religious broadcasting, which we held recently – namely the need for a series of talks which would take some of the more abstruse theological doctrines and show what sort of difference they make, both to thought and to conduct. This seems roughly in line with what you had in mind, and I wonder if we could explore it further sometime.
2. Could you suggest anybody to take over our monthly review of recent religious books? The Dean of St Paul's is at present tackling this, but he ought to be given a rest in the autumn, and we are very keen to get somebody younger to take on the job. The whole thing seems to have got into

a bit of a rut and needs a fresh mind on it. The talks are on Sunday afternoons, from 4.45 – 5.00 in the Home Service – usually on the fourth Sunday in each month. (Is this a job, by any chance, you would like to do yourself?)[16]

Paper must have been in short supply at The Kilns because most of Lewis's letters at this time are typed or hand-written on tiny strips of paper. Fenn can't help but comment on it:

If I may say so, your passion for paper economy exceeds anything my imagination can grasp! I should like to talk this project over with you. Would it be any use my trying to arrange to come to Oxford sometime next month? Our available periods are all pretty well mapped out until well into the autumn, and some of them are a little uncertain by reason of rival claims. But, in any case, I should very much like to have a talk, and not only about this particular matter.[17]

Perhaps to underline the point even more and to show his responsible stewardship – or maybe he had run out of paper – but Lewis replied verbally via an acquaintance called Frank Woods. Fenn was still putting pressure on Lewis to take part in The Anvil and asked him if he could manage to come to London on 19 July, for a recording of a session, together with Canon Cockin (Anglican), Father Andrew Beck (Roman Catholic) and W.A.L. Elmslie, Principal of Westminster College, Cambridge. The plan was to meet at 6 p.m. for a preliminary discussion and then arrange 'a batting order', record half an hour's discussion from 7.15–7.45, have supper and then hear the play-back. He included the questions received from listeners to be tackled that night.[18]

Lewis agrees to the arrangements. With characteristic good humour, he abandons his usual letter-box strip of writing paper for a whole sheet, sent uncut. Not only that, but he leaves four inches by six inches of blank paper.

And what about paper economy now? I trust I can do a handsome thing when put on my mettle.

P.S. You may use the margin of this letter for any purpose you like.[19]

The extravagant use of a whole sheet of writing paper uncut was just an amusing aberration. Lewis's next letter is written by hand in tiny lettering worthy of a medieval monk writing in Carolingian minuscule.[20] Lewis comes up for the first time with his proposed list of topics. They are:

1. The doctrine of the Trinity [part 1]
2. The doctrine of the Trinity [part 2]
3. Creation
4. The Incarnation, suggested title 'The Human element in God'
5. The Two Natures
6. The Resurrection, suggested title 'The defeat of death'
7. The Ascension, suggested title 'The promotion of man'[21]

Relations between the BBC and Lewis are back on an even keel. A meeting is arranged in Oxford between Fenn and Lewis. It would appear that Lewis was finally to join the panel and take part in *The Anvil*. Fenn wrote confirming acceptance of Lewis's proposal for the forthcoming series.

It was good to see you again on Monday, and I was glad that 'The Anvil' seemed to be going well, at least up to the time when I had to leave. This is to confirm the provisional arrangement we came to – namely, that you will give a series of seven or eight talks on 'Christian Doctrine', on Tuesdays, January 18, 25, February 1, 8, 15, 22, March 1 and, possibly, 8. The talks will probably be at 7.30 p.m. or thereabouts. We should be glad to see the scripts in good time in case of any hitch, though I don't imagine we are likely to quarrel violently over them. If you could let us have them sometime in November we should be grateful.[22]

The best-laid plans can sometimes go adrift in broadcasting. While Fenn's letter implies that Lewis did take part in *The Anvil* – 'The Anvil seemed to be going well' – we would expect the definitive account to be found in what are known in the BBC as P-as-B's, which is short-hand for Programmes-as-Broadcast. C.S. Lewis's name does not appear in the records as having taken part in *The Anvil* at all, throughout the series. On 19 July, it was pre-recorded for transmission on the 22nd. The contributors were Canon Cockin (Anglican), Father Beck (Roman Catholic), Rev. Dorothy Wilson (Free Church) with Rev. James Welch in the Chair. This is one fewer contributor than normal, seeming to suggest that either Lewis did not make it or dropped out. The only surviving record or proof that Lewis *did* take part that night is a dog-eared script kept by Walter Hooper, which shows a characteristically lively contribution from Lewis.[23]

There was another blow. On 19 August, Fenn delayed the next series of Lewis's broadcast talks. Another series on 'Science and Religion' looked likely to be ready by the beginning of the new year. The BBC wanted to schedule them on Tuesday evenings from 4 January till 8 February inclusive. This would push back Lewis's talks to 15 February to 28 March.

Why are they so short?

Six weeks later, Eric Fenn revealed the first signs of concern that Lewis might be slipping behind schedule in his preparation of the talks.

I am wondering very much how you are getting on with the talks on Christian Doctrine. Could you let me know where they now stand and how soon it will be possible for you to let us see the result of your labour. We may have to ask you to begin a week later than is at present suggested: – i.e. on February 22nd instead of February 15th. You could still have seven talks if you want them. On the other hand, if it proves more convenient to do the job in six, that would at the moment be a possible alternative. If you do seven, beginning on February 22nd, it would carry you to April 4th.[24]

He needn't have worried. The reason for the silence is that Lewis cannot get hold of a typist to convert his long-hand version of the scripts.

Much relieved, Fenn asked Lewis to give the manuscript to a colleague, Nat Micklem, to bring up with him on Sunday next, when he has a broadcast in London, and asked him to give it to his colleague Mr Beales for him. That avoids trusting it to the post. This meant that Beales, who was a Roman Catholic, was the first to see the manuscript. He was a valued member of the religious broadcasting team and one who regularly acted as studio producer for Lewis, but not the one who was normally the first to see his scripts. It prompted a memo fired off to Eric Fenn. The detail and the length of this note demonstrates the attention to detail that the production process necessitates.

These seven Talks were handed to me yesterday by Micklem. Lewis had given them to him to deliver, as they are in long-hand and he didn't want to risk them in the post. They are quite up to standard, and one just has to take off one's hat to them. But one or two points:

In Talk Two (the Trinity) I think he misses a step. I feel that half way through the Talk, they will sit up and say, 'half a jiffy. Which of us started this query about more than one Person in God? I didn't; and I'm wondering what put it into *your* mind to suppose that there might be?' This will bother them, and in thinking about it they may miss the next few lines. I think he needs to 'suggest' it in their minds, first, that it is worth asking about the Three Persons.

My other point is that, while he deliberately sets out to give a course, he cannot count altogether on full continuity of listening, and accordingly it might be better still to open each succeeding Talk not by saying, 'Last time we did this . . .', but beginning right off with the first concrete example he is going to use – state it, and come back to it again in its proper place in the argument.[25]

Three days before Christmas, Fenn follows up the memo from Beales by writing to Lewis directly. A much bigger problem has arisen than Beales's suggestion for refining the script. Why are they so short?

Thank you very much for the manuscripts which arrived safely by the hand of Dr Micklem. We'll get them copied, and send you our comments and any suggestions for revision when we have got a typed script. I like them immensely, and think that, as usual, you have achieved a quite astonishing degree of clarity in a very difficult subject. One or two of your analogies seem to me to need a little scrutiny or possible qualification – but of that, more anon.

The thing that chiefly worries me is that, so far as I can make out you have worked to a 10-minute script, and not a 15-minute. The average length appears to be about 1,150 words, which is what we usually allow for a 10-minute talk. There are two ways out of this – we can either keep them as 10-minute talks, and give away the other five to some other programme, or you could expand each by another 600 words. Would you think this over and let me know which course of action you would prefer? The difficulty is, of course, that each is complete as it stands, and the possibility of

> expansion varies from script to script, but we could make
> suggestions about this if you like.

Lewis did not let this unwelcome news disrupt his Christmas. He waited until the day after the Boxing Day Bank Holiday, 27 December, to respond. Writing by hand in blue ink, he expressed his exasperation at his own failure to time the scripts properly.

> I could kick myself for not having used my 15 mins. to the full. . . . . I suppose your threatened 'scrutiny' of some of my analogies (the very word has a sinister sound suggesting scrooge, screws, screwtape, scraping and Inland Revenue) may lead to at least 600 additional words in some cases. But, as you know, I'm very biddable when it comes to the point.

Knocking the script into shape

The longest letter sent by Eric Fenn in three years as C.S. Lewis's producer was the one dispatched on 29 December, 1943. It's an important letter for a number of reasons. It shows the depth of the relationship that the two men had built up over three years and three series of programmes. Fenn as producer held nothing back – he tells Lewis exactly what he thinks of the script and how it can be improved. It also confirms again just how much support the production process at the BBC gave to its contributors. No detail is spared on how to turn around what was a difficult problem – expanding ten-minute completed scripts into fifteen-minute talks, without the joins showing.

No matter how good a writer might be – whether they be T.S. Eliot, J.R.R. Tolkien, J.B. Priestley or C.S. Lewis – writing for radio is not the same as writing for the printed page. The words have to make sense right away, because the listener does not have the luxury of a second chance. There are no pages to be turned back to check a passage again. Moreover if a broadcaster does not engage his listener, the listener will go away, retune to another station or just turn off the radio. The radio producer is trained to detect the weak spots and to put them right, to cut out the superfluous and to clarify anything that is not readily comprehensible. Normally, the kind of debate recorded in this letter is what would have taken place when the two men met in Oxford to run through the scripts. The content of this letter is unusual in the detail it reveals and the role played by the producer in making Lewis a better writer for radio. It helped to hone Lewis's style into something lean and direct, giving his writing a sharper edge. Here is the full text of what Eric Fenn wrote to C.S. Lewis.

Please reply to: Box No. 7, G.P.O. Bedford
Reference 03/R/JEF   29th December 1943
My dear Lewis,
I am enclosing herewith a typed script of your seven talks. This is not the final copy, but one we have had made in order to avoid sending a precious manuscript backwards and forwards through the post for revision purposes.

In my last letter I indicated how much we like the whole set, but warned you I had some misgivings about length and about some of your analogies. Taking our appreciation for granted, here are some suggestions, humbly submitted to your wisdom.

1) Length: So far as I can tell, after carefully checking the length of each script, they work out like this:-

1) 1,180 words	4) 1,350 words
2) 1,160	5) 1,200
3) 1,300	6) 1,200 words
7) 1,130 words	

We usually reckon 1,750 words for a 15-minute talk. A simple exercise in arithmetic therefore, indicates that you need about another page of a typed script in each case.

As indicated in my last letter, there are two possible answers to this conundrum – we can either keep them as 10-minute talks, or expand them to 15 minutes. If we do the former, we shall have to cut numbers 3 & 4. We should very much prefer to expand them if you can bear to do so. What we can't do with any comfort is to arrange for a 15-minute talk, then occupy only 11 minutes of that time!

2) *Arrangement:* On the suggestion of expanding the talks to 1,750 words, we should like to suggest in some, if not all cases, that you begin with one of your most striking illustrations, and then go back to it later in the script at the appropriate place in the argument. This would mean a certain repetition (though in two rather different forms) but it would have the advantage of catching the attention of people who have not heard the previous talk, and of etching that particular illustration into the mind.

For instance, in No. 3, if you begin with the illustration about the candle – which does in large measure focus what you are trying to say all through the talk – and then went on with your argument as at present, taking up the candle metaphor again at the appropriate place, this might provide an effective opening for the listener who has not heard the previous talk without damaging your argument.

I don't want to insist on this, I realise that you are deliberately doing a consecutive series and expecting the listener to accept the fact. At the same time, you can't rely on the complete absence of the more casual listener (indeed, one hopes that he will join in in increasing numbers, and anything you can do to temper the wind to the shorn lamb the better).

3) One or two suggestions about the individual scripts and places where some expansion might help to make your arguments clear:-

1) I wonder if you might profitably expand paragraph 3,

especially the last sentence, which people may not get at first hearing.

2) I wonder if it might be clearer if you took a second example of the way in which lower forms are taken up into higher forms from the biological field – i.e. the way in which inorganic matter is built into animal life and animal life combined with consciousness in man. The 'cube' is a most illuminating metaphor but it is inevitably static.

3) First about this candle. This is one of the metaphors I am not quite sure about. Doesn't it open a flank to the scientist (or pseudo-scientist) unless rather carefully dealt with? There is a sense in which 'the light is there before the flame' – i.e. there is a centre of radiant energy, which in certain conditions of temperature becomes visible as flame. Anyway, I find that the illustration set my mind questioning it and tended to hold up my thoughts in the rest of the talk (but that may be the way I am made).

I wonder if it might not be well to forestall criticism that this is 'a very complex and bewildering conception of life' by an aside of some length, showing how very complex and bewildering a 'scientific' account of the simplest action is. (I mean the kind of thing Edington does so well about a scientist's account of his own action in walking into a room). Yet nobody questions the scientific mind or feels that he has an odd way of describing a 'simple' experience.

One more point on this – aren't you a bit hard on the people who say 'Love is God?' Is that really what they mean?

4) I think you need to expand the point about 'human solidarity'. We have so completely lost this idea (except in a Marxist sense), that you need to take time to establish it – and it is quite vital to any understanding of the practical bearing of your chief argument.

5) I wonder if this might not be the place to say a bit more about the Christian community? With the exception of one or two references, you don't seem to mention this at

all, and the scripts give, therefore, an impression of a purely individualistic approach. In this one, for instance, you are thinking all about one man in relation to God, and not at all about the connection this always establishes with other men. I do think it would strengthen the series to say something more about the Church and it would come naturally after your insistence on human solidarity in No. 4.

6) The only suggestion here is that you should go back at some point to your statement in the first paragraph that this is 'the whole of Christianity'. This will be so surprising a statement to many people that it would help if about two-thirds of the way through you go back to that and rubbed it in again.

7) This appears to be the shortest of the seven – about 600 words less than it might be.

I have a feeling you could, with advantage, expand paragraph 2 to make clearer how good things go bad, and possibly a bit more about the process whereby this happens.

Then I am not sure about your analogy of salt. The trouble is that salt is a totally different substance from the material it flavours, whereas you are stressing the likeness of character and the way in which this likeness makes room for difference. However, this may not be a frightfully important point.

Forgive this inordinate length. We should be grateful if you would look at the scripts in the light of these comments and make whatever adjustments may seem good to you. We are prepared to buy them as they stand, but should prefer that each one should be expanded to the length of our programme.

Kind regards, and good wishes for 1944,

Yours sincerely,

EF

(Eric Fenn)

Two days later, on New Year's Eve, Lewis caught up with his correspondence and gives Fenn his answer. Yes, he has made up his mind to use the full fifteen minutes and expand each script to the required duration. No, he warned Fenn not to be disappointed if he does not adopt all the suggestions put forward by the BBC.

> All that about organisms, for instance – I cd do it for a Bampton Lecture but this d-d [damned] colloquial style is so intrinsically honest that I can't conceal *in it* my ignorance of what really does happen in an organism! And the Church – it's difficult to go on long about that without raising the denominational question. But I'll peg away.

Where the earlier series had seen a relatively smooth process from conception to treatment to preparation and script and then to broadcast and transmission, this series was hitting problems from the start. But both Lewis and Fenn knew it had the making of something good, if only Lewis could solve the problem of the length of each talk without destroying their integrity. A lot of work was needed on Lewis's part but 'peg away' he did.

Notes

1   Interview with Walter Hooper, 28 October 1999
2   Interview with Jill Freud, 19 November 1999
3   BBC Written Archives file R34/759/1 Policy Religion Conferences File 1 1939–1943, letter, 11 May 1942
4   Rose Macaulay (1881-1958) was a novelist, essayist and poet. Her father had a distinguished academic career at Cambridge and translated the writings of Herodotus. She began writing from an early age, starting with *Abbots Verney* in 1906. *The Lee Shore* in 1913 established her reputation. Her novels included *They Were Defeated* (1932), and *The Towers of Trebizond* (1956). She was a great traveller and even in her later years, was an all-the-year-round swimmer.
5   Macaulay, Rose, *Letters to a Friend*, Collins, 1961, Volume 1, p. 239 ff.
6   Ibid. Volume 2
7   Wolfe, Kenneth M., *The Churches and the British Broadcasting Corporation 1922–1956*, SCM Press Ltd, London, p. 207 ff.
8   10 March 1943

[9] 8 April 1943
[10] 12 April 1943
[11] 23 April 1943
[12] 29 April 1943
[13] 4 May 1943
[14] 6 May 1943
[15] 7 May 1943
[16] 11 June 1943
[17] 18 June 1943
[18] 28 June 1943
[19] 1 July 1943
[20] It is believed that the use of small lettering in medieval manuscripts arose during the era of Charles 1 of France at the turn of the eighth and ninth centuries, when parchment was in short supply in the monasteries. The Carolingian Renaissance saw a flowering of manuscript writing, preservation of the classics and the development of illuminated manuscripts. But with the parchment running out, the lettering became smaller and smaller, with less reliance on capital letters. The writing style that resulted is known as Carolingian minuscule.
[21] 16 June 1943. 'The doctrine of the Trinity' is in the letter for topics one and two.
[22] 21 July 1943
[23] See *Appendix* 3.
[24] 8 December 1943
[25] 20 December 1943

CHAPTER SIXTEEN

A Pox On Your Powers

∾∾

In January 1944, C.S. Lewis began the arduous process. He had to convert seven ten-minute talks and stretch them to fifteen minutes. The trick was to do it without allowing the listener to spot the joins. At risk was the flow of the argument. Lewis was not finding it easy. Some interpolations are not very 'artistically dovetailed', he warned Fenn.[1] One compensation was that the process had given Lewis a title for the whole series. It was to be called *Beyond Personality*. Eric Fenn appreciated the extra paragraphs for the script but was not yet convinced by the title.

> I think it might be better to have a quite plain descriptive title, such as 'What Christians Believe about the Nature of God' or, if you prefer it, 'Beyond Personality – what Christians Believe about the Nature of God'. What I can't quite see is how your intriguing subtitles would then fit into the billings, but I think it is specially important in this series to let listeners know plainly what they are in for. Would you think this over and let me know how you feel about it?[2]

Lewis wanted to keep the sub-headings but was flexible on the choice of main title. He would approve any of the following:

What Christians think God is like
What is God like? The Christian answer
Beyond Personality: or the Christian God[3]

Fenn went to Oxford on 22 January to dine with Lewis and settle any outstanding issues. While he was making good progress with Lewis on the fourth series of broadcast talks, his colleague, A.C.F. Beales, attempted yet again to get Lewis to take part in the next series of *The Anvil*. This would follow up an 'on air' campaign to explain the Christian faith to listeners – the department's own 'mission'.

> At our staff meeting this week we decided to resume *The Anvil* towards the end of this quarter, as an immediate means of following up the 'Mission'. Dr Welch has asked us to write to you and to Canon Cockin, Mgr. R.L. Smith, and Professor C.H. Dodd, the four speakers whom we should like to take part in the first few Anvil broadcasts, with Welch himself in the chair.
>
> As the quarter's broadcasts proceed, questions arising out of them will come in from listeners. We shall be most grateful if you will send us, in due course, all the questions which you find in your correspondence, whether you get them in the form of direct questions, or in the form of difficulties or points which can be rephrased as questions. This will be the material on which *The Anvil* sessions will be based.

Beales leaves Lewis under no illusion as to the commitment. There would first be two or three trial recordings 'to reach a technical standard adequate for broadcasting' on Monday nights. The format for the actual recordings was to meet at 6 o'clock for a preliminary discussion about the evening's work, to record between 7.0 and 8.0 o'clock, then to have supper in the restaurant. After that, the panel would listen to the recording being played back 'so that we could judge it ourselves'. Lewis's reply has not survived, but again he said no to the BBC. Beales did not hide his disappointment.

> Many thanks for your card about *The Anvil*. Bad luck. They will all be very disappointed when I tell them. I wonder whether you could do it if we changed the recording evening? Since there is nothing sacrosanct about Monday beyond the fact of sheer tradition.[4]

At the end of the month, Eric Fenn issued a contract for the *Beyond Personality* series. Lewis was offered ten guineas and one pound expenses per talk and seven railway vouchers (Oxford/ London) return. On 8 February, Eric Fenn alerted Lewis to yet another significant change:

> There is a rather serious hitch about the time of your talk. It is a long story connected with the change over on February 27th in our Forces Programme, which has involved radical readjustment of the Home Service. The net result is that our Tuesday talk has to be put at about 10.20 p.m. from February 22nd onwards. I explained to the powers that be that this was extremely awkward for you, and attempted to get permission to broadcast from Oxford, but on security grounds, outside broadcasts of that kind have been cut down drastically – so I am afraid we are in a bit of a hole! We don't like recording talks, and it always drops the temperature in the audience when they hear that it is a recording, but this may be the only thing left to be done. If you possibly could do even some of them 'live' from London at that time (it would mean spending the night in town) we should be enormously grateful, but if this is impossible, we would record the whole seven talks, which I suggest might be done in two, or possibly three recording sessions.

Eric Fenn's tone is apologetic but unbending.

> I really am extremely sorry about this, and we have tried every conceivable method of getting round it, because I know how very awkward it is for you – but there we are!

C.S. Lewis was furious and writes a blistering reply. Even in his anger, his humour flashes through. His usual greeting *My dear Fenn* is abbreviated to Dear Fenn.

> Pox on your 'powers'! Who the devil is going to listen at 10.20? If it is possible . . . cancel the whole thing for this spring and put it on later in the year. If not – a talk at 10.20 means catching the midnight train and getting to bed about 3 o'clock. Well, I'll give *three* under those conditions. The rest you'll have to record.
>
> If you know the address of any reliable firm of assassins, nose-slitters, garotters and poisoners I should be grateful to have it. I shall write a book about the BBC – you see if I don't! gr-r-r-r!![5]

Eric Fenn's reply two days later empathises with Lewis and his growing frustration with the BBC. Fenn does not make the mistake of offering any concessions however. He knows where the lines are drawn:

> Thanks for your letter. I can assure you that if I had known any reliable firm of assassins, nose-slitters, garotters and poisoners, I should already have made full use of them myself! This business has made me understand anew why the term 'grey matter' is so frequently used of the brain – the point being that it describes the state of affairs when something has gone far beyond turning the hair grey, and penetrated well beneath the scalp. However, there comes a point beyond which one has to give up the struggle while not throwing away the record.

He falls back on the old BBC maxim, a tradition of the elders in the Corporation which affirmed that 'the later the hour, the more intelligent the audience'. The solution of recording one at 9 p.m. and broadcasting another talk live at 10.15 p.m. seemed the best compromise:

> I take my hats off you for being willing to do three of these things 'live'. I can imagine nothing worse than arriving in Oxford in the middle of the night (except arriving in Bletchley). I think the simplest thing is the following arrangement, if you don't mind spreading out the agony, instead of getting it over in one go: –
> February 2nd – record No. 2, and broadcast No. 1
> March 7th: record No. 4, and broadcast No. 3
> March 21st – record Nos. 6 & 7, and broadcast No. 5

Making and begetting

It would be nice to think, but impossible to prove, that some of the strain Lewis was encountering in getting these programmes to air had an influence on the writing. There is a directness of approach in the talks which is not short of outright aggression by Lewis. From his opening sentence of the first talk, Lewis lays down the gauntlet.

> Everyone has warned me not to tell you what I am going to tell you in these talks. They all say 'the ordinary listener doesn't want Theology; you give him plain practical religion'. I don't think the ordinary listener is such a fool. I think any man who wants to think about God at all would like the clearest and most accurate ideas about Him which are available. You're not children: why should you be treated like children?[6]

In this first talk, *Making and Begetting*, Lewis gives an indication of the kind of response he used to receive to his talks at RAF camps. He refers to an old hard-bitten officer who had felt God's presence out in the desert and therefore had no time for dogmas and doctrines. To him such explanations were petty and pedantic and unreal. Lewis told the listener that he can understand why such a genuine experience might provoke that reaction. Looking at the Atlantic from a beach is not the same as seeing it on a map – the first is personal, the second is the accumulation of masses of experience. Doctrines are not God – theology is like the map. A single experience of God does not lead anywhere. Feeling the presence of God in flowers or music does not give you eternal life. Going to sea without a map is not very safe! So theology is practical too.

Without an understanding of theology the statements made about Jesus in the Bible and by himself are hard to make sense of. He takes 'begotten not created' from the creed as an example and explains its meaning. To beget is literally 'to be the father of', whereas to make is a creative act, just as a beaver makes a dam, or a man a radio. This is not the same as a man begetting human babies or a beaver little beavers. A statue has a man's shape but is not alive. Likeness to God exists in all things in one sense, but it is not spiritual life. Here Lewis distinguishes between the Greek words zoë and bios. Zoë is the spiritual life from God from all eternity – bios is the biological life that is subject to decay and to death. Christianity is about the transformation from one into the other. It is as if, Lewis suggests, we are the statues in a sculptor's studio – and a rumour is going round that one day some of us might come to life.

Each of these talks was published in the BBC's magazine *The Listener*, the first of Lewis's four series to have each script published the week after broadcast transmission. One listener was offended by Lewis's statement that you will not get eternal life just by feeling the presence of God in flowers or music. W.R. Childe of Leeds argued that such a feeling *is* eternal life. 'He [Lewis] may prepare his faggots [bundle of sticks for burning] for the usual heresy hunt in which Christian dogmatists in the past so often liberated their suppressed intellects and passions.' He cited William Blake's poem about seeing heaven in a wild flower and holding infinity in the palm of your hand. 'If Mr Lewis could tell people how to do that, he might make a real contribution to religious progress.'

C.S. Lewis felt this criticism could not go without a response. Alongside the script of his third talk in *The Listener*, was placed Lewis's reply. Although admitting to be no judge of his own lucidity, Lewis is equally offended as Mr Childe, seeing no cause for such accusations in a difference in theological opinion:

> I take it very hard that a total stranger should publicly accuse me of being a potential torturer, murderer and tyrant – for that is what Mr Childe's reference to faggots means . . . If he can find any passage in my works which favours religious or anti-religious compulsion I will give five pounds to any (not militantly anti-Christian) charity he cares to name. If he cannot, I ask him for justice and charity's sake, to withdraw his charge.[7]

Mr Childe was stung into a further letter in which he absolves Mr Lewis 'from the charge of preparing faggots in the literal sense' but considers the image an obvious one for what he calls 'odium theologium' from which 'I cannot acquit him'.

> In fact in the long run nature, art and philosophy all harmonise with the deepest elements in Christian doctrine. But I am sorry to have to say that in my judgement the effect of Mr Lewis's propaganda is to isolate Christianity, as it is isolated for instance in the poetry of Milton, in a sort of vacuum totally impervious to any ideas except those of theological origin.[8]

He pleads for Lewis to abandon 'the sublime but preposterous melodrama of *Paradise Lost*' and to embrace Blake's *Jerusalem* and Shelley's *Prometheus Unbound* to see what is really meant by the spirit of life.

The Three-Personal God

The second talk again makes a bold start. 'Christians', Lewis states, 'are the only people who offer any idea of what a being that is beyond personality could be like'. When people speak of God being beyond personality, they are implying that God is impersonal or less than personal. For something that is more than personal, then the Christian idea is the 'only one on the market'.

The idea of being 'absorbed' into God is wrong – it would be like a drop of water disappearing into an ocean. Human souls taken into the life of God remain themselves but even more so than before in Christian theology. It is like three dimensions. In one dimension, a line can be drawn. In two you can manage a square. With three, it can become a cube of six squares. In more complex levels you gain, you do not lose. In God's dimension there is a being who is three persons while remaining one. When a man says his prayers, he is praying to God, aided by Christ through whom God is known and God is also the motive power within him. So in prayer man is being caught up into the higher kind of dimension – being pulled into God, by God, while still remaining himself.

Theology started when along came a man who claimed to *be* God. Those who met him believed in him. They saw him after he was killed, formed a community and then they found God inside them, making them able to do things they hadn't been able to do before.

The doctrine of the three-dimensional God, the Trinity, came later when they worked it all out. So in this simple way Lewis made the link between experimental knowledge and doctrine, between what we can work out and getting to know more from our lives. He argued that complexity is itself an indication of truth. The instrument through which we see God is our whole self. Some of us are more disposed towards God than others. Lewis uses strong language to describe other faiths, language which today would be considered offensive. However, it is important to remember the context. This was 1944. The world was beginning to hear of the atrocities carried out by the Japanese towards prisoners-of-war. With such news on the radio, it was possible to understand that a man who is not 'clean and bright' could only have a blurred, distorted view of God. They are – as it were – looking at God through a dirty lens. And that, says Lewis, is why 'horrible nations have horrible religions'.

In *The Listener* nobody took issue with Lewis's disparaging comments on other faiths. Two writers did comment on the Trinity. F.J. Webb from Cranwell considered it 'a little too ingenious of Lewis' to imply that if we accept the validity of experimental knowledge, then 'we must accept the theological superstructure that the Church has built upon it'. Harold Binns in Bournemouth questioned the historical foundation of Lewis's assertion, quoting another scholar who accused the church of appropriating the 'divine triads' of Egyptian systems. Surely, he asserts, the origin of the Trinity must remain a mystery.

The problem of time

Time and Beyond Time is the title Lewis gives to the next chapter of the published version of the broadcast talks. However, for listeners in 1944 it formed the opening of the concluding talk in this series, *Beyond Personality*. In the *Listener* it was called *The New Man*.

Lewis must have received many letters asking the same question in order to devote a talk to the answer, but he does so here. The question was, how can God attend to millions of prayers addressed to him simultaneously? The answer? Time for God is not linear as it is for us. God is not *in* time. For him life is not one moment following another with a past leading to the present into the future. There is not a 'time' when prayers are said and answered. For him, time is always present. 'He has all eternity in which to listen to the split second of prayer put up by a pilot as his plane crashes in flames.'

Lewis was able to reflect on his own struggle with this before he became a Christian. He battled with the idea of God sustaining the universe at the same time as he was incarnated as a baby in Palestine. He had assumed that Christ's life in God was in time – as if God is alive when his human existence lies with a future to come for thirty-three years before it becomes his past. Not so. Christ's earthly life cannot be fitted into this life, as God is beyond space and time. We see a particular period in time and space – God intervening in history. But God has no history – he is too *real* to have one. Lewis is at pains to explain that such thinking is not in the Bible or any of the creeds, but is a Christian idea of long-standing. You can be a perfectly good Christian without it.

Good infection

The title of this third talk in the broadcast series describes the purpose of man. In *The Listener*, he calls it *The Whole Purpose of the Christian*. Jesus became a man 'in order to spread to other men the kind of life He has – by what I call "good infection"'. Every Christian is to become a little Christ. Lewis reached this conclusion after explaining the nature of the relationships within the community of God. God the Son is, as he illustrates it, always streaming forth from the Father like light or heat from a fire; like thoughts from a mind. The Son is the self-expression of the Father.

The Father-and-Son perfectly describes the relationship between the first and second persons of the Trinity. 'God is love' only makes sense if God contains at least two persons – love is what one person has for another. God is not static but 'a dynamic, pulsating activity, a life, almost a kind of drama'. Lewis dares to use a phrase that might seem irreverent to some listeners, describing God as a kind of dance. The third person, the Holy Ghost or Spirit of God, is more shadowy to grasp. If the Father is out there in front, and the Son is standing by your side, then the third person is inside you, or behind you. The whole point of this is for Lewis to explain that the entire pattern of the three-dimensional Christian life is to be played out in each of us. 'We all have to enter that pattern and to take our place in that dance.' To do that you must draw close to God. You don't get wet by staying away from the fountain – you need to be close enough to feel the spray of the water. 'There is no other way to the happiness for which we were made.'

The series hits home

Lewis is well into his stride. The talks had a continuity, despite the tampering with the script, and seemed to flow well. But regrettably, Eric Fenn felt the pre-recorded ones were not as fresh and spontaneous as those delivered live. He felt he had perhaps been too generous to Lewis. What was missing was the rehearsal of the pre-recorded script.

> Looking back I think I was wrong not to cause you to rehearse the whole of the recorded script before recording it, but I was anxious to avoid undue botheration for you, especially as you were bothered with a cough. We could, however, have timed it better had we gone right through it . . .[9]

The next talk in the series returned to Lewis's preferred pattern of drawing profound truths out of sublimely simple illustrations, as shown in the title: *The Obstinate Toy Soldiers*. Every child likes to imagine what fun it would be if their toys could come to life. But what if you actually could turn a tin soldier into a real little man? Suppose he didn't like it? The tin soldier may not like being turned into human flesh. He may, Lewis suggests, think you are killing him. In fact, he'd do all he could to prevent it.

The second person in God, the Son, became human; an actual man with a hair colour, a weight and speaking a language. Not only that, but before becoming a man, God became a baby and before that a foetus inside a woman's body. In this way humanity arrived among the tin soldiers. After being betrayed and killed, the human in him could actually come to life again – because it was united to the divine. It was as if one tin soldier, like the rest of us, had become fully alive.

The analogy breaks down there because for mankind, the whole of humanity is affected as a result. Humanity is already 'saved' in principle. We can express this in different ways and apply different biblical phrases – of Christ dying for us, of being forgiven, or being 'washed in the Lamb'. Lewis is untroubled by these – all are true. He urges listeners to get on with whichever formulation best works for them and says 'don't start quarrelling with other people' because they use a different formula to your own.

Let Us Pretend, the fifth talk, speaks of transformation. Transformation has to do with prayer. This talk encouraged the listeners to pray. The 'Lord's Prayer' is a good place to start. Just to say 'Our Father' is to put yourself in the place of a son of God:

> To put it bluntly, you're dressing up as Christ. If you like, you're pretending . . . a piece of outrageous cheek. But the odd thing is that He has ordered us to do it.

The dynamic at work is that of Christ himself and God turning that pretence into a reality as it happens. God is beginning to inject his spiritual life into us as we pray to him. He is beginning to turn the tin soldier into a living man – but the part in us that fights this is still 'tin'. We humans are 'carriers' of Christ to other people. People who were not Christians helped bring C.S. Lewis to Christ, but mainly it will be Christians who bring others to Christ. That's why the Church matters, the whole body of Christians showing him to one another. Human beings will let us down, but Christ does not. Hence the biblical phrases of 'putting on Christ' or 'being born again'.

By the time the fifth script appeared in *The Listener,* those who were enjoying Lewis's talks were provoked by the earlier correspondents to come to his defence, though by no means always agreeing with him. Alfred Olswang begins with an interesting assessment of Lewis as a broadcaster.

> Mr C.S. Lewis is an adroit expounder of his ideas and I have enjoyed and been stimulated by them . . . He is so positive in his manner, and with the convincing assurance of a good salesman very, very nearly sells his idea of what God is. Mr Lewis is apparently one of those people whose whole mind and character is in the right condition, because he is certainly in possession of a lot of knowledge. He knows just how God works, and the idea that God, who is all mighty, finds it impossible to show Himself to people in a different state of mind and character is a flaw in 'almightiness' that does not trouble Mr Lewis . . . If it were not that Mr Lewis was expounding the Christian idea of the Absolute, I would probably have thought that he was explaining Agnosticism. I don't think Mr Lewis should let the cat out of the bag even that much.[10]

Backlash

As the series proceeded, two things happened. First, another broadcaster, NBC in America, wanted a version of it. Secondly, the audience reaction became, in some cases, overtly hostile. Fenn writes:

> Herewith the script of your last talk for recording next Tuesday. We are also having dealings with the NBC about

> your broadcast of No. 6 for them, and hope this goes well.
> I thought last Tuesday was quite admirable, and so did the
> people I was listening with, but you do make some people
> angry don't you? (i.e. your old friend the psychologist in
> Glasgow has obtained some asbestos paper and is writing
> on it in vitriol!). All good wishes for the next dose . . .[11]

The audience research was based on the reaction of a sample to
the second talk. The number listening was quite good for that time
of night but the effect of the later hour in reducing the audience
size was greater than Eric Fenn had expected.

> But the most important single fact is the sharp division you
> produce in your audience. They obviously either regard you
> as 'the cat's whiskers' or as beneath contempt, which is inter-
> esting; and ought, I feel, to teach us something, but I can't
> quite think what![12]

Lewis wasn't worried by such divergences in opinion on him,
remaining sagely convinced that they were far more a reflection
on his subject matter than on him: '. . . it's an old story, isn't it.
They love, or hate.' [13] Walter Hooper even thinks Lewis read criticisms in the hope they would do him good, rather than treating
them over-sensitively.[14] He knew that what he received would be
the extremes of abuse or praise, or the listener would not have
bothered to write. 'Replies,' he informed Fenn, 'except in a real
rigorous high-brow controversy, are always a mistake.' Ultimately,
he wasn't shy of providing the hard answer to difficult questions
– that God by his very nature is 'the rock bottom, irreducible Fact
on which all other facts depend'. We cannot ask if he could have
done it another way. 'It is what it is and that's an end of the
matter.'[15]

Audience Research

The war had created a whole new set of conditions for listeners, and aroused new needs and interests. The Listener Research Department of the BBC investigated these in a scientific and practical way. Every day a cross-section of the public, consisting of a sample of 800 people, was interviewed by a staff of part-time field-workers, employed by the British Institute of Public Opinion. The daily sample was carefully graded to ensure that all types of listener were included in appropriate proportions. At each interview the previous day's listening was carefully recorded. In the first two years of the survey's existence, nearly 600,000 interviews had been conducted.

Listening figures do not tell you very much on their own. Producers also wanted to know if programmes were considered good or bad, and why. Therefore, the research was supplemented by listening panels who were questioned about the programmes they heard. When recruiting these panels, the BBC asked for 3,500 volunteers. Over 12,000 listeners offered their services to the BBC. The volunteers took the role very seriously. One remark typified the co-operation the BBC received and gives a sense of the spirit of the British at war. A shop assistant in a north-east town wrote:

> I am extremely sorry not to be able to complete this form this time. As a result of enemy action I have been unable to make the usual inquiries, but will begin again next week, when we open a new shop.[16]

It was from such research that Eric Fenn discovered that the amount of consecutive listening from one talk to the next was lower than he would have expected. Without the continuity of the series, the individual talk out of context could leave the listener plain confused or 'intrigued or puzzled by them'.[17] None of this undermined Fenn's confidence in the series. On the contrary he told Lewis he was 'not really at all depressed about this evidence of public reaction'. He had been pretty certain the series would get a mixed reception from the start, but the departmental consensus was that it was still right to produce it.

Hard or easy?

The sixth talk in *Beyond Personality* asked the blunt question – is Christianity hard or easy? If we take our natural self as the starting point, then we find we are faced with increasing demands from morality and what we sense to be right. In this realm of thinking we will either give up trying to be good or be unhappy. The more we obey our conscience, the more it seems to demand of us. Lewis argued that the Christian way is quite different, both harder and easier. Half measures will not do. Christ wants us. In Lewis's typical no nonsense way he describes the attitude as one that says 'I have not come to torment your natural self, but to kill it'. Christ sometimes said the way was hard, sometimes easy. Lewis draws upon the worst wartime analogy to drive the point home.

> Christ says, 'Take up your Cross' – in other words, it's going
> to be beaten to death in a concentration camp. Next minute
> he says, 'My yoke is easy and my burden light'. He means
> both.[18]

Change must come at the root of our being: if you remain a thistle, you won't grow figs. Hacking away at the branches is not enough. The real problem of the Christian life, Lewis suggests, hits us first thing in the morning when we wake up. We have to shove back all our wishes and hopes which rush at us, and listen to the other, quieter, voice. And keep letting it in, all day.

From such moments the new life begins to flow. Like an egg, we must be hatched or go bad. This is the whole of Christianity – there is nothing else. When we are drawn into Christ, other things begin to go right. 'The bad dream will be over; it will be morning.' It is hard to imagine a more simple or powerful picture of the Christian faith than the one Lewis conjures up here – the new day, morning that follows after the bad dream.

The concluding talk in the series began with the conundrum of how God hears so many prayers simultaneously, described earlier. This is, incidentally, the only talk in all four series of Lewis's broadcast talks of which the recording survived intact. This one was pre-recorded and is preserved in the BBC's Sound Archives. Listening to it today, there appears no loss of freshness from the fact that it did not go out live. Lewis had by now mastered the difference between live broadcasting and recording 'as live'. His voice carries its full, deep authority and enthusiasm. The listener is carried along into Lewis's irresistible flow like a stick carried along a fast-flowing stream, as he talks of moving from being mere creatures to sons of God. When people ask what is the next step after evolution, for the Christian the next step has already appeared. The new kind of man appeared in Christ, who, instead of coming up from nature came down from a world beyond all nature, a world of light and power. Lewis urges the listeners to give up themselves and so to find their real selves. He ends the series with a plea from the heart and a hard choice for the listener: 'Look for Christ and you will get Him, and with Him everything else is thrown in. Look for yourself, and you will get only hatred, loneliness, despair and ruin.'

The BBC was pleased. Despite the many delays and the inconveniences to Lewis of the later time slot, once again he had proved that he was able to cut through the ether and provoke a strong response. Eric Fenn was certainly appreciative.

Now that your last talk in the series has been safely launched into the air, I should like to write and say thank you for the whole series – the more so as the change of time means considerable extra inconvenience. I do think they've been very good, and have stirred up a lot of interest, as well as making some people angry. You will remember that, when we first discussed the idea, you wondered how the Great British Public would react – whether the evidence to hand applies to the G.B.P. at all widely it is difficult to say, but at least the reactions have been interesting, and complacency has been quite in question! Anyway, we should all like you to know how very grateful we are, and that, when you feel the urge upon you again, we shall be happy to oblige (on the understanding that, if the urge comes from us you will at least consider it!).

This series, more than its predecessors, was accident-prone. A memo from Eric Fenn to Maurice Shillingford in the BBC's Presentation Department, apologised for 'an erroneous announcement' at the end of one of the talks.[19] They trailed a talk by James Welch on the results of the special Sunday broadcasts last quarter but the talk was postponed and Fenn had completely forgotten. 'I write to accept responsibility for it in advance, so that Presentation Department doesn't get any additional kick! I do apologise.'

Lewis himself was not free from mishaps either. It was bad enough that he had to extend all seven scripts by five minutes. But he also forgot to return his contract. The Contracts staff wrote to him on 20 April to chase it: 'As we have never received back from you your signed acceptance of this contract, we have been unable to make you the payments due for these talks.' Lewis is forced to admit he had lost it. He wrote: 'I am sorry to say that I *do* appear to have lost the contract, and would be obliged if you would send me another. With apologies for my stupidity.'[20]

Notes

[1] 5 January 1944
[2] 6 January 1944
[3] 9 January 1944
[4] 7 January 1944
[5] 10 February 1944

[6] Any quotations from the first edition of *Beyond Personality*, like this one, are taken from *Beyond Personality – The Christian Idea of God* published by Geoffrey Bles, London, 1944

[7] *The Listener* Vol. XXXI no. 791 dated 9 March 1944, p. 273

[8] *The Listener* Vol. XXXI no. 792 dated 16 March 1944, p. 301

[9] 28 February 1944

[10] *The Listener*

[11] 17 March 1944

[12] 23 March 1944

[13] 25 March 1944

[14] Interview with Walter Hooper, 28 October 1999

[15] Lewis prepared an article (not retained by the BBC, sadly) intended for *The Listener* to answer his critics. It did not hit the right tone, in Fenn's opinion. Others in the religious department agreed with him, and thought it far too long to appear in *The Listener*. A flavour of it did survive in a three-page addition to the published edition of the series, *Broadcast Talks*.

[16] White, Antonia, *BBC at War*, BBC pamphlet 1942, p. 26

[17] 31 March 1944

[18] Taken from the text of *Beyond Personality* carried in *The Listener*, 30 March 1944, Volume XXXI no. 794, p.356

[19] 7 April 1944

[20] 25 April 1944

CHAPTER SEVENTEEN

'We understand and we regret . . .'

∽◦∾

The BBC made its third attempt to sign up C.S. Lewis for *The Anvil* panel discussion series.

> 'The 'Anvil' broadcasts duly began last Sunday, and will run for eleven weeks. We are going ahead with the recordings each Monday night. We are using this 'Anvil' series, as you know, to deal (amongst other things) with questions thrown up in listeners' minds by the Addresses and Talks that were broadcast in our special 'Mission' last quarter.
>
> Now, we have had sent in a number of questions arising out of your talks on 'Beyond Personality'. We are wondering – and Welch has asked me to write to you to find out – whether, after the end of May, you could find time to give one Monday evening, and take part in two 'Anvil' recordings for which we would use these questions. [1]

The proposed timetable was even more demanding than before. Contributors were required to arrive at 4.00 p.m. followed by the first discussion of questions until 5.00, tea till 5.30, recording first session from 5.30–6.30, discussion of second session from 6.30–7.00, recording second session from 7.00–8.00, supper from

8–8.45, and playback of both sessions till 9.45. This added up to six hours at the BBC to record the programme. Moreover . . .

> If you can do this, and if, in addition, you cared to stay the night in London rather than go back at 9.50, we could easily book you a room at the Berners [Hotel]. If there is any chance that you can help us in this and you will let me know, I will send you a list of the questions arising out of your talks, from which the body of these, your seven questions, would provide the two sessions.

Lewis did not find it hard to refuse. After four series, he had said all he wanted to say and broadcasting had lost its allure for him. It was 1944, the students were beginning to return in larger numbers and Lewis found his diary filling up. His earlier broadcast talks had been published in slim books and were readily available. The problem for the BBC was that other broadcasters had now cottoned on to the existence of this Oxford academic who spoke about Christianity in a jargon-free and entirely original way. One such telegram came from Australia addressed to Mr R.S. Lee, the Overseas Religious Broadcasting Officer of the BBC. They wanted the BBC to either rebroadcast the series or to get Lewis to repeat it, just for them. Without consulting Lewis, Lee replied that he would be willing to approach him.

> SUBJECT YOUR DESIRING REBROADCAST WE WILLING ASK HIM REPEAT SERIES MORAL CONDUCT FOR TRANSMISSION PACIFIC WEEKLY SUNDAYS 0615 BEGINNING 19 NOVEMBER STOP AWAITING YOUR SOONEST REPLY BEFORE CONTACTING STOP LEWIS UNLIKELY UNDERTAKE NEW SERIES NEAR FUTURE STOP

Lee followed up the telegram to Australia with a long letter to C.S. Lewis. Over two pages, he introduced himself and put the case. He began:

You will not know my name, but I am responsible for religious programmes broadcast in all the Overseas Services of the BBC ... I am getting inquiries from the Director of Religious Broadcasting in Australia about the talks that you did in the Home Service. He is anxious to use them, but no series has been fully recorded. I have had no information yet in response to my queries as to whether copies of the broadcast as published are on sale in Australia or New Zealand, which we cover in the same service. It is rather against our policy to repeat broadcasts which have been published, except in very special circumstances, otherwise I would simply invite you to repeat one of the series for the benefit of all our listeners overseas.

I know that Dr Welch has told you that he would be glad to have a fresh series of talks from you whenever you feel ready to do them, and that you have not recently said anything to him about further talks. In spite of that I am writing to invite you to do a series for our Overseas Services, that is our Regional Services to the Pacific (Australia and New Zealand), to Africa, and to North America, as well as in our General Overseas Services directed to our forces abroad, and to English-speaking listeners in other parts of the world. This gives a complete world coverage. I wonder whether you will be willing to contemplate doing another such series, and starting in, say, about six weeks' time. If need be you need not break fresh ground but cover some of the ground you have already been over. If you are willing to consider this suggestion I would very gladly come to Oxford and talk it over with you at any time that suited you. I hope you will. I believe that it is very important for us to broadcast from Britain the best thought that we can, particularly on religious matters, for many people throughout the world are looking to Britain for leadership in religion.[2]

The reluctant broadcaster

Unfortunately for Mr Lee, C.S. Lewis had no desire to repeat himself.

> It would be rather difficult to give a series covering old ground, as all my previous talks have been published in book form: I could not make them *sound* like fresh talks.[3]

More to the point, as Lewis was aware, six weeks' notice was not long enough. Six months would have been better. He would have done well to give a firm refusal. But by even the mere suggestion that more notice would help, he left himself open to further approaches. They came thick and fast. Mr Lee demonstrated all the persistence you'd expect from a determined producer used to getting his own way. The next day the attack resumed.

> Thank you for your letter of the 6th. I realise the force of what you say about covering old ground, and I would not have asked you had we not had special enquiries from Australia. I have not yet heard from them in reply to my cable as to whether they wanted the talks in the form in which you gave them originally.
>
> I would be very pleased indeed to have a new series from you in six months' time, and may I close with that offer now. It would fit in most conveniently if you could begin a series of talks on the Sunday after Easter, that would be April 8th, 1945, which is the six months you asked for. Would you please let me know when you have given it some thought what general subject you would like to tackle, and about how many talks you think you would want to do.

Meanwhile, Australia was expecting Mr Lee to deliver! From Ivan Smith dated 19 October 1944:

TELEGRAM/CABLE FROM SYDNEY
IVAN SMITH YOUR P51444 THANKS APPRECIATE
REPETITION CS LEWIS SERIES MORAL CONDUCT
WEEKLY 0615 SUNDAYS BEGINNING 19 NOVEMBER
WE RECORDING FOR RELAY STOP

Lee wrote again to Lewis at once telling him that he received the cable from the Australian Broadcasting Commission saying that they would appreciate a repetition of his series *Christian Behaviour*, which they would record for rebroadcast on the National Stations. He wondered if Lewis would be willing to record the talks as he gave them originally, so that the BBC could satisfy their request. He very much hoped that he would do them, and be ready to give the first one on 19 November. His dubious carrot was allowing for three extra minutes of talk, not to mention the anticipated world-wide appreciative audience.

> I would like to be able to cable the Australian Broadcasting Commission to say that you are doing the talks, so I would be grateful for an answer as soon as you have considered the matter. Of course you would get appropriate fees and your expenses paid for re-doing these talks.

With Pandora's Box opening up wider by the day, C.S. Lewis managed to write a firmer rejection letter this time around, reiterating that he could not speak on what already existed in print. The last thing he would want would be for listeners who had read the book to feel they had been cheated. He remained circumspect, however, about the possibility of something new the following year.[4]

Lee's response was more sympathetic than before. He told Lewis that he quite understood his reasons for not wanting to do the old broadcasts again. But he added that the Australian people will be 'disappointed, but it will mitigate their disappointment if I can promise them in the near future a new series of talks from you.'[5]

He offers another incentive, that any new series would be broadcast by the Home Service as well as the overseas services. Lee cabled Australia with another half promise that . . .

> WE HAVE NOW APPROACHED LEWIS WHO UNWISHES REPEAT PUBLISHED MATERIAL BUT PROMISES CONSIDER FRESH SERIES COMMENCING SUNDAY AFTER EASTER STOP WILL CONFIRM LATER STOP

C.S. Lewis now recognised that Mr Lee would not go away and was going to keep up the pressure for a new series until he delivered it or gave a definite refusal. He was also aware that Eric Fenn would not be pleased to receive a series from Lewis as a by-product of a commission from the Overseas Services of the BBC. So it was important to re-establish the link with Welch and Fenn. At this point Lewis apologised for wasting their time and finally refused the Overseas Service. In the past he had something new to say when broadcasting – and this time he hasn't.

> All success depends on not pumping something up – it must come of its own accord. If and when I feel I've got a new head of that particular kind of steam, I'll write to Fenn. I'm sorry you should have been kept waiting.[6]

The Lewis series that never was

If Lewis thought for a moment that his letter would deter Mr Lee, he was wrong. Lee set aside Lewis's refusal as if swatting a fly. Worse still, he decided that he would personally resolve Lewis's writer's block by coming up with a scheme for a fifth series of talks. On 11 December 1944, he revealed his hand to C.S. Lewis, whom he had never met. His audacity is breathtaking. He told Lewis he was attempting to draw up a schedule of six talks for broadcast on the Sundays during Lent in the BBC's Pacific, African, North American and General Overseas services.

At the risk of appearing to pester you, I am writing now to ask whether you would possibly feel inclined to undertake to do all these talks. I know that when you said you felt you had a subject on which you would like to talk you would let me know, but I hope that this series may possibly interest you, and I would certainly be very pleased if you should feel inclined to undertake them. The talks would be each of thirteen minutes duration and you could record them at your convenience before Sunday, February 19th, the first Sunday in Lent. The schedule is briefly as follows:

1) *The Sin of Man.* Why is consciousness of sin remote from the modern mind? What is the nature of sin and of original sin? Is sin only sickness needing therapy, not repentance? What are the most damaging sins? Can one man save himself? Some historic attempts to do so. This should set the problem for number two.

2) *God's Plan for Man.* God had a plan for man of full and free fellowship with Himself and every man. How do we know this plan? The witness of evolution and history. The value of negative evidence supplied by man's failure. The evidence of revelation, specially in Christ. What does God do in answer to man's sin? God is not passive but active. This prepares for number three.

3) *The Incarnation.* God's historic answer. The reality and fullness of the incarnation; the assertion of love as supreme not only in personal life, but as controlling the material organisation of community fellowship. Could Jesus only become Saviour by incarnation? Was His death necessary to win men back to God?

This prepares for number four.

4) *The nature of Christ's sacrifice.* Different forms of sacrifice. Pagan, Jewish. The meaning of sacrifice. False con-

ceptions of God and His purpose for man. Christ as the fulfilment of sacrifice. Atonement through Christ. Historic explanations of atonement. Its manifestations. This leads to number five.

5) *The Life in Grace*. What is grace? In what sense is it supernatural? Grace and nature. How do we get it? How do we keep it ? Does it mean sinlessness? If not, what does it mean? How does it manifest itself in us?

6) *Christ the Lord of Life*. This should sum up the others. What did Christ believe Himself to be? Is the church 'the extension of the incarnation'? Is his kingship in this world; if so what gives it to him? The mission and the achievements of the historic church. What is Christ's claim upon the modern world? How can we make it effective? What are the alternatives to it? Is there a place for Christianity in a world at war, or for a world at war in Christianity.

Those are rough notes that I have been putting together as a guide to the kind of things that might be discussed. I hope it will interest you.

To compound the impertinence, Lee did not even sign the letter himself. His secretary initialled it in his absence. If he really imagined for a moment that C.S. Lewis would be swayed by such a proposal, he was deceiving himself. Losing patience now, Lewis wrote a courteous but curt answer, pointing out that since Lee had made all the suggestions, anything coming from them would not be Lewis's; and, 'it overlaps too much with talks I have given already.'[7]

The letter does the trick and Mr Lee finally got the message. It did not prevent him from trying once again eight months later. In so doing, he made a colossal gaffe. He wrote to Lewis at Oxford but said he was not yet sure whether or not Lewis had 'taken up your Professorship at Cambridge' – a piece of newspaper gossip that had no basis in fact – yet. He invited Lewis on this occasion to contribute one talk in a series in the overseas networks dealing with the Bible. Lee invited Lewis to write talk number four on 'The Bible as literature' which would be broadcast on 4 November.[8] As it happened, Lewis had coincidentally been thinking of trying to do something popular about the Bible but knew the timing was impossible. He adds, peremptorily, that 'the Cambridge Chair is a newspaper rumour and untrue'.[9]

Disillusioned

So nearly eighteen months after his last programme for the BBC, Lewis has turned down every subsequent invitation to broadcast. He simply had nothing more to say on the radio. The war had by now ended, taking away with it the context of spiritual immediacy that had first inspired James Welch's invitation. The experiences of Lewis's fourth series – the long journeys, the pressure of pre-recording one talk before delivering another talk live, getting home in the middle of the night – had all left a sour taste. From being a joyful and exhilarating experience, broadcasting had become a tiresome chore. Moreover, the letters did not stop pouring through his letterbox. The BBC was becoming a nuisance, never taking no for an answer and persistently coming up with new ways to re-invent the wheel. Lewis was disillusioned with broadcasting.

The gate is open

With the BBC's Religious Broadcasting Department in danger of losing contact with one of its most valued contributors, Welch wrote another invitation to Lewis, to return to the microphone at any time of his own choosing with anything he wished to say. This was an extraordinarily generous invitation. Welch writes in his usual elegant style.

We should always be anxious to make space for you in our

religious talks programme. It is some time since we had a series of broadcast talks from you, and a great many listeners are anxious to hear you again. Have you anything you would like to say during May, June or July of 1946? It has been suggested, e.g. that a series of talks by you on Religious Experience would be of very great help to many listeners. Do please feel free to put up ideas to us whenever they come to you.[10]

C.S. Lewis appreciated the tone of the letter and its offer, but his life had moved on with the end of the war, and the arrival of the first intake of post-war students was taking its toll.

I am hoping to try the microphone again in the next few years if I may, and am glad to hear that the gate is still open. But this year and next, work will be so fast and furious at Oxford (the full tide of the demobbed pupils is now upon us) that nothing can be done.[11]

James Welch sends Lewis a two-sentence response: 'We understand and we regret. But remember, the gate is always wide open.'[12] Once a contributor has established a reputation as a broadcaster, the name goes into the contact books and will inevitably resurface.

Over the next few years, more approaches were made. An old friend from Oxford, R. Campbell, sought Lewis's advice on which passages from Milton he would recommend for a radio anthology. Lewis writes to him with a perfect mix of suggestions, aware what will not work ('give P.R. [Paradise Regained] the go-by') and how to make something work well. For instance, on 'But when their hearts were jocund and sublime' he insists that Campbell 'persuade someone to thump it out like Vachel Lindsay, and not moan or murmur.'[13] Campbell is grateful. Lewis's selection 'fits in beautifully'.[14] He speaks of very happy memories of Lewis, Warnie and Tolkien and sends greetings.

In October 1946, Lewis was contacted by Major General Sir

Ian Jacob, later to become Director-General of the BBC. At this stage in his career, Jacob was Controller of the European Service. With the post-war reconstruction under way, this was an area of critical strategic importance. He asks Lewis to write a series of new weekly commentaries. The commission itself is a fascinating commentary on the times.

> Our plan is to obtain each week, from an authoritative writer, a short study of some of the major problems under-lying the current news. The intention is to go deeper than the immediate event and to analyse the causes which give that event its proper perspective. We shall be broadcasting this new series to Europe as a feature in which, week by week, an independent commentator of distinction in this country freely analyses and discusses the problems of our time. These talks will be given a leading place on all our language broadcasts each week. I should like to broadcast in this series a consideration of the decay of religion in the past century – if you can give any facts to show that it has been decayed – and of the effect in secular terms: the violence, rapacity. And general loss of civilised values which have resulted. It seems to me that one would not want to be too sweeping, but that precise indications could be given to suggest that civilisation has suffered greatly from its unreflecting tendency to abandon vivid religious belief.[15]

Though intrigued, Lewis gives a flat turn-down.

All offers refused

The list of those who wrote to Lewis but were turned down is long and distinguished. Producer Mary Treadgold used Mrs Charles Williams to give her a personal introduction to Lewis. She came to see him in Oxford to 'to discuss the possibility of an autumn broadcast with you'.[16] Mr Lee tried yet again in May 1947, obviously made desperate by repeated requests from overseas for Lewis on air. He received the now customary rejection. Ronald Lewin of the BBC Talks Department requests a piece on the writer Malory for the Third Programme of the BBC.[17] The rejection is in the post the next day, citing the pressures of work.

James Welch left the BBC in 1947 and was succeeded by the Acting Director of Religious Broadcasting, the Rev. K. Grayston. It is evident from his letter how the thinking of the department had moved on, no longer just bolstering the faith of those for whom the experience of war had been shattering or appealing to those outside the faith; the target is now 'the puzzled'. These are those who fall outside the normal reach of the Churches but are agnostic and open to reason. Grayston has an idea how to reach these people.

We think we shall begin by trying to expose the basic difference between the Christian and the secularist points of view, and then deal with some of the divergences of thought and conduct that spring from these views. The forms in which this is done must make an appeal to the many 'puzzled people' who are often only aware of the superficial levels of the conflict, as well as to those with trained minds.

It had not yet been decided whether these programmes would go out on the Home Service or the more highbrow Third Programme. Interestingly, just as it was *The Problem of Pain* that drew C.S. Lewis to the attention of James Welch in 1940, seven years later it is the publication of Lewis's book on *Miracles* that attracts Welch's successor. It convinced him that Lewis would 'enable listeners to see what are the issues involved'. [18] Lewis responded with his now automatic reply – pleading pressure of work at Oxford. He writes wishing the proposal every success, but saying unequivocally that he cannot possibly spare the time.

C.S. Lewis's broadcasting days were virtually behind him now. He had neither the time or the stomach to take this on. A memo is filed away for posterity in the registry of the Controller of BBC Talks . . .

> The files about the Tuesday evening discussions are at present on their way back to London from West Region, but I am told by A.D.R.B.'s [Rev. Grayston] Secretary that only one letter has been written to C.S. Lewis, an invitation to take part in the discussions. No reply was received from him, so later Mr Waller apparently telephoned him, to ask if he were willing to take part, and was told that Mr Lewis was going to undertake no more broadcasting work for two years, owing to the great pressure of other things he had to do.[19]

Tempted back by degree

What does eventually succeed in tempting Lewis back to the microphone is an invitation to write a short three-minute introduction to a dramatisation of his book *The Great Divorce*. This was pre-recorded on 27 February 1948 and first broadcast on 9 May. Lewis's fee was three guineas.

His self-imposed exile from broadcasting broken, if only by three minutes, the invitations to do more keep coming. There are more approaches from the overseas services of the BBC. One originated from Lillian Lang in the BBC's New York offices, then at 630 Fifth Avenue in Manhattan. A letter sent to J. Warren McAlpine of the BBC's North American Service in London poses a question.

> The Federal Council of Churches is making inquiries concerning C.S. Lewis who has given numerous talks on BBC. Apparently his new approach to religious subjects is causing considerable interest in this country. Would it be possible

JUSTIN PHILLIPS

to send us a script of one of his recent talks together with
a list of the subjects he has covered? It is entirely possible
that, after examination of the script, the Federal Council of
Churches might consider the inclusion of a talk by Mr Lewis
on one of its network programmes.[20]

Lillian Lang reveals that the idea to find out about Lewis came
from Charles Taft, President of the Federal Council of Churches.
The Council's interest in Mr Lewis was due in large part to letters
which Mr Taft had received from friends in England. Ivor Thomas
of the BBC's Overseas Programme Services sent her a memo
spelling out the difficulties of getting C.S. Lewis to do anything
just now.

I find that C.S. Lewis has not broadcast for about two years,
and I am told that, in spite of repeated requests, he has
informed us that he has no intention of broadcasting for
some time to come as he is very much preoccupied with
his academic career. I am therefore unable to send you a
script of a recent talk, but the broadcast talks he did some
years ago have all been published in booklet form . . .

Although that proposal came to nothing, in March 1948, Lewis
was presented with another opportunity to talk about the work of
his dear friend, the late Charles Williams.[21] The same idea resur-
faced 18 months later, with an added incentive for the BBC. Not
only did they want someone to relate Williams' life. They also
wanted to grab the opportunity to record Lewis broadcasting for
the archives. Amazingly, the BBC archives had only one brief
recording of Lewis's voice in its permanent collection.

Lewis is neither swayed nor flattered:

T.S. Eliot would do it better and carry more weight with
that audience. There's also Miss Sayers. But if it comes
down to me or nobody, I will do it. [In his own hand] I am

273

v. busy and not v. well and wd. like to be passed over provided this wd. not miss a chance of helping C.W.'s sales.[22]

Within the archives is a sheet with some hand-written scribbled
notes between two BBC staffers, Mr D.F. Boyd, who began the
war as Assistant Programme Director in Manchester and Ronald
Lewin, the Talks producer. On 18 November, Boyd asked Lewin
for any news of Lewis's response. Lewin sent Boyd a copy of Lewis's
suggestion of T.S. Eliot. Boyd was not convinced by the recommendation, and simply concluded that it would be best to abandon
the idea altogether: 'Let's not bother about books'.[23] Lewis was
contacted to this effect out of courtesy. His protest arrived the
next day.

> But I have not made myself plain. I can and I will do a talk
> on Charles Williams if you can't, or don't want to get anyone
> else to do it. Indeed I have drafted it already, on the chance
> that the people whom I suggested might refuse.

The talk went ahead and was broadcast on 11 February 1949. After
that, only three other BBC broadcasts by C.S. Lewis survive. In
April 1955, Lewis delivered a two-part series called *The Great
Divide*, a re-assessment of the main division between old and new
Western culture. In September 1961, a one-hour Portrait of Charles
Williams lists Lewis as one of the contributors (reversioning his
earlier contribution). His last programme for the BBC was a talk
on John Bunyan's *The Pilgrim's Progress*, broadcast in November
1962, almost exactly a year before his death. There were no more
theological series after the three wartime sets of talks. Lewis did
not believe in repeating himself.

Radio blamed for leprechaun shortage

Despite all that his four series of talks for the BBC had achieved – most notably the lasting legacy of *Mere Christianity* – there is evidence that Lewis was disenchanted with radio and with much of the mass media.

It comes out in his correspondence.

The main reason why Lewis seldom returned to the microphone after the war is that it was in his writing for the printed page that he felt most comfortable and in control. Writing for radio meant dealing with a host of producers who would suggest changes or improvements that Lewis found tiresome. The BBC had created for him a new audience and transformed him into a national figure. His books had no difficulty in finding their public. In 1952, the four series of BBC talks were brought together as *Mere Christianity*. Lewis added an introduction and a few minor changes, but the book is substantially the collection of talks he first gave on the radio.

There was another reason why his broadcasts became increasingly rare. He was not a great radio listener, apart from following the news bulletins. The broadcasting medium seemed increasingly trivial to him. In his books and his correspondence, references to radio listening are usually negative.[24] For instance, in *The Screwtape Letters*, the senior devil writes another diabolical letter to young Wormwood. He tells him how he detests both music and silence, implying that both are forces for good:

> . . . no square inch of infernal time has been surrendered to either of those abominable forces, but all has been occupied by Noise – Noise, the grand dynamism, the audible expression of all that is exultant, ruthless, and virile . . .we will make the whole universe a noise in the end.[25]

If noise was seen by Lewis as a devilish device to distract us from the seeking of God, then he saw radio as contributing to that noise.

When an American schoolgirl wrote to him seeking tips on how to write, Lewis gives her seven pieces of advice. The first is to turn off the radio. The second is to read all the books she can and the third is to write with the ear, not the eye. Reflecting a lesson from his broadcasting career perhaps, he advises her to hear every sentence she writes as if it were being read aloud. He then tells her to only write about what interests her, to take great trouble to be clear, not to throw any work away but save it in a drawer; not to use a type-writer and to be sure she understands every word she uses.[26]

Why turn the radio off first of all? Because if you want to avoid God, avoid silence and solitude, live in a crowd and keep the radio on.[27] The radio, he says, was invented to destroy solitude.[28] In less serious mood, he even blames radio for driving away the lep-rechauns from Ireland![29]

All this adds up to a feeling on his part that radio contributed to the noisy environment that helped keep people away from the silence and solitude in which God is sought and the mind is most free to explore truth. Radio was a distraction from this. In the war years he saw its true value. As he grew older, his appreciation of its contribution withered away. He was no kinder to television than to radio. In a letter to Mrs John Watt, written in 1958, he is glad to say that he doesn't often watch it. But Warnie, who sometimes watches a friend's television set, observed that television portrays progress as an inevitable process and assumes that the important thing is to increase man's comfort at all costs.[30]

Regretful but too busy

The BBC never completely gave up hope of persuading C.S. Lewis to broadcast again but the interval between approaches begins to widen as the refusals piled up. In February 1949, he turned down the invitation to give five or six talks on *The Problem of Pain*. In April, the 400th anniversary of the Book of Common Prayer was commemorated and the BBC approached Lewis once more. He felt that the topic would take him quite out of his depth. The third request that year – to write a twenty-five minute talk for a Radio 3 series on the poetry and philosophy of Edmund Spenser – was also declined. Two years later, in February 1951, a series on literary work in progress was being put together. Lewis, then working on *The Oxford History of English Literature*, was invited to be one of the contributors. Again he refused, not wanting to steal any thunder from the book. The next idea the BBC came up with for Lewis was to be one of two participants in a discussion on the nature of evidence in July 1951. Again he turned it down.

It was not until December 1952 that the next approach came. The American network CBS planned a series to be presented by Edward R. Murrow called *This I believe*. This was an opportunity for Lewis to talk about his faith, ten years after his first wartime broadcasts. The invitation came from producer Keith Kyle, later a distinguished BBC news reporter. Lewis declined as he was 'snowed under'. Nevertheless, he assured the BBC in 1954 that he still had hope of someday talking into the microphone again.[31]

The long list of refusals was only briefly interrupted when he agreed to the broadcast of his Inaugural Lecture at Cambridge University which was so well received that the programme was repeated by the BBC in May and June 1955. This was an oasis in a broadcasting desert for Lewis. The opportunities continued to abound, but only two other proposals lured him back: an interview about Charles Williams, and a discussion about children's writing, both in 1962. It is surprising that he even agreed to this at a stage in his life when he was dogged by poor health. His last letter to the BBC on 17 January 1963, just ten months before his death, is poignant.

> I am afraid I am not well enough to undertake a talk at present.
> With thanks and regret.
> Yours sincerely
> CS Lewis

Notes

[1] 20 April 1944
[2] 3 October 1944
[3] 6 October 1944
[4] 13 October 1944.
[5] 16 October 1944
[6] 23 October 1944
[7] 15 December 1944
[8] 29 August 1945
[9] 31 August 1945
[10] 22 November 1945
[11] 24 November 1945
[12] 26 November 1945
[13] 16 August 1946.
[14] 23 September 1946
[15] 30 October 1946
[16] 22 May 1947
[17] 4 June 1947
[18] 24 September 1947
[19] 10 December 1947
[20] 16 June 1948
[21] 20 March 1947
[22] 17 November 1948
[23] 22 November 1948
[24] Goffar, Janine (ed.), *C.S. Lewis Index – Rumours from the Sculptor's Shop*, Solway, La Sierra University Press, California, USA 1995 and Solway, London 1995, pp. 519–520
[25] Lewis, C.S, *The Screwtape Letters*, Geoffrey Bles 1943 (dedicated to J.R.R Tolkein), and now published by HarperCollins.
[26] 14 December 1959 in Hooper, (ed.), *Letters* p. 485
[27] Lewis, C.S., *Christian Reflections*, chapter 14 par. 17–18
[28] Lewis, C.S. *The Weight of Glory*, Macmillan Publishing, New York , 1965 Chapter 7 par. 2
[29] 8 September 1956 in Lewis, C.S., *Letters to an American Lady*, Eerdmans, Grand Rapids USA, 1967
[30] 30 October 1958, in Hooper, (ed.), *Letters*, p. 475
[31] 3 November 1954

CHAPTER EIGHTEEN

The Legacy

≈

How does the making of *Mere Christianity* appear with the wisdom of hindsight? Why is there still so much interest in the life and achievements of C.S.Lewis, Dorothy L. Sayers and their Christian literary counterparts?

The legacy of C.S. Lewis extends well beyond the repository of books, most of which are still in print and continue to sell in sufficient numbers to make any author blush. Numbers vary, but in the year 2000 some estimates put worldwide sales of Lewis's books at over 200 million copies in more than thirty languages. The legacy extends beyond the world of academia where Lewis's achievements as a literary scholar are still recognised and valued. His greatest influence is arguably within Christian culture and ethos, where his stature as the outstanding popular theologian of the last century is unchallenged. More than that, from within the Christian culture his thinking has extended more widely still through those who have read his books and absorbed his ideas and insights into their own beliefs.

The literary legacy

Professor James Como opened a collection of essays on C.S. Lewis in 1978 with the observation that Lewis's reputation would 'soon' become so established that 'his literary impact will be recognised by scholars and teachers to such an extent that its importance shall be quite taken for granted.'[1] Como was right. Lewis's insights into particular phases of English literature remain unmatched in their acuity, according to *The Oxford Illustrated History of English Literature* a decade later.[2] Whatever Lewis's standing as an academic might be, his contribution to English Church history is also receiving recognition long after his death. Adrian Hastings, Emeritus Professor of Theology in the University of Leeds, gives C.S. Lewis and Dorothy L. Sayers more than an honorary mention in his classic of modern Church history, *A History of English Christianity*.[3] Between them the names of Lewis and Sayers crop up over thirty times.

Wartime innovation

Hastings considers that on the literary front, the war was 'the golden age of that Anglican lay literary and theological foursome', whom he names as C.S. Lewis, T.S. Eliot, Dorothy L. Sayers and Charles Williams. The most critical time in the war saw a flourishing of Christian writing of a high order. In 1942 alone, as Lewis wrote *The Screwtape Letters* and Sayers worked on *The Man Born to be King*, Archbishop William Temple wrote *Christianity and Social Order* and T.S. Eliot wrote *Little Gidding*. Christopher Dawson's *Judgement of the Nations* rejected totalitarianism in all its forms and called for co-operation with other Churches and democratic principles. Hastings recognises that the BBC had a key part to play:

From such titles it is obvious enough that the most critical phase of the Second World War was a time of very considerable Christian literary creativity but of a very unsectarian sort. The BBC was its natural medium.

In time of war, people needed to be kept in touch with the world of thought, imagination and ideas more than ever. Escapism had its place in the world of entertainment, but a nation at war needed food for its intellect and its soul as well as for its body. The BBC acknowledged freely that religion, art and science were not luxuries but basic needs.[4] With so many people cut off from libraries, churches, concert halls, lecture-rooms and theatres, the BBC stepped into the void. Leading thinkers and people of ideas could be brought into the home by the microphone.

But this required something of a revolution in the perception of what religious broadcasting was. Barriers and conventions had to be broken down. C.S. Lewis was party to the great revolution in religious broadcasting pioneered by the BBC's Director of Religion, Rev. Dr James Welch. Welch had the vision and Lewis and Sayers were two of the key instruments to break the mould.

The effect of war on religious broadcasting was remarkable. First, it broke down the barriers between the many different forms of Christian worship in Britain. It became more important to find the common ground than to stress the differences. With his strong personal commitment to Church unity before the war, Eric Fenn's contribution to this process cannot be over-estimated.

One national day of prayer exemplified this breaking-down of denominational boundaries. Archbishops of Canterbury, Wales and the Primate of All Ireland addressed the whole nation side by side with the Moderators of the Church of Scotland and the Free Church Federal Council, together with the Roman Catholic Cardinal-Archbishop of Westminster. A Lutheran pastor, a French Protestant, an Anglican clergyman and a member of the Eastern Orthodox Church broadcast in turn a programme on Christian unity. Before the war, to hear an Anglican Archbishop and a

Congregationalist speaking in support of a papal encyclical from Rome would have seemed bizarre. The war changed all that. Christians of all denominations found a solidarity in the face of an enemy who had declared war on Christianity as much as on democracy and liberty of thought and belief. Radio provided the perfect medium to demonstrate this. James Welch summed up the 'radio effect' perfectly.

> The religious services of all denominations are heard by all; each denomination learns from the others. Listeners feel they are sharing in a Christian, not merely a denominational service; suspicions and misunderstandings are removed . . . and there is a growing sense that, though some differences are great, yet the things we have in common are far greater.[5]

Audience research confirmed that the number of Roman Catholic listeners who did not tune in to Protestant services and vice-versa was small. The vast majority did not discriminate between broadcast religious services on denominational lines. A highly potent factor in determining whether or not a broadcast service was left on or switched off was the type of hymn with which it opened.[6]

Another effect of the war – one to which Lewis contributed hugely – was that religious programmes finally broke away from the old 'Sundays only' tradition. They began to make contact with people's ordinary daily lives. They did this through new programmes like *Lift Up Your Hearts*, a morning talk just before the eight o'clock news. The idea came from Scotland and revived the practice of a few minutes of meditation or spiritual reading to start the day in a different way.

Innovation was much easier in wartime. The BBC opened up a spiritual front with the creation of what became known as the *Big Ben Silent Minute* at nine o'clock each evening. A campaign started after the National Day of Prayer on 26 May 1940. On 28 October 1940, the BBC Governors agreed to arrange for the minute to be signalled by the chiming of Big Ben each evening from Armistice Sunday on 10 November 1940. Its purpose was to 'enable the people of the whole nation and of the world to submit themselves and the cause of Right in penitence and in unity to God, realising that we ourselves can do nothing'.[7] It was non-sectarian, inclusive and available to men and women of good will everywhere. The campaigners urged that all listeners use the minute to unite in strength and let it be a 'mighty influence for good, so that darkness shall be replaced by the light of the Christ presence in our midst'. Who would dare say that this daily act of silent meditation or prayer was not another powerful weapon opened up by the BBC in wartime that encouraged persistent prayer?

Lewis helped to establish within religious broadcasting the importance of the fifteen-minute broadcast talk as an effective medium for communicating ideas on the radio, in the wake of its leading secular exponent J.B. Priestley. Over time, alas, the fifteen-minute broadcast talk has all but disappeared from national speech radio. It has survived in a shortened form, but few broadcasters in the modern era can sustain a fifteen-minute slot. The great exception would be Alistair Cooke whose *Letter from America* on BBC Radio 4 and the BBC World Service can fill a quarter-hour with ease. BBC has introduced variations of the format – with correspondents bringing a letter from Moscow or wherever – but the days of *Postscript* or the series of quarter-hour talks have long gone. People no longer sit around the radio in the evenings as they did in the wartime era when there was no television.

Radio 4's *Thought for the Day* – not fifteen minutes but barely three minutes – is one lasting tribute to Lewis's approach. Many of its most popular speakers are drawn from the Church of England. At the turn of the century a hard-hitting direct approach to current issues much in the spirit of C.S. Lewis is exemplified by the Rt. Rev. Richard Harries, Bishop of Oxford, and Rt. Rev. James Jones, Bishop of Liverpool. Lay members have their voices heard too, men and women such as Elaine Storkey, President of Tearfund, and Synod member Christina Rees. Talks such as these are still capable of creating media outcry on occasion. There are few battles fought by the BBC that have not been fought before.

There was a definite increase in public approval of broadcast religious services over the first three years of the war. Most notably, the biggest gains were among men and young people, the groups normally least interested in religious worship. A Listener Research Report conducted in October 1943 revealed that 52% of listeners said they were keenly or mildly interested in religious broadcasting: an increase of over 10% in three years. Those who described themselves as 'indifferent' had fallen by 7% in the same period to 23%, and those who said they were 'hostile' numbered 4% less, at 25%. The BBC concluded that half of the audience of religious radio were not church-goers.

War had thrown things into sharp relief. It marked a return to the simplicity of received doctrine but communicated it in new ways. Lewis was one of the pioneers. Sayers, too, paved the way for innovative communication. In her case, the portrayal of Jesus Christ as a living, breathing, fully human person, the very incarnation of God, represented a paradigm shift. The old taboo of not allowing Christ to be portrayed as less than divine, whose voice could not be heard, of whom any impersonation was outlawed, was broken. Without Dorothy L. Sayers there may have been no *Godspell* or *Jesus Christ Superstar*. Hollywood may have been stuck, as it was for the next decade, with Christ as a shadowy figure, seen but seldom heard. Not perhaps until Franco Zeffirelli's *Jesus of Nazareth* was Christ portrayed on film with the same realism as Dorothy Sayers had achieved on BBC Radio.

Nobody is pretending that the relationship between the likes of Lewis and Sayers and the BBC was always an easy one. Both writers were driven to distraction by the control exercised by the producers, by the sudden changes of plan and by the internal politics as scripts had to be cleared and sometimes widely circulated before getting anywhere near the studio. All this they found incredibly frustrating. Yet both owed a debt to the BBC and were pleased to acknowledge its role as commissioner, patron, encourager, supporter and facilitator.

In his BBC Religious Broadcasting Department James Welch had created a stable for developing new broadcasting talent. He found the best raw material among writers, not among the clergy. His unique gift was to see the latent potential and to bring it on to the air. He fervently believed in the truth of the gospel and the need to broadcast it to as many people as possible as clearly as he could. The creative input of the BBC made a significant difference to the end product. Would C.S. Lewis's broadcast talks have had the same impact without the input of James Welch and Eric Fenn? Would *Mere Christianity* ever have been written without the impetus given by the vision and Christian zeal of James Welch? Would *The Man Born to be King* ever been broadcast without the skill of Val Gielgud? One cannot know for certain but I doubt it very much. At the same time, it was the brilliant writing, the assured theology and the ability to communicate to the ordinary listener that made these programmes what they were. In that sense, the BBC's role was that of the enabler. The God-given talent lay with Lewis and Sayers.

Breaking the ecclesiastical tyranny

C.S. Lewis's own contribution to this remoulding of religious broadcasting was considerable and significant. He helped to establish that it was perfectly acceptable to have Christian theology explained by a layman – Christian belief was not the monopoly of the ordained clergyman or priest. A layman could speak with equal authority and avoid the elephant traps.

The 'ecclesiastical tyranny' of the BBC was broken. Lewis proved that a layman could be more effective than an ordained person in communicating simple Christian truths. By so doing, Lewis restored an intellectual respectability to Christianity in a culture which thought it had rejected it and left it behind. He rendered complex doctrine and ideas comprehensible. He demonstrated that Christian teaching and values were still relevant to the most complex ethical dilemmas. He revealed that at the heart of Christianity was the person and work of Jesus Christ and that only in relationship to Christ did the world begin to make sense.

To the Christian in the pew, Lewis's writings of Christian apologetics are compelling in their intellectual rigour and spiritual clarity. For the seeker after truth, Lewis is still able to prise open that door of faith that follows the corridor of doubt. On the basics of Christian doctrine, there is a timelessness and lucidity to his ideas. His command of English and sharpness of mind bring an edge to areas where other writers get lost in muddiness. On explaining core Christian thinking – from repentance to prayer, pride to passion – he is the teacher helping his occasionally dim pupils to understand it for the first time.

Through Lewis, a Christian orthodoxy that is non-denominational yet true to biblical Christianity, has permeated far and wide. This is an important legacy to the Church today in a postmodern society. With British spirituality taking on more of a consumer mentality, with a pick-and-mix of beliefs available and with each seen as offering a version of truth, Lewis's assertion of absolute truth that can compete with and defeat inferior versions is invigorating. There is a direct honesty of approach established by Lewis which remains compelling in today's culture. However, as soon as that theology is applied to issues like churchmanship or women's ordination, he reverts quickly to being a man of his own time.

It is hard to imagine how Lewis would be at home in the modern Church where so many of his most ardent admirers worship. How would he have coped with modern low-Church movements that have rejected formal institutional Christianity for more fluid structures based on home-churches or cells or networks nurtured on the Internet, so-called cyber-churches? It is hard to see him reacting with anything less than scepticism to the excesses of the modern Church movements. The renewed emphasis on God the Holy Spirit he would welcome, so long as it was not to the detriment the three-personality God. His lifestyle in the war years, of the tweedy conservative Oxford academic living with his brother with an old friend's mother, her daughter and evacuees, is one that has long gone. Even today, his love of smoking his pipe and drinking a pint of beer in his favourite pub can cause difficulties for some of his more conservative admirers in the United States, though seldom a problem for those in Europe.

Why has Lewis's appeal endured?

This juxtaposition between the Christian principles he exposes with such crispness and his own churchmanship and mind-set, was summarised by theologian Professor James Packer[8] at the Oxbridge '98 keynote lecture to commemorate the centenary of C.S.Lewis.[9] Though Lewis claimed to be no more than a 'mere Christian' layman, according to Packer Lewis was 'identifiably a High Church Anglican, orthodox and mainstream'. To what does Packer attribute Lewis's popularity and near-iconic status?

> Since Lewis spoke so forthrightly for mainstream Christianity, and since historic evangelicals belong to the mainstream, it is hardly surprising that for many Lewis has something like icon status, despite his smoking and drinking, his belief in purgatory and his quiet but decoded sacramentalism, his use of the confessional to keep himself honest, his non-inerrantist view of Scripture, and his unwillingness to speak of penal substitution and justification by faith alone when affirming forgiveness and salvation in Christ. What evangelicals most love in Lewis is his depiction of Aslan, the Christly lion of Narnia; his strong defence of supernaturalism, personal new birth, Christ's return to judgement, the reality of Satan, heaven, and hell, and the certainty that we are inescapably en route for one or the other . . .

This viewpoint is reinforced by Lewis's dislike of secular modernity, of 'Christianity-and-water' religion which offers a liberal dilution of biblical certainty. Though adopted by evangelicals as 'one of us', as Packer puts it, Lewis himself was a 'Christian for all Christians'.

Packer cites the heritage of Plato, Athanasius, Augustine and Aquinas, Thomas Traherne and William Law as among the seminal influences on C.S. Lewis. I'd have added Richard Baxter and Richard Hooker to that list. A parallel can be drawn between C.S. Lewis's enduring popularity and the influence of Richard Hooker long after his successful defence of broad Christianity in the debate at the Temple in London in 1585. Against Hooker stood Walter Travers, champion of the narrower Calvinist puritanism against the perceived threat from Catholic Europe. Travers wanted to return to the purity of the primitive church. Hooker, like C.S. Lewis, was rooted in the understanding gained from Aristotle, Augustine, Aquinas and Calvin himself. He argued that differences enriched the Anglican tradition. 'Be it that Peter has one interpretation, and Apollos has another; that Paul is of this mind, and Barnabas of that. If this offends you, the fault is yours. Carry peaceable minds. And you may find comfort by this variety.' Lewis, I suspect, would have muttered a loud Amen to that aspiration.

The debate was ended by Archbishop Whitgift. In 1586, Travers was banned from preaching. Hooker went on to write *Ecclesiastical Polity*, one of the most influential explorations of doctrine of the Anglican church. (He was admired by Laud and by Richard Baxter, whose writings gave Lewis the title for *Mere Christianity*). Samuel Pepys read it at the recommendation of a friend who had become a Christian after reading it. There are echoes here of the influence *Mere Christianity* continues to have over those who read it. Lewis, like Hooker, glorified in the diversity of traditions that the Anglican communion embraces. He succeeded in avoiding the labels that other Christians might try to pin upon him by always trying to find the common ground, that which unites Christians, and seldom strayed into the areas that divide.

Transformation

It was the BBC wartime broadcasts which showcased Lewis's unique approach to the wider English public. At one level the invitation to Lewis from the BBC had been just another call on his time. At another, it was an incredibly formative period for Lewis that was to shape his future. One in which the discipline of the broadcaster taught him how to write for the ordinary person, in a direct and popular way. Radio created for Lewis a new audience that no amount of teaching in a university or talking to RAF camps could ever reach. In accepting the invitation from James Welch, he was not to know that the broadcast talks would themselves transform his reputation. Nor could he have known how the correspondence they would generate would change his life. Just as he would play an integral part in transforming religious radio in those crucial war years, he too was changed irrevocably, to the point where popular success began to impinge on the rest of his life.

Rational imagination

Charles Colson has argued that Lewis's move from Magdalen College, Oxford, to the chair of Medieval and Renaissance Literature at Magdalene College, Cambridge, was critical to get Lewis away from the in-fighting and academic snobbery at Oxford, where popular success was treated with grave suspicion. Colson said Lewis was 'smart enough to realise that to be arrayed against the faculty at Oxford would involve him in a ground war all the time against intellectuals who held a naturalistic view-point, and that he might not succeed'. Lewis could bypass all of that by appealing instead to the imagination. Colson concluded: 'He devoted himself to penetrating the imagination, which is perhaps a more effective way to reach the culture. People are moved by moral literature more than they are by moral exposition.'

Lewis's own conversion demonstrates the harmony he found

between the power of his imagination and the irresistible logic of rationalism. His ability to reconcile the two was an abiding quality. To his old friend Bede Griffiths it was this 'union of rigorous critical intellect with rich poetic imagination that ... gave Lewis's Christian apologetics such an extraordinary force'.[10] James Packer describes it in this way: 'Deep inside him was a pictorial, dramatic, poetic, story-forming imagination of a Celtic type, childlike in its directness and simplicity and colourfully vivid in its verbalising'. Possibly the best example of this is of course Narnia, which continues to capture the imagination of children and adults alike.

Lewis's centenary

In Britain, the way in which the centenary of C.S. Lewis was marked in 1998 only served to confirm that it is C.S. Lewis the creator of Narnia that the British like to celebrate, rather than Lewis the academic, the popular theologian or Christian apologist.

On 21 July, the Royal Mail issued a series of special stamps entitled 'Magical worlds'. The 26p stamp featured *The Lion, the Witch and the Wardrobe*. Around the actual anniversary of Lewis's birth (29 November 1898), his step-son Douglas Gresham hosted a three-week nationwide tour in fourteen venues of an evening of words and music entitled *Jack – A Musical Portrait of C.S. Lewis*. A deluxe leather-bound edition of *The Lion, the Witch and the Wardrobe* and the other Narnia stories went on sale for £150. The Royal Shakespeare Company presented an adaptation of *The Lion, the Witch and the Wardrobe* and England's most famous toy shop, Hamleys in Regent Street, held a special C.S. Lewis 100th birthday party. Children were invited to draw greeting cards inspired by the Narnia books in a competition. Celebrities queued up to name it as their favourite story including contemporary pop stars Geri Halliwell, Liam Gallagher of the band Oasis, as well as Peter Mandelson, the former British government minister.

The reaction of the British press was divided on whether we should be celebrating Lewis or consigning him to history. An article assessing his legacy in celebratory mood stood in stark contrast to one writer's attack on his contribution in the *Guardian* newspaper called 'The dark side of Narnia'. *The Times* in London, meanwhile, had a retrospective assessment with the picture caption 'A pilgrim comes out of the Shadowlands'. Most interesting was the sub-editor's headline: 'Americans are putting us to shame by championing the works of C.S. Lewis in his centenary year'.[11]

It seems ironic that an academic from Oxford and Cambridge should be remembered in Britain primarily as a children's novelist, and only receive more representative recognition on the other side of the Atlantic. For the centenary the California-based C.S. Lewis Foundation organised a two-week event opening in Oxford and closing in Cambridge. Clive Davis, writing *The Times*' article, notes how this event tried to get behind the 'cosy image' of Lewis the storyteller to a more complex view of his achievements as literary critic, polemical novelist and popular theologian. As well as lectures from various Lewis experts, there were also performances of various kinds. Actor Joss Ackland, who portrayed Lewis in the BBC film production of *Shadowlands,* re-enacted Lewis's inauguration lecture at Cambridge. Actor David Suchet, best-known in Britain for his portrayal of the Agatha Christie detective Poirot, read out Lewis's sermon *The Weight of Glory*. Susan Howatch, whose Starbridge novels are perhaps the most accomplished Christian fiction of recent years, took part as well.

The vast majority of the 600 who attended had flown over from the United States, reflecting a marked difference in how Lewis is perceived. The article suggested that in the United States, 'a country that takes its religion seriously', Lewis is regarded as a writer of consequence. Whereas in England, 'indifference is the order of the day as far as mainstream Christianity is concerned', and maintained that 'Lewis's reputation has suffered accordingly, especially among the opinion-forming classes, who are all too ready to relegate him to the children's corner'.

Another paper, *The Sunday Times*,[12] in its Lewis Centenary feature, observed that 'in America – to the amused bafflement of British theologians – Lewis's religious writings have so caught the adult imagination that his work has become one of the most potent forces of modern Christianity'. The American *Christianity Today* magazine, in calling C.S. Lewis the Aquinas, the Augustine and the Aesop of contemporary evangelism,[13] certainly cannot be faulted for under-statement.

The divergence of opinion could be partly attributed to timing. The rise of the post-war evangelical movement in the United States happened at the same time as *The Screwtape Letters* and *Mere Christianity* began to have a wider impact. Lewis gave the movement an intellectual under-girding and respectability. In post-war Britain there was a strong desire to escape from the paternalistic government, from messages identified with wartime and immediate post-war austerity.

Lewis and the other Christian writers had rehabilitated the Christian faith and given it a massive intellectual thrust into British culture as a whole, but Lewis was still to find that his children's fiction held broader appeal to the British post-war consciousness than his apologetics. There is substance in the charge that in England, Lewis has suffered from type-casting as a children's fiction writer. Narnia has served him well, in terms of prolonging the longevity of his reputation among new generations, but has also damaged his reputation by confining him to that genre.

Where *The Times* suggested that Americans were putting the English to shame in their celebrations, *The Guardian* asked: 'Why are we marking the centenary of C.S. Lewis's birth with parties and competitions? The books of this "tweedy medievalist", says Philip Pullman, were reactionary and dishonest.[14] Pullman won the Carnegie Medal in 1996 for his novel *Northern Lights* and is a leading writer of fiction for children. He finds the Narnia cycle one of the most 'ugly and poisonous' things he's ever read.[15] For him, the idea of killing off all your characters (in *The Last Battle* in a railway accident) is anathema. 'To slaughter the lot of them, and then claim they're better off, is not honest storytelling: it's propaganda in the service of a life-hating ideology.' The article ends: 'I haven't the slightest doubt that the man will be sainted in due course: the legend is too potent. However, when that happens, those of us who detest the supernatural, the reactionary sneering, the misogyny, the racism, and the sheer dishonesty of the narrative method will still be arguing against him.'

Some of Lewis's admirers share Pullman's concern that the legend of Lewis makes it harder to assess his work with the objectivity Lewis himself would expect. Dr Bruce L. Edwards, Professor of English at Bowling Green State University in Ohio, has written numerous essays on Lewis published in the public domain on the Internet. He is concerned, in view of the countless books on Lewis's life and work since his death in 1963, that 'ironically' Lewis might eventually suffer the same fate as others he himself 'rehabilitated' during his career.

> Surfeited by volume after volume of analysis, paraphrase, and critique, Lewis's own canon may be dwarfed by secondary sources, an attitude he opposed all of his life in reading others. As it stands, both his fiction and theological writings have been endlessly and hyper-critically explored, creating a trail of footnotes and asides long enough to camouflage the essential viewpoints and facts about his life – thus discouraging even the most diligent student of Lewis.[16]

Professor Edwards would be right if admirers of Lewis were simply to read *about* him and not read what he wrote. The sales of his works suggest that books about Lewis do generate more interest in returning to what Lewis himself had to say. The purpose of this book has been to put *Mere Christianity* back into its proper context as a formative influence in the history of religious broadcasting. Through the medium of radio, C.S. Lewis offers cogent arguments for Christian verities, able to withstand any amount of intellectual testing even in the middle of the Second World War. If readers of this book are not inspired to want to read *Mere Christianity* for themselves and to draw their own conclusions on the subject matter of the book, then this author will have fallen short.

It seems that even at the time of the centenary of his birth, the jury is as divided over C.S. Lewis as it was when the first listeners wrote in to the BBC with letters of adulation or anger. Lewis's ability to polarise his audience is undiminished after sixty years. However, there is no disputing the fact that he continues to influence those who read his popular theology just as profoundly as he touched the lives of those he met.

The continuing impact of Lewis and his writing

One of the least expected tributes came in a profile of the great drama critic Kenneth Tynan, carried in the *Daily Telegraph*.[17] Tynan is credited with 'injecting himself into the veins of the British theatre' as one of its most articulate, outspoken and influential critics. The first volume of his diaries is full of gossip and indiscretion, including extra-marital affairs. One of the 'more surprising and generous tributes' paid by Tynan is to his old university tutor, C.S. Lewis. As a tutor, he considered Lewis to have the best attributes of Dr Johnson and G.K. Chesterton without their vices. Lewis's mind is 'Johnsonian without the bullying and Chestertonian without the facetiousness'. What touched Tynan most was Lewis's generous help when he went to see him after being jilted by his fiancée on the eve of their marriage in 1949. Lewis was most kind to Tynan, letting him defer sitting his finals by six months. Then he 'got on with the Christian business of consolation'. Tynan records that 'as I listened to him, my problems began to dwindle . . . I had entered his room suicidal and I left it exhilarated'.

At the time of the centenary *The Sunday Times* carried an extract from *Mere Christianity* – the section on pride – in a full-page feature with one of the longest headlines to appear in the paper. 'This man is a pizza millionaire. He's smiling because he is giving £600m to charity and devoting himself to God. He is doing so because he read this book by C.S.Lewis'. The headline appears over a composite photograph – with *Mere Christianity* on the right, superimposed on the picture of Thomas Monaghan, founder of Domino Pizza, one of America's most successful companies. After reading Lewis's analysis of pride, Monaghan decided to divest himself of his fortune. It began with selling his private helicopter, the Rolls-Royce and Bentley limousines, the yacht and his collection of Frank Lloyd Wright artefacts. He went on to sell most of his stake in Domino Pizza. He is expected to spend most of his money building more Catholic schools in the Americas, according to the article.

In the forty years since his death, the question has been asked, 'Who is the new C.S. Lewis? When will we have the next Christian writer who can straddle popular theology and fiction with such ease?' Prof. James Packer ended his Lewis Centenary lecture with the question: 'Who follows, now, where Lewis led?'[18] The fact is that no-one is forthcoming.

C.S. Lewis was unique. His brand of Anglican and yet nonpartisan conservative theology has kept his appeal broad indeed. He was that rare breed of Christian polymath whose interests and skills as a communicator in a range of media have secured his legacy and made him an almost impossible act to follow. His work has stood the test of time and looks set to be just as potent in the new century as in the old. The influence of Lewis pervades a good deal of popular culture. It will go on attracting interest so long as his books remain in print, his ideas are tested and each new generation discovers his writings, his faith and his corpus of Christian apologetics, that stemmed in part from his neglected career as a broadcaster.

Reluctant fame

All over the world, there are hundreds of societies dedicated to exploring and perpetuating Lewis's work, as any quick Internet search will reveal. His iconic status, in some quarters, is assured. Lewis himself would have hated all the fuss. He had no time for personality cults.

He was not motivated by money or fame or attention. The quantity of letters that poured through his letter-box after the BBC talks was a constant burden to him. His inspiration was never the work itself, but the desire to do his part for God. 'Ever since I became a Christian, I have thought that perhaps the best, perhaps the only service I could do for my unbelieving neighbours was to explain and defend the belief.'[19]

At a papal audience, Walter Hooper found himself discussing C.S. Lewis with Pope John Paul II. At the end of the meeting, the Pope gave his own summary of Lewis's achievement. Lewis, he said, knew what his 'apostolate', his divine calling, was. There was a long pause when Hooper thought the Pope had finished. Then the Pope added 'and he did it'. He saw Lewis as having a God-given task and doing it. For C.S. Lewis it was really very simple. Hooper thinks Lewis felt that you just do these things because you are given them to do.

> I'm sure he must have prayed a lot about it too. I think he must have found that this was something that he should do. I think also he felt that at wartime when people were sacrificing their lives, at least those who are left comfortably off at home in a nice college should do what they can. He didn't think his gifts were the highest gifts – they were the only ones he had.[20]

That collaboration with the BBC transformed religious broadcasting. With the guiding hands of James Welch and Eric Fenn, C.S. Lewis was transformed in a four-year period from a little-known Christian writer to the most widely-celebrated Christian apologist on both sides of the Atlantic. A more than useful writer was refined by the intensity of the radio production process into one of the most effective Christian communicators of his or any

JUSTIN PHILLIPS

other time. From the modest beginning of a series of broadcast talks emerged a classic best-seller.

There is no doubting Lewis's talent was already there. However, the grooming it received at the hands of professional broadcasters and fellow Christian believers honed it into something uniquely effective. A new audience discovered Lewis. The talks were published and eventually brought together in *Mere Christianity*, opening up a new frontier for the Christian gospel that is widening by the day. After sixty years, *Mere Christianity* has lost none of its power. It continues to transform the lives of those who read it. There is no reason why it won't continue to be potent for decades to come. Its success is not just because of Lewis's unique skill as a communicator but because of the person he writes about. Christianity without Christ is just another dogma. *Mere Christianity*, with Christ at its heart, remains C.S. Lewis's most important contribution to contemporary thought.

Notes

[1] James T. Como, an associate professor of rhetoric and public communication at York College, at the City University of New York, brought out a collection of essays and memoirs, *C.S. Lewis at the Breakfast Table and other reminiscences.* A Harvest Book, Harcourt Brace & Company, New York, 1992 edition. The quotation comes from the preface.
[2] Rogers, Pat, (ed.) *The Oxford Illustrated History of English Literature*, Guild Publishing, London, Oxford University Press 1987, p. viii
[3] Hastings, Adrian, *A History of English Christianity* 1920–1990, SCM Press London, quoting from the 1991 paperback edition
[4] White, Antonia, *The BBC at War*, BBC pamphlet 1942, p.18
[5] Ibid.
[6] BBC Written Archives Centre, BBC Listener Research Report LR/2138 October 1943 on the structure of the civilian audience for broadcasts of religious services. The figures indicated a distinct increase in public interest, most pronounced among precisely those listeners to whom religious services would normally hold least appeal – men of all ages and young people of both sexes.
[7] *The Spiritual Front, the origin and significance of The Big Ben Silent Minute*

Observance. A three-penny pamphlet. This quotation is taken from the 20th edition, completing 132,000 copies, published June 1945 by the Big Ben Council.

[8] Professor Packer is the Sangwoo Youtong Chee Professor of Theology at Regent College, Vancouver.

[9] Professor James I. Packer's keynote address, *Living Truth for a Dying World – the message of C.S. Lewis,* was reprinted in *Articulate,* the journal of the Arts Centre Group, Volume 2 1999, ISSN 1461–1465.

[10] Como, op. cit. p.17

[11] *The Times,* London, 5 August 1998, Arts section p. 28. Article by Clive Davis.

[12] *The Sunday Times,* London, 4 October 1998, section 1 p.14. Focus article by Tom Rhodes and Margarette Driscoll

[13] September 1998 edition

[14] *The Guardian,* London, 1 October 1998, pp. 6–7. Article by Philip Pullman.

[15] Pullman cites various criticisms from 'slapdash' mythology (a view he attributes to Tolkien) to an American critic John Goldthwaite who allegedly 'lays bare the misogyny, the racism, the sado-masochistic relish for violence that permeates the whole cycle'. This is his summary (not mine) of John Goldthwaite's 'powerful and original' study of children's literature, *The Natural History of Make-Believe,* Oxford University Press, 1996.

[16] Dr Bruce L. Edwards, Professor of English, Bowling Green State University, Ohio in *C.S. Lewis: A Modest Literary Biography and Bibliography* to be found on the Internet.

[17] *The Daily Telegraph,* London, Tuesday 1 August 2000, p. 17. Article by Philip Delves Broughton, *Tynan, his wife and other women.*

[18] Ibid.

[19] Lewis, C.S., *Mere Christianity,* Preface p. vi , Fount, HarperCollins, Centenary edition 1997

[20] Interview with Walter Hooper, 28 October 1999

ACKNOWLEDGMENTS

∽◦∾

To write a book like this is not just a labour of love. It depends on the help and support of people, too numerous to mention, whose encouragement and practical assistance make such an enterprise possible. Without the support of my colleagues at the BBC's Written Archives Centre in Caversham, this book would not have been possible. They have put up with regular visits from me over the last two years, seeking ever more obscure files from the archive. Jacquie Kavanagh, the Written Archivist, has been endlessly patient, assisted by Gwyniver Jones, James Codd, Neil Somerville and other archivist colleagues with Marion Fallon's administrative support. Vicky Mitchell of the BBC Commercial Agency gave me sound advice and Christine Slattery, BBC Television Archivist, gave me the Eric Fenn transcript from the oral history archive.

Walter Hooper, literary advisor to the C.S. Lewis Estate, kindly agreed to write the preface to the book and getting to know Walter has been a delight. His guidance was much valued. In the BBC's Photographic Library, Mary Portalska did much picture research and Bobbie Mitchell cleared permissions. I am grateful to Simon Milner, The Secretary of the BBC, and his predecessor Christopher Graham (now Director-General of the Advertising Standards

Agency) and my personnel manager, Moira Richards, for their support.

Arthur Strong, the National Portrait Gallery, and representatives of Norman Parkinson's estate, all assisted with provision of photographs.

Finally, there are those who let me interview them, told me stories, let me borrow their books, prompted questions and added hugely to my source material. They include (in no particular order) Lady Freud, Professor Jean Seaton, Leonard Miall, Dr Bill Hague, Diana Moxon, Angela Raby, Christopher Dean, Betty Baker, Michael Barton, Robert Baylis, Joan and Douglas Osborne, Quentin Phillips and Vera Phillips. It was in Camilla's Bookshop in Eastbourne, my favourite second-hand bookshop, where I found many early wartime editions of Lewis and Sayers and BBC Handbooks. I am indebted to all my publishing team at HarperCollins, especially the enthusiasm and friendship of senior editor Amy Boucher-Pye and publishing director James Catford. It was James who first persuaded me that there was a book to be written on Lewis at the BBC. Last, but not least, deepest thanks go to my long-suffering and much loved family. My daughters Laura Treneer, Rhiannon, Isabelle and Bryony Phillips put up with their father being tied to a computer most weekends for over a year. Deepest thanks go to Gillian, my wife, to whom the book is dedicated. She has been endlessly patient and supportive and made important suggestions. To all who have assisted, named and unnamed, thank you and blessings.

Justin Phillips
December 2000

Following the death of the author, his family would like to add their thanks to David Brawn and Dominic Kingston at HarperCollins, the BBC and the C.S. Lewis Estate for the support and encouragement which has enabled this book to go ahead.

APPENDIX 1

The BBC Sound Archives

∾∾

The BBC Sound Archives has five surviving recordings of C.S. Lewis's talks. Only one of his wartime broadcast talks survives.

Programme	Date	Duration	Content
1. 'Beyond Personality'	21 Mar. 1944	14 mins	The last of a series of weekly talks under the title 'Beyond Personality'. The talk covers difficulties people have with prayer – the next step in evolution to change from mere creatures to sons of God.
2. 'The Great Divorce'	27 Feb. 1948	2 mins	C.S. Lewis reads the prologue to *The Great Divorce*.
3. 'Charles Williams'	11 Feb. 1949	18 mins	C.S. Lewis's critique of fellow-writer Charles Williams, stating that many contemporary critics were wide of the mark. Williams seems to know of another world.

| 4. 'The Great Divide' | 1 Apr. 1955 | 37 mins | Lewis argues that the hitherto accepted 'great divide' between the Middle Ages and the Renaissance is a fallacy. A reassessment of the division between old and new Western culture. |
| 5. 'Pilgrim's Progress' | 16 Oct. 1962 | 26 mins | A talk on *Pilgrim's Progress*, illustrated with extracts read by Vivienne Chatterton and Michael Spice. The first in a series on six classics. He considers its content and style, says it's a misconception that it is biblical, considers 'its unpleasant side' and thinks its sense of 'intolerable terror' adds to its significance. It has a unique quality – an allegory based on life in Bunyan's day but pre-occupied with the spiritual life. |

APPENDIX 2

The History of *Mere Christianity*

∽∾

This shows the history of *Mere Christianity* as it progressed from radio broadcast talk to separate publication, series by series towards amalgamation in book form in 1952.

1. *Right and Wrong: A Clue to the Meaning of the Universe*

Broadcast on the BBC Home Service on Wednesdays between 7.45 and 8 p.m. An extra programme was added on Saturday, September 6 to respond to letters from listeners. The talks were first published in Britain in 1942 as *Broadcast Talks* and a year later in the United States as *The Case for Christianity*.

BBC Broadcast Talk	*Broadcast Talks* and *The Case For Christianity*, Book 1	*Mere Christianity* Book 1
1. 'Common Decency', Aug. 6, 1941	1.	'The Law of Human Nature'
2. 'Scientific Law and Moral Law', Aug. 13, 1941	3.	'The Reality of the Law'

3. 'Materialism or Religion', Aug. 20, 1941	4.	'What Lies Behind the Law'
4. 'What Can We Do About It?', Aug. 27, 1941	5.	'We Have Cause to Be Uneasy'
5. 'Answers to Listeners' Questions', Sept. 6, 1941	2.	'Some Objections'

2. *What Christians Believe*

Transmitted on the BBC Home Service on Sundays from 4.45 to 5 p.m.

BBC Broadcast Talk	*Broadcast Talks* and *The Case For Christianity*, Book 2	*Mere Christianity* Book 2
First Talk, Jan. 11, 1942	1.	'The Rival Conceptions of God'
Second Talk, Jan. 18, 1942	2.	'The Invasion'
Third Talk, Feb. 1, 1942	3.	'The Shocking Alternative'
Fourth Talk, Feb. 8, 1942	4.	'The Perfect Penitent'
Fifth Talk, Feb. 15, 1942	5.	'The Practical Conclusion'

3. *Christian Behaviour*

The third series went out on the Forces network on Sunday afternoons between 2.50 and 3 p.m. It was this series when things began to go wrong. Lewis had prepared his usual fifteen-minute talks only to discover they were five minutes too long for the time allocated. Each had to be drastically pruned. The cuts were restored in the first published version, *Christian Behaviour* (1943) with some further revisions for *Mere Christianity*.

BBC Broadcast Talk	*Christian Behaviour*	*Mere Christianity,* Book 3
First Talk, Sept. 20, 1942	'The Three Parts of Morality'	1. 'The Three Parts of Morality'
	2. 'The "Cardinal Virtues" '	2. 'The "Cardinal Virtues" '
Second Talk, Sept. 27, 1942	3. 'Social Morality'	3. 'Social Morality'
Third Talk, Oct. 4, 1942	4. 'Morality and Psychoanalysis'	4. 'Morality and Psychoanalysis'
Fourth Talk, Oct. 11, 1942	5. 'Sexual Morality'	5. 'Sexual Morality'
	6. 'Christian Marriage'	6. 'Christian Marriage'
Fifth Talk, Oct. 18, 1942	7. 'Forgiveness'	7. 'Forgiveness'
Sixth Talk, Oct. 25, 1942	8. 'The Great Sin'	8. 'The Great Sin'
	9. 'Charity'	9. 'Charity'
	10. 'Hope'	10. 'Hope'
Seventh Talk, Nov. 1, 1942	11. 'Faith'	11. 'Faith'
Eighth Talk, Nov. 8, 1942	12. 'Faith'	12. 'Faith'

4. *Beyond Personality: The Christian View of God*

Transmitted on the BBC Home Service and published two days later in the BBC's weekly magazine, *The Listener*. For this series, the BBC and Lewis reached a compromise arrangement to reduce the burden on Lewis of the late-evening live transmission. Talks 2, 6 and 7 were pre-recorded and the remainder broadcast live.

BBC Broadcast Talk	*The Listener*	*Beyond Personality*	*Mere Christianity* Book 4
1. 'Making and Begetting', Feb. 22, 1944	1. 'The Map and the Ocean', Feb. 24, 1944	1. 'Making and Begetting'	1. 'Making and and Begetting'
2. 'The Three-Personal God', Feb. 29, 1944.	2. 'God in Three Persons', March 2, 1944	2. 'The Three-Personal God'	2. 'The Three-Personal God'
		3. 'Time and Beyond Time'	3. 'Time and Beyond Time'
3. 'Good Infection', March 7, 1944	3. 'The Whole Purpose of the Christian', March 9, 1944	4. 'Good Infection'	4. 'Good Infection'
4. 'The Obstinate Toy Soldiers', March 14, 1944	4. 'The Obstinate Toy Soldiers', March 16, 1944	5. 'The Obstinate Toy Soldiers'	5. 'The Obstinate Toy Soldiers'
		6. 'Two Notes'	6. 'Two Notes'
5. 'Let's Pretend', March 21, 1944	5. 'Let us Pretend', March 24, 1944	7. 'Let's Pretend'	7. 'Let's Pretend'
6. 'Is Christianity Hard or Easy?', March 28, 1944	6. 'Is Christianity Hard or Easy?', March 30, 1944	8. 'Is Christianity Hard or Easy?'	8. 'Is Christianity Hard or Easy?'

		9. 'Counting the Cost'	9. 'Counting the Cost'
		10. 'Nice People or New Men'	10. 'Nice People or New Men'
7. 'The New Man', April 4, 1944	7. 'The New Man', April 6, 1944	11. 'The New Men'	11. 'The New Men'

Details of the American editions taken from www.discovery.org/lewis/mchr.htm.

APPENDIX 3

The Anvil

∞

The Anvil was a regular programme conducted by the Reverend Dr J.W. Welch, Director of the Religious Broadcasting Department of the BBC. The following session was recorded on July 19, 1943 and transmitted July 22 from Broadcasting House, London. Only C.S. Lewis's answers are given as spoken over the air (see p. 231).

WELCH: Good evening, listeners. This is the Anvil in session again, with two old friends, Canon [F.A.] Cockin of St Paul's Cathedral and Father Andrew Beck, a Roman Catholic priest. And we welcome tonight the Reverend Dorothy Wilson, who has been Minister-in-Charge of the Muswell Hill Congregational Church, and also Mr C.S. Lewis, known to many of you through his broadcasts and his books. We hope to discuss and possibly answer four questions tonight, and the first is this. "Will you please tell me what really happens when a person dies? Have you any proof or is it only faith that we shall meet our loved ones again?"

[Canon Cockin pointed out that, even if it sounds brutal, the New Testament emphasis is on the importance of meeting God, not on meeting those we loved on earth.]

WELCH: Lewis, do you want to . . . ?

LEWIS: Well, yes. I was going to say very much what Cockin has said, so as he's said it for me, I'll confine myself to this, to try and make it sound a little less brutal. I fully agree with him that as long as you are thinking of God as merely as a sort of bridge by which you can get to your loved ones you're on the wrong track. But that doesn't mean of course that you can demand of a woman who's just lost her only son, say, that she's to alter her feelings and start caring more about God than about him. That's probably impossible. But if you will go to God just as you are, fully admitting that you care about Him very little, and put yourself in His hands, if you're even ready to be made to care and leave Him to work, He'll do the rest. And there's no question of anyone wanting you to love your son less than you do. God wants you to love him more. You will love him more than you do now when you've learnt to love God most. Because, of course, whatever we think, we really don't know much about loving until we're in touch with love Himself.

WELCH: . . . The second question . . . is this. "When the war began, I heard many parsons talk of courage, and they said you can't be brave unless you are a Christian. I can't believe this is true. What do the Anvil members think?" Now what do you think, Lewis?

LEWIS: Well, I think the parsons who said that were talking bosh! It's perfectly obvious that you can have courage without being a Christian. Lots of Nazis are courageous, lots of animals are courageous. I think the real point is: what sources you're getting your courage from. Because, of course, all sorts of things will make a man brave for the time being. Alcohol, ignorance of the danger, anger, self-respect, human loyalty, and love of God. But they're not all equally good sources.

WELCH: . . . Well now, the third question is, I think, an important one . . . "Could the Anvil tell me how to set about reading the Bible. I know that the Genesis account is untrue, and some Old Testament miracles are legendary. Now I hear parts of the

New Testament were inserted in the fourth century, that Matthew didn't write the first Gospel, not Paul the epistle to the Hebrews, and so on. Well, what are we to believe? I've no time to be a scholar like the parsons. Can the Anvil please help me? I want to read the Bible, but I just don't know what to believe." Now Lewis, you're a teacher, can you . . . ?

LEWIS: Well, I'd like to say straight away that if this man knows the Genesis account to be untrue I'm wondering where he's picked up his information because I don't know anything about that from human knowledge – I believe it to be true. But I'm not a biblical scholar so I can't go into the question. All I am in private life is a literary critic and historian, that's my job. And I'm prepared to say on that basis if anyone thinks the Gospels are either legends or novels, then that person is simply showing his incompetence as a literary critic. I've read a great many novels and I know a fair amount about the legends that grew up among early people, and I know perfectly well the Gospels are not that kind of stuff. They're absolutely full of the sort of things that don't come into legends. Take one simple example. The passage in which Our Lord is scribbling in the dust before He gives His answer about the woman taken in adultery. Nothing whatever comes of it, no doctrine has ever been based on it, it has no point at all; there's no conceivable reason why anyone should ever have written it down, unless he's seen it happening. From first to last the things strike me as records of fact. And, in my opinion, the people who think that any of the episodes in the Gospels are imaginary are the people who have no imagination themselves and have never understood what imaginative story-telling is. But of course I'm not a biblical scholar.

[Miss Wilson mentioned that, even if it were true that Bacon wrote the plays ascribed to Shakespeare, it is the plays themselves that are important.]

LEWIS: There's just one point, since Miss Wilson mentioned Bacon and Shakespeare. I should like to say from my own subject of

English literature that when I began they were playing with English literature just the same sort of thing they do with the Bible. *Henry the Sixth* was supposed to be by about six authors and they could tell which scene was by which. Well, that nonsense is all being blown away as far as I can make out in all subjects except Biblical criticism.

WELCH: . . . Now I do want to pass to the last question – it's so important . . . "Why does God allow suffering?"

[Canon Cockin suggested that suffering resulted from people of evil wills, that which is necessary in a surgical ward, and natural disaster. He was followed by Father Beck who mentioned the view of the Archbishop of Canterbury – that suffering was inseparable from a perfect life, and evil inseparable from an imperfect one.]

WELCH: Lewis, do you accept that?

LEWIS: Well, no, I'm afraid I'm very old-fashioned and simple here. I think in this world as it is, suffering is necessary for our cure and the cure of the whole universe, just like in Cockin's surgical ward. But I don't think you would need the cure of suffering nor the legs cut off unless something had gone wrong. And I think all the suffering in the world comes in the long run from evil wills. A great deal of it obviously comes from evil human wills, such as the war. But the things that are wrong in nature, I think, come from the evil wills of being older and stronger than men. In fact, devils, if you like to use the old-fashioned word. It's not a popular view now – it was the view taken by Christ of the woman who was deformed. He said Satan had bound her. I think we are living in a world that has gone wrong. So that I would say that all suffering springs from wickedness in the long run, though not all from human wickedness.

INDEX